Voyage of No Return

NORMA PLANK

© June 2008 Carlisle Press

All rights reserved. No portion of this book may
be reproduced by any means, electronic or mechanical,
including photocopying, recording, or by any
information storage retrieval system, without
written permission of the copyright's owner, except
for the inclusion of brief quotations for a review.

ISBN 10 digit: 1-933-753-07-2
ISBN 13 digit: 978-1-933-753-072

Text design: Amy Wengerd
Cover design: Ann Troyer
Cover art: Lisa Weaver
Printed by: Carlisle Printing

Carlisle Press
WALNUT CREEK
2701 TR 421
Sugarcreek, OH 44681

Introduction

After six generations, this story has been preserved and still continues to be popular in the Plank families. While some imagination was needed to weave the true facts together in this story, most of the names and all the dates come from historical records.

The story you are about to read is built around the following true facts.

Johan Melchior Blankenburg was kidnapped from Holland, and then sold as an indentured servant, but his Mennonite ancestors are thought to have come from Switzerland during the Reformation. Of course there is no way we can know all that was said and done, but the story stays close to the time period and actual things that happened to indentured servants according to personal records and historical facts.

According to the preserved records, Johan and his wife, Margaret, a young married couple, went to the port of Rotterdam, Holland, to bid farewell to friends who were leaving for America. The captain told them his ship would not leave until the next day. He graciously invited Johan and Margaret to stay, free of charge, with their friends on board his ship during the night. They agreed. During the night, while they were fast asleep, the ship set sail. The Blankenburg couple (they were later called Plank) awoke in the morning to find that they had been kidnapped. The captain had tricked them so he could fill his ship and then sell them as indentured servants when his ship docked in America.

Years later, Johan's great-great grandson, one-armed David Plank (son of Bishop David E. Plank), wrote some words similar to the following: "When Johan got up the next morning and looked out over the ocean there was no land in sight. Johan decided it was too far to swim, too deep to wade, so there was nothing to do but come to America."

Upon arrival in Philadelphia, they were sold as indentured servants to pay for their passage. The ship's list clearly shows that Johan Melchior Blankenburg left Rotterdam in the summer of 1767 and arrived in Philadelphia in October on the ship *Minerva*. Johan and the other foreign men signed the required statements of loyalty and renunciation on October 29, 1767, at the office of Thomas Willing. Being illiterate, Johan placed his mark (X) beside his name, which someone had written for him. The name "John Melchior Planckenberg" is listed as a 1767 immigrant. Because Johan's fare had not been paid, he returned to the ship to wait for a buyer who was in need of a servant's help.

Johan's wife, Margaret, gave birth to their first child, Jacob, while waiting on board the *Minerva* in the Philadelphia harbor. Baby Jacob was born November 6, 1767.

According to the preserved indenture papers, on November 27, 1767, Johan was first sold to Jason Cloud. He worked for him a little over one year. Then Jason sold the rest of Johan's indenture to Howard Hughes for the remainder of the time. I believe Mr. Hughes was a cruel master, because Johan or possibly Colonel Jacob Morgan paid Howard Hughes the sum of five pounds so Johan could be free. That five pounds was enough to pay for a year of service, but Johan owed Howard Hughes for only five more months of service. Johan even gave up his rightful "freedom dues", which was quite a loss. The freedom dues varied from colony to colony, but I found an example in my research. In Maryland, the "freedom dues" consisted of one new suit of broadcloth or jersey, one new shirt, one pair of new shoes and stockings, and a wool cap. Also to be furnished were two hoes, an ax, three barrels of corn, and fifty acres of land. Women servants got a similar amount of clothing and land and a year's supply of corn.

A son, Christian, was born during Johan's time with Howard Hughes. Christian is the bloodline through which my husband, Donald Plank, was born.

The records tell us Johan farmed for "Colonel" Jacob Morgan. As a free man, he worked for him during the Revolutionary War and possibly for the rest of his life. The "Colonel" was very concerned about the high taxes, which England was demanding on tea and other items. He was also present to sign his name to the indenture document (making it legal) when the indenture changed owners—from Jason Cloud to Howard Hughes.

Personally, I'm glad they came to America, because if they hadn't, I wouldn't have married my husband, Donald Plank. Donald's first wife, Doris Good, died in 1987, and in the same year I lost my husband, Marion Hartman, to cancer. Donald and I married June 3, 1989. It was then that I heard this fascinating story of his grandfather—six generations removed.

A history book gave me the true story of Elizabeth Hanley, who left for America to escape an undesirable marriage and was then indentured —exchanged for a yoke of oxen to pay her passage. Also, many people were taken to America from the overcrowded prisons in Europe and then sold as indentured servants to pay for their passage. Many children were kidnapped for the same purpose. Then, too, there were some examples too cruel to mention in this book.

After much thought and research, this story started to take shape in my mind. I have my husband and Darlene Bonvie, a sister in the Lord from Nova Scotia, to thank for the great encouragement they were to me. They urged me to get started and to keep going. They spent time proofreading and giving helpful criticism. Others who were a great help with editing and giving helpful suggestions and encouragement were: Roger Berry, Mrs. Dan (Sandy) Wengerd, Mrs. Dan (Diane) Freed, Mrs. Stephen (Lydia) Good, and Mrs. Raymond (Elizabeth Ann) Shenk.

We trust this story helps the reader to have a greater faith in God. May He receive honor and glory; He alone is worthy.

Mrs. Norma Plank

Genealogy of Johan Melchior Blankenburg

1. Johan married Margaret
Children: Jacob, **Christian**, John, Barbara, Margaret, Peter (Amish Minister) Lancaster County, PA

2. Christian married Barbara (Yoder)
Children: Joseph, Jacob, Martha, Christian, John, Magelene, Barbara, Isaac, **Samuel**

3. Deacon Samuel Plank married Juliana (Hertzler)
Children: Joseph, **David**, Leah, Elizabeth, Martha, Barbara, Juliana, Samuel, Mary

4. Bishop David Plank married Mary (Hertzler)
Children: Samuel, **Salome**, Levi, Mary, Elsie, Lydia, Anna, Catherine, Juliana, David (one-armed Davey)

5. Salome Plank married Samuel B. Plank
(Plank from OH married a Plank from MO)
Children: Marion, **Ira**, Fred

6. Ira Plank married Laura (Kanagy)
Children: Floyd, Oren, Roy, **Donald**, Dwight

7. Minister Donald Plank married Doris (Good)
Children: Donna, David, Diane

Because of illiteracy, the name Blankenburg was changed through the years from Blankenburg to Blanckenburg to Blanck to Planck to Plank. When a Dutchman says Blank, it sounds like Plank, so possibly that is how it got changed. Johan Melchior Blankenburg could neither read nor write.

Contents

1. Life Without Father 1
2. Grootvader's Memories 7
3. New Jobs for Johan and Hilda 13
4. Good-bye to Grootvader 19
5. The Singing Gardener 23
6. A New Song 27
7. Susie is Encouraged 33
8. Welcome Aboard! 39
9. Tricked! 45
10. Midnight Departure 53
11. Pete the Unbeatable 59
12. Where Two or More Are Gathered 65
13. What Now, Captain? 71
14. Caught! 77
15. New Life for Pete 85
16. The Hero of Haarlem 91
17. Epidemic! 97
18. Burial at Sea 103
19. Unseen Hands 109

20. God Gives Direction 115

21. "Land, Ho!" 123

22. The Captain Shows Mercy.....................131

23. Baby Joys 137

24. Surprise Visits.......................................143

25. One Man, Two Oxen, and God.............151

26. Captain Keeps His Promises 157

27. New Home for Elizabeth 163

28. Welcome, Elizabeth 171

29. Settling In 181

30. Tommy Goes to School........................187

31. We Meet Again 195

32. Temptation Met and Refused................203

33. Yet Another Life 211

34. A Friend Indeed 217

35. Good-bye, Allie 227

36. Promise Made, Promise Kept 235

37. Winds of Change 241

38. Life Renewed 247

39. It's Moving Time Again 253

40. Letters from Home! 263

Bibliography..273

chapter one

Life Without Father

Johan (Yo-han) Melchior Blankenburg, a muscular 21-year-old, hunched forward on a one-legged milking stool, his head pressed against the warm flank of a cow. He softly sang a hymn as he milked the last of his eight cows, a typical herd for an Anabaptist farmer in Holland in 1765. As always, Johan enjoyed his early morning chores, but his singing suddenly died away as deep thoughts took over. *Here I am, 21 years of age, and there seems to be no way to make enough money to have a home of my own. I'd like that, but I guess I shouldn't get too concerned because I haven't met anyone I would want for my wife. I'll pray about it though.* He smiled as he finished stripping out the last of the milk. Getting to his feet, he set the milk aside, then reached forward and unchained the cow, giving her a gentle pat on the neck. Pushing his thick blond hair back from his damp forehead, he watched her amble out to join the other cows that were eating lush grass on the polder.

Johan carried the buckets of milk from the barn to the spotless milk house. Removing his wooden shoes at the door, as the Dutch custom was, he quickly slipped into a pair of cloth slippers and carried the milk over to the worktable. Carefully he strained the milk and poured it into twenty shiny brass pails with swinging metal handles. He placed them into a trough of fresh, cool, running water. Great flapping windmills pumped the water into the trough, after which it ran out the overflow pipe to a nearby canal.

Johan had worked up a healthy appetite and was looking forward to a good breakfast as he slipped into his shoes and headed for the house. An aroma of sausage and pancakes met him as he opened the kitchen door.

He sniffed appreciatively and said, "Good morning, Mother. Sure smells good in here."

"Well, it's ready," she replied, "so let's eat. Come, Greta and Hilda, leave your spinning and knitting and come to the table. Johan is in a hurry to deliver the milk and butter to his customers."

Since his father's death three years before, Johan had been the man of the house, so as they all sat down, he said reverently, "Let us pray." Each one prayed silently and Johan ended with "Amen."

"Greta," queried Johan as he speared a plump sausage with his fork, "how much butter do we have? I hope there is some extra, because Dame Hummel would like three pounds instead of the usual one pound. I believe she said she's getting company from Leyden."

"Yes, Johan, the cows are giving a lot of cream these days. You never saw such lovely yellow butter. And the cheeses, you should see them. Hilda is twelve now and old enough to be a good help, so we have a dozen balls of cheese nearly ready to sell. They look and smell so good." Greta handed the butter and syrup to Johan for his stack of pancakes.

"Good!" exclaimed Johan, looking at his smiling mother. "Not only because there is extra butter, but the way the girls work together is wonderful." Turning to his sisters, he continued, "After Father died, Mother and I made all the butter and cheese, but not anymore—thanks to you girls."

When the meal was over, Johan pushed his chair back and got to his feet. "Well, it's time to deliver the milk," he said as he jerked off his slippers and put them on a low shelf by the door.

"Johan," said Hilda, springing to her feet, "may I help you harness the dogs? They are so well trained I could even run your milk route."

"Sure, Hilda, I'll be glad for your help," agreed Johan, chuckling as they headed for the barn. "But I'm not sure you're old enough to handle the dogs; at least not when they meet another dog team that's determined to fight. The other day I saw two teams in a fight. What a mess they made of the produce—vegetables were flying everywhere. One of the squash flew out and clouted one of the dogs on the head. That was enough for him. He yelped loudly and decided to tend to his own business. He and the rest of his team tucked their tails between their legs and struck out at high speed for safer territory."

"Oh, Johan, that must have been a funny sight," laughed Hilda, her eyes dancing. "You helped the poor man pick up his vegetables, didn't you?"

"Yes, I arrived just in time to help him gather his scattered produce.

The tomatoes were done for, but the other things came through in fair shape. Now, if you'll hold these three dogs, I'll slip the harness on them." Johan's fingers flew as he buckled each strap. Connecting the harnessed dogs to the milk cart, he stopped and watched Hilda as the dogs crowded close, licking her hands. "Looks like they really like you, Hilda. The dogs are well trained, so maybe some day when your work isn't too pressing, I'll see if you can drive the milk route. I'd go along, of course, and see if you really can handle these dogs."

"Oh," squealed Hilda, clasping her hands with delight, "I'll work extra hard so we can have a trial run soon."

They placed the full milk containers and small tubs of butter into the cart, and Johan took up the driving lines.

As Johan spoke to the dogs, Hilda watched his every move. With a hearty, "Thank you, Hilda," and a wave of his free hand, he was on his way.

By 9 A.M., Johan returned home with the empty milk pails rattling in his cart. Many men would have ridden home in the cart after the milk was sold, but not Johan. He believed the dogs would become bad tempered if he overworked them.

After unloading the empty pails at the milk house, he loaded up four large stone pails with their stone lids. He drove his team a short piece down the road to buy some boiling water from an old woman who made her living by tending great fires of peat which flamed beneath her shining, water-filled copper tanks.

"Good morning, Dame Bowman! How are you this fine morning?" greeted Johan. "Do you have some boiling water for me?" He glanced at the group of ragged-looking children crowded around the old lady.

"That I do, but I reckon you'll have to wait your turn. These poor, hungry *kinder* (children) haven't had their breakfast, and their mothers are waiting for them to bring home a bit of burning peat and a jar of hot water for their gruel," explained the grinning old woman, showing her few remaining teeth.

"Do you mind if I help you?" asked Johan.

"Why no, lad," agreed the astonished old woman, sitting down with a sigh. "That'd be a great help to an old woman the likes of me."

For the next fifteen minutes, Johan was busy lifting small burning blocks of peat into stone pails and hot water into similar pails. For these two items, each child gave the old woman a Dutch cent. She kept her stivers and cent pieces in a large pocket in her gathered skirt.

Johan sadly shook his head as he watched the ragged, undernourished children struggle with their small stone pails. They tried to hold their pails of hot water and burning peat as far out as possible with their bony little arms.

Poor little kinder, thought Johan with a sigh. As he filled the large containers in his cart, he purposed in his heart: *Never will I let strong drink touch my lips. Full well I know the reason for the plight of most of these poor little kinder.*

Steam rolled up from the boiling water as each container was filled. He quickly capped the pails with stone lids so very little heat or water would be lost on the way home.

As he walked over to pay the old woman, she was shaking her head. "Johan, my lad, why are you so different from other men here about?"

"What do you mean, Dame Bowman?" asked Johan, with a hearty laugh. "I've got a head, two arms, and two legs like other men, haven't I?"

"You know that's not what I mean. I've never seen a man so kind. What makes you so different, Johan?" She was in earnest, waiting for an answer.

Johan hesitated as the color rose in his cheeks. "Dame Bowman, I serve a God who is very kind and who asks His children to be kind also. I'm one of His children, you see."

"Thank you kindly, Johan, for telling me. I've been meaning for some time to ask you." Her voice trembling, she added, "I suppose I've waited too long to be one of His children."

"Oh, no, Dame Bowman, it's God's will that everyone should become one of His children—no matter the age. I attend the little church about a mile up the road. It sits close to the canal. You are invited. Will you come?"

"Yes, I promise to come if I'm able to be there," said the old woman as she pocketed Johan's coins.

"I'll be waiting for you at the church door next Sunday," promised Johan with a smile. "See you there."

A few minutes later he was singing in the milk house while scrubbing the milk pails in hot, soapy water. After rinsing them, he placed them upside down on racks to dry. Now the pails were prepared for the next morning's milking. The Saturday evening and Sunday milk was always used later to make butter and cheese, making it unnecessary to sell milk on Sunday.

He turned his head as his mother opened the door. "Do you need my help, Johan?"

"I'm almost finished, but thanks for asking," he replied, flashing his mother a smile.

"I wish you'd step over and visit *Grootvader* (Grandfather) a bit—at least for an hour. He gets so lonesome since *Grootmoeder* (Grandmother) passed away," encouraged his mother.

"Sure, I'll do that. I always enjoy talking with him. He understands me so well and reminds me so much of Father. I'm so grateful for the many Scriptures and poems he has helped me memorize. I'm just thankful he's still with us."

"Yes," agreed his mother, "he's a wonderful blessing to us all. He's had nearly eighty fruitful years, so we may not have him much longer."

Johan slipped into his wooden shoes and headed down the road, whistling a merry tune. As he got close to Grootvader's house, he was surprised to see him outside. He was sitting in his chair, placed alongside the white cottage.

Waving his hand, Johan shouted, "Good morning, Grootvader. Why are you sitting out here? Isn't it a bit cool and damp for you so early in the morning?"

"It's not too bad. You see I'm wearing the heavy lined blouse your grootmoeder made for me. I was feeling a mite lonesome for her, so I decided to come out here and enjoy her tulips. You know she set great store by them and never allowed a weed to spoil their beauty. When I sit just so, I can reach out my hand and touch her tulips and I'm not quite so lonesome. Just an old man's foolish notion, I suppose."

"No, Grootvader, I'm glad when you share your feelings with me. It helps me to better understand what a great love you and Grootmoeder shared."

"Yes, Johan," he agreed, "our love was great for God and for each other. It saw us through many hardships in this life, and our love grew all the stronger because of them. I've shared many of our experiences with you, but I'll tell you more when you have time."

"I have at least an hour, Grootvader, and I always enjoy hearing about your experiences."

"Well, if you're sure it suits, Johan. I thank God for my memories of bygone days. They are precious treasures and a great comfort to me, especially since I'm here alone."

"Let's go inside, Grootvader, where it's a bit warmer and you can sit in a more comfortable chair," said Johan. He reached out a strong arm to steady the elderly man as he got to his feet and they started for the cottage.

chapter two

Grootvader's Memories

"Johan," Grootvader began when they were both settled in comfortable chairs, "I feel burdened today. Maybe it's because I have a feeling I won't be around much longer, or maybe it is because I have such a burden for you young people. It's probably a mixture of the two. Anyway, I'm seeing more and more that life is very short and very uncertain. None of us know what we may face in this life. I just hope if the going gets tough sometime in your future, Johan, you'll remember what your forefathers went through because of their faith in God. I pray it may strengthen you, that you may ever be faithful to God, no matter what comes."

"I have purposed in my heart, Grootvader, to live for God all the days of my life, no matter what I may have to suffer," declared Johan.

"Johan, those words make your forefathers' sufferings worthwhile." After shifting to a more comfortable position and placing his feet on a footstool, Grootvader continued. "I hope you don't tire of the things I speak of often—the things of the past. You don't, do you?"

"Oh, no, Grootvader," Johan replied quickly. "I enjoy hearing your stories. Actually, I'd like to hear more of your own childhood and life. It's been a while since you've told me about that."

"I'll do that," Grootvader replied, with a pleased but sober look in his eyes. "I'll never forget my childhood in Bern, Switzerland, where I was born and raised. We were rich farmers. We lived in great comfort with plenty to eat and very nice clothes. We drove expensive horses and carriages. When I was in my teens, my family became acquainted with a group of Anabaptists. These people had a great love for God and were willing to suffer much to uphold what the Bible taught. They were kind and willing to help anyone in need. We became good friends and when they invited us to one of their secret meetings, we went."

"Weren't you afraid of being caught?" inquired Johan.

"Oh, yes, it was never far from our minds, but our longing to know God was greater than our fear of the authorities. We were determined to possess the peace and joy which the Anabaptists had. I personally saw some of these godly souls joyfully singing while being brutally treated on their way to be burned at the stake. Others were drowned, beheaded, and hanged from the gallows. They stepped forward with a smile on their lips, praising God that they were accounted worthy to suffer for Jesus' sake. Their persecutors were unable to drive out the love of God that burned in their hearts."

Grootvader cleared his throat and continued, "The Anabaptists did not set their hearts on the treasures of this earth, for they had pitched their tents on the shores of eternity. Their faith had a firm foundation. Persecution could not shake their assurance in the promises of God nor strip them of their reward. God was their all in all, and He gave them grace to bear their suffering without fear."

Johan leaned forward with clasped hands, listening as Grootvader told of terrible sufferings of the past.

Grootvader paused with a faraway look, then continued. "Johan, all this shedding of innocent blood did not take place without fruit. Many were moved to think seriously about eternity, and Anabaptists began popping up everywhere. So much so that the authorities began killing the Christians at night so people would not be influenced by their joyful deaths."

Suddenly Grootvader gasped and clutched his chest. His face turned pale—his lips blue.

"Grootvader!" exclaimed Johan, springing to his side, "you've overtired yourself. Maybe you should stop and continue another day."

"No, Johan, I feel better now," he said, smiling faintly. "Please sit down and I'll continue."

Johan watched Grootvader's face closely as he continued telling the story.

"In some places the prisons and dungeons were full of Christians. They lived on bread and water and there was no heat or fresh air in their damp, moldy cells. Many died there. Their persecutors thought this would dampen and extinguish the fire of God, but the prisoners sang loudly and rejoiced, causing their enemies to fear. Many Anabaptists who were not in prisons fled for their lives to other countries where they were offered a place of refuge. They left all their possessions behind except what they could carry. Two places of refuge were Alsace in France and Palatinate in Germany."

"Grootvader," interrupted Johan, "did your family continue to attend the secret meetings?"

"Yes, we did, Johan, and I have never regretted it. We were convinced that the Swiss Mennonites were right in what they were doing and believing. We, of course, had been baptized as babies, but we wanted to become one of their group, so we requested 'believer's baptism'. We knew it might mean imprisonment or death, but we were willing to suffer for Christ's sake."

"How old were you at this time, Grootvader, and were you married?" asked Johan.

"I was around 23, and had been married only one year, but my dear Gretel was one hundred percent in agreement with our decision to join the Swiss Mennonites and to be rebaptized. We had learned to truly love God. Remember, Johan, if you want to have a happy marriage, never marry an unbeliever. You must both love God with all your heart."

"I know you're right, Grootvader. I've been praying for God's leading," Johan confided.

"That's good, Johan! I've been praying about it too, because I want you to have a happy Christian home."

"Thank you, Grootvader. I'm glad you're praying about my future. You have been like a father to me. While my father worked long hours on the dikes, you helped me memorize many Scriptures and poems, and I'm very grateful," said Johan, with deep emotion.

"And you are like a son, like my dear son Henric." Grootvader stopped and brushed a tear from his eye. "Johan, those memorized Scriptures and poems hidden in your heart will help you not to sin against God." Grootvader's eyes were shining with love. "Will you pour me a cup of tea? I'm not used to all this talking and my throat is dry."

Johan set a cup of tea on the stand beside his grootvader, who took the cup eagerly and drank deeply. "Ah, that's better. Now I'm ready to finish my story." He cleared his throat and continued. "News had reached the Mennonites in Holland that a fresh outbreak of severe persecution was being endured by the brotherhood in Switzerland. They were deeply touched, and through their relief organization, they contributed 50,000 guilders to help the oppressed flee to a country of refuge. Holland opened its doors to any of us who wanted to come."

"But Grootvader," asked Johan, "how were you able to get away from those who wanted to persecute you?"

"I'll tell you. Soon after Holland had made this decision, two brethren from their country met with us in a secret meeting. They said if we were willing to leave our farms and possessions behind, they would give us enough financial aid so we could flee to Holland. More than 400 Swiss Mennonite refugees, including both Gretel's and my parents and most of our brothers and sisters, agreed to leave all and trust God to take care of us in a new country. We were advised to break up into smaller groups of fifteen to twenty for safety's sake. This time of flight was doubly hard for my dear Gretel because she was nearly due to give birth to our first child—your father. I hesitated, but Gretel insisted that we must go. She didn't want her condition to stand in the way of religious freedom. We had to travel at night, sleeping during the day in deserted barns, or sometimes in the woods or in caves. To make a long story short, Henric, a very husky child, was born in a deserted barn. From there on, for several days, five brethren offered to help me carry my wife and baby on a makeshift stretcher made of a sturdy blanket wrapped around two sapling poles."

"Oh, that would have been hard for Grootmoeder," sympathized Johan, "and for you too, because I'm sure that you were continually thinking of the possibility that the Anabaptist hunters might appear and capture your group."

"Yes, it was a tense time, but we clearly felt God's presence. One group was caught and taken to prison, but there were 400 of us Swiss Brethren refugees who made it safely to the harbor, and were loaded onto four ships. On August 2, 1711, we docked at Utrecht in Holland. We were oh, so happy, but so very poor. All 400 of us knelt there on the shore and thanked God. We knew God had been with us this far and would continue to be our faithful guide. Always remember, Johan, that God is completely trustworthy, no matter the circumstance. It has been 56 years since we began our life in Holland and I am already seeing some decline in some of our churches. So far, it seems, our own church has retained their 'first love' for God and His Word." With eyes brimming with love, Grootvader said, "I do not regret our move, my son, when I see your staunch faith in God. I'm sure many and maybe all of my grandchildren would have lost their lives or faith if we had stayed in Switzerland. We are no longer rich like we once were in Switzerland, but we are rich in faith. Do you enjoy life in Holland, my son?"

"Why, Grootvader, you forget, I was born here in Holland. That's all I've known, and yes, I enjoy life here. I just wish it weren't so hard to get ahead financially. It's true the herd is building up and we're now milking eight cows, but even though we sell milk, cheese, and butter, and raise tulip bulbs for sale, we still struggle to lay some money aside for anything special. If only Father hadn't died from the accident on the dikes."

"Ah, yes, Johan, I greatly miss your father too, but God in His wisdom knows what is best, and we must continue on and trust Him." Grootvader hesitated as he gently rocked his chair back and forth. Then he glanced at Johan with a tender smile. "You were talking about money for something special. Could that something be like you taking a *vrouw* (wife) and starting your own home? That takes money, doesn't it? Eh?" Grootvader chuckled as Johan flushed and didn't reply.

"Well, Johan, I may have good news for you. Just yesterday, your good friend, Jacob, said Mynheer (Mister) Voosterman is looking for a hardworking Dutch gardener for the beautiful grounds that surround his mansion and summerhouse. I believe you could do the work, for it seems everything grows under your care. Caring for your cows and delivering milk with your splendid dogcart doesn't take all of your time, and your sisters are good at making the cheese and butter. Would you be interested in having an extra job?"

"Yes, indeed, Grootvader, I'm very much interested in the job. I could get up an hour earlier and be free to work for Mynheer Voosterman by the stroke of nine bells."

"Ach vell, you'd best not be wasting your time talking with me then, but hurry home and discuss it with your mother and sisters. If they're agreed, maybe you should go right over to him and offer your services," encouraged Grootvader.

"Oh, I will, and thanks for speaking again of those wonderful memories from your past. These times we spend together are precious to me. I'm sure the things you have told me will help me to keep my trust in God if I should meet with hard times in my life."

While reaching for his cup of tea, Grootvader saw a piece of paper lying on the stand. He picked it up and said, "Johan, I almost forgot to tell you; an old friend stopped by a few days ago and gave me this poem, which was written by Charles Wesley, an English preacher. You have always been good at memorizing Bible verses as well as poetry and I've heard you making up tunes and singing the poems. This poem has moved me to tears and I would like for you to listen while I read it and maybe the Lord will give you a tune to go with it."

Slowly, haltingly, with Grootvader's limited reading abilities, the first verses were read.

"Jesus, lover of my soul,/Let me to Thy bosom fly,/While the nearer waters roll,/While the tempest still is high:/Hide me, O my Saviour, hide,/

Till the storm of life is past;/Safe into the haven guide,/O receive my soul at last."

After the rest of the poem was reverently read, Johan exclaimed, "Oh, Grootvader, that poem is wonderful; it nearly sings itself. How I wish I could have had enough schooling so I could read it."

"I knew you would appreciate it. I'll help you memorize it, Johan."

And so the gray head and the blond head set their hearts to the task of memorizing that great poem. When the work was completed, Grootvader said, "I'm pleased and satisfied that you have learned it well. Now if you will help me to my couch, Johan, I think I'll sleep awhile."

"I hope I haven't tired you too much, Grootvader," said Johan gently.

"No, Johan, I'm happy and satisfied with what we've accomplished during your visit."

After Johan had assisted him to the couch, he hurried home and discussed the possibility of an extra job with his family, who agreed enthusiastically.

chapter three

New Jobs for Johan and Hilda

Johan arrived at the Voosterman mansion and knocked gently on the door.

A servant opened the door and said, "Yes?"

"May I speak with Mynheer Voosterman, please?" asked Johan.

Soon a middle-aged gentleman appeared and commanded gruffly, "State your business."

"Mynheer, my name is Johan Blankenburg. I hear you are in need of a gardener to take care of your garden and beautiful grounds that surround your lovely home. I came to apply for the job."

Johan saw the man looking him over with a critical eye.

Finally, the gentleman spoke slowly. "You're probably strong enough, but do you know how to care for gardens and flowers? Have you any experience?"

"Yes," said Johan, "I take care of our large family garden, and we also raise tulips. We sell the flowers as well as the bulbs. I enjoy working with plants. You are welcome to come to our home and look at our gardens, if you wish."

"I suppose I'll have to take your word for it," came the gruff reply. "My wife's very ill and I can't—oh, well, never mind."

"Do you mean you will hire me then?" Johan asked eagerly.

"You may work for two weeks, and if your work is satisfactory, you may count on the job. Come to work next Monday; my present gardener will show you what is expected. That will be his last day of work here. I want you to know, young man, I expect promptness and good work from you, but don't expect me to pay the highest wages. Are you still interested?"

"Yes," agreed Johan. "I'll be here Monday morning at the stroke of nine bells." Then his voice turned serious with tender concern. "I'm very sorry about your wife and I hope she'll soon be well, Mynheer."

"Good day!" was Mynheer Voosterman's abrupt reply as he closed the door with force, completely ignoring Johan's concern over his sick wife.

Johan turned his steps toward home. *Mynheer Voosterman seems to have a cross nature, but it's a job and I'm happy for it. I guess I can't expect very high pay though. I wonder why he didn't seem pleased when I showed concern for his wife. I suppose he thought a stranger, a servant at that, is not worthy to show sympathy to such a rich man. I must remember to stay in my place.*

After working hard in the garden and tulip field that evening, Johan shared the good news with his family, who rejoiced with him.

"Johan," said his mother, "you are 21, so I insist that you keep the money you make at Mynheer Voosterman's for yourself. Someday you'll want a home of your own."

"Thank you, Mother," agreed Johan. "I'm sure there will be enough money coming in for you and the girls, so I'll do as you say." He glanced at Hilda and chuckled. "What's wrong with you, Hilda? You look as if you're about to burst. Out with it."

"Well!" exclaimed Hilda, exhaling a gusty breath. "I thought you'd never get done talking about your fine job. I just wanted to say that I did extra work today and I'm ready to try my hand at delivering the milk in the morning. Mother said she is willing for me to try."

"You must be extra careful with her, Johan," cautioned his mother. "I don't want any harm to come to Hilda."

"I'll take the best of care, Mother. I have the rest of this week to teach her all about it, and I have a feeling she's going to do a fine job. But, Hilda," said Johan, turning an earnest face toward his sister, "I don't want you to feel pushed into this, because I'm willing to get up an hour earlier so I can get to my job on time."

"Don't you worry, Johan. I'm determined to learn how to handle the milk route, so don't even consider losing an hour's sleep. I'm so excited, I suppose I'll be the one losing sleep—at least tonight," giggled Hilda.

"All right, Hilda. Tomorrow we'll give it a try," agreed Johan. "I'll do the milking, but you may come out and learn about straining the milk and pouring it into the brass pails and setting it to cool while we eat breakfast."

He gave a noisy yawn, stretching his arms above his head. "Well, I think I'll head for bed."

Johan spent more time than usual on his knees that evening. *Thank you, Lord, for the blessings of a happy family. It was hard when Father left us, but you are continually showering us with many other blessings—like this nice job as gardener and Hilda's desire to learn the milk route. I can see your hand in it all.*

Lord, you know how I long for a Christian wife, who loves you with all her heart and could also love me and be willing to share my joys and sorrows. I'm willing to wait on your leading, dear Father, for I know your choice will be best.

The next morning Hilda joined Johan in the milk house. They strained the milk, poured it into pails, and set it to cool in the milk trough. They hurried in for breakfast and were soon outside, ready to harness the dogs.

"I'll hold them this time," offered Johan. "You can place and buckle the harness."

Hilda harnessed the dogs with very little help and slowly drove to the milk house. They loaded the pails of milk and Hilda drove the dogs and cart out onto the road with Johan walking by her side.

Johan reached out, tapped the long leather whip sticking upright through a loop on the cart's sideboard, and said, "Hilda, never forget to take this whip with you when you're out delivering milk. Always keep the whip in this handy holder, just in case you meet some dogs that try to fight your team. Remember, you must hit hard enough so they'll know who is boss."

"I thought about that, Johan," Hilda replied with a smile, "so yesterday I practiced using the whip on a stump beside our barn. I tried to prepare for any dog fights."

"You're some girl, Hilda," said Johan, shaking his head. "You really mean business about taking over this delivery route, don't you?"

"I sure do," Hilda replied. Then she gasped, "Look!" Another dogcart was rapidly approaching, pulled by a bad-tempered team of dogs—snarling through bared teeth.

Hilda stopped the team at the edge of the road and grabbed the whip as the quarrelsome team headed straight for the dogs. Just before the two teams tangled, she brought her whip down hard, sharply nipping the feisty lead-dog on his nose. He gave a surprised yelp and dashed with his barking companions to the other side of the road, making their shouting driver trot to keep up.

"Well," said Johan, doubled over with laughter, "you certainly passed your test with flying colors. Practicing with the whip on that old stump really paid off. I couldn't have done better myself. Hey, are you all right? You look mighty pale."

"I—I think I'll be fine. I'm just a bit excited," said Hilda, suddenly flushing with pleasure at Johan's concern and praise.

As they passed the first house, Johan pointed, saying, "Look, Hilda, a big stork is nesting on the wagon wheel they've placed on their roof for that purpose."

"Johan, do you believe, like most Hollanders, that when a stork builds its nest on a roof, it will bring good luck to the people of that house?" Hilda studied her brother's face earnestly.

"No, I don't," replied Johan. "We know God made the stork and I think they are nice birds, but I believe God alone—not the stork—has control of the happenings in our lives."

"I thought you'd say that and I believe the same." Then she nodded toward the canal on their right. "Look over there—a group of our church ladies is doing their weekly wash. It's a lovely day to wash and chat with friends."

Suddenly all the women stopped and stared hard at Hilda. Janyce, her best friend, stuck her hand high above the women and waved. Hilda gave a quick wave before turning a corner and disappearing from their view.

"Now they're going to have something new to talk about," said Johan with a chuckle.

After finishing the stops on that side of the road, they turned the dog team and started back. Five stops later, their milk delivery was finished and Hilda finally had enough nerve to ask, "Johan, do you think your good friend Jacob Boekman is interested in our Greta? I saw him watching her on Sunday and Greta blushed."

"Really? I think Jacob would be embarrassed if he thought his desires were so obvious that Greta's younger sister observed his intent," Johan chuckled. "But you may as well know. You are right. Jacob has asked to come calling on Greta. Does that please you, Hilda?"

"Yes and no—there's no one I'd rather see Greta marry, but how I'll miss her if she leaves our home. She's so good and patient and fun to work with."

"Life is full of changes, so we may as well adjust cheerfully to them," encouraged Johan.

As they came near to Grootvader's cottage, Johan said, "When I visited Grootvader yesterday, he didn't seem to be feeling the best. Run in and see how he is while I take the dogs on home and then go after hot water to wash the buckets."

Johan watched as Hilda skipped happily between the rows of red tulips by Grootvader's house, then he hurried on home.

Later, when Johan was returning home with jars of hot water, he glanced up the road and was startled to see the *Aanspreeker** leaving his uncle's house. *Hm-m-m, I wonder who could have died? Mother will surely know.* He quickened his steps as he hurried his dogs along.

---

* Aanspreeker: one who dresses in black, notifies family and friends of a death, and attends funerals.

chapter four

Good-bye to Grootvader

Johan had just finished placing the last clean bucket on the rack to dry when his mother burst through the door. "Oh, Johan," she sobbed, "Grootvader has passed away. Hilda got there in time to hold his hand and hear his last words. She ran home to tell me and then returned to stay with the body while I ran to notify the Aanspreeker. I just got back. How we'll miss him!"

Johan pulled his weeping mother to him, patting her comfortingly. "Don't cry, Mother, you know how lonely he was for Grootmoeder, and he had such a longing to see his Saviour. I'm glad you sent me over there yesterday. We had such a special time together. I'll never forget it," said Johan, with an emphatic shake of his head.

"Why, Johan, that must have been what Grootvader was referring to in his last words."

"What were his last words, Mother?"

"Hilda said his chest was giving him terrible pain, but he said, 'The most important thing you can ever do is to be faithful to God, Hilda.' Then he gave a big sigh and said, 'I'm so glad I talked with Johan yesterday. It was such a blessing. Get him to tell the whole family what we talked about.' Then he gave a contented sigh, smiled, and was gone. Do you know what he meant?"

"Yes, Mother," Johan said with deep emotion, "I'm sure I know. When our whole family comes together before the funeral, I'll tell them the things he shared with me—how God was faithful to them all their life, even when things were difficult and hard to understand. He had a great concern for the church and especially our family. He felt, and I agree with him, that his story will encourage us to stay close to God."

The Blankenburg family came together in the afternoon to prepare Grootvader's body for the funeral, which was to take place the following day. When Jacob Boekman asked whether he could be of service to the family, Johan told him it would be very helpful if he would do the evening and morning milking and also deliver the morning milk.

After laying their dear one into a homemade casket, they carried him the short distance to the Blankenburg home, which was bigger than Grootvader's little cottage.

Hilda ran back and gathered a nice bouquet of Grootmoeder's red tulips and placed them in a vase beside the casket.

"I'm glad you thought of that, Hilda. May I have just one of the flowers to place in Grootvader's hand?" asked Johan.

"Sure, but why do you want to do that?" queried Hilda.

"I'll explain in a moment, Hilda."

Then Johan stood up and faced his family. He spoke around a lump in his throat. "When I was over at Grootvader's house yesterday, he said he was so lonesome for Grootmoeder that he often sat at a place where he could touch her tulips. He said it helped him to be less lonesome. So I thought it would seem right to place one of her tulips in his hand. We all know they had a special love for each other. I'm glad they'll never be parted again and they're with their Saviour whom they both loved so well."

Pausing to gain control of his emotions, Johan continued, "Grootvader's dying request, while Hilda was holding his hand, was that I should tell you what he shared with me yesterday."

The family listened quietly as Johan told about the concerns Grootvader had expressed and of the hardships Grootvader and Grootmoeder had endured because of their faith and love for God.

"Then just before I left," Johan said, "Grootvader shared a wonderful poem which a close friend had given to him a couple days before. He helped me memorize it and then encouraged me to put a tune to it. I'll try to sing it." Johan cleared his throat and began. "Jesus, lover of my soul, Let me to Thy bosom fly. . ."

When the song ended, many eyes were moist. How true it was—Grootvader had flown to his Saviour's bosom.

That evening their church family and community friends came to show their last respects for a dearly loved brother in the church. There were those who came prepared, as the custom was, to sit up the whole night in the room with the body. The time was spent in singing and there was plenty of food for any who might be hungry. Also, there were periods of weeping as one or another recounted precious memories.

In the morning, the whole family gathered to walk behind the donkey and cart that would carry their loved one to the church for the funeral service.

After several days, the Blankenburg family settled back into their usual pattern of daily living, but in their hearts they were still grieving. Grootvader had filled a very important part in their lives.

During the rest of that week, Hilda proved she was well able to deliver the morning milk with the dogcart. She was enjoying every minute of it, and even Mother and Johan were satisfied that she was fully capable.

On Monday morning at the stroke of nine bells, Johan appeared promptly for work in the beautiful gardens of Mynheer Voosterman.

The gardener, who was unlocking the tool shed, looked up and smiled as he saw Johan approaching. "So you're hoping to be the new gardener. I believe your name is Johan. Right?"

"Yes, that's right," assured Johan. "And you're supposed to teach me what is expected from a good gardener. I'm determined to do my best."

"That's good. I'm glad to hear it. Here, take these clipping shears," he said, handing them to Johan. "We'll get started right away."

They were busy all day, snipping here and clipping there, weeding, digging, and planting.

When the day's work was finished, a servant approached Johan and said, "Mynheer Voosterman would like to talk with you."

"I'll be right there as soon as I hang this last tool in the shed," agreed Johan.

Now what does he want? Johan wondered as he walked rapidly toward the house where the master was standing in the doorway.

"I believe you wished to speak to me, Mynheer Voosterman?" inquired Johan.

"Yes, I was wondering if you might know of some woman who would be willing to work here during the summer months—to can and preserve fruits and vegetables from our gardens?"

"No, I don't know of anyone, but I'll ask around and maybe I can find someone for you," offered Johan.

"I want it understood that it must be a woman who is hardworking, dependable, and knows how to do a good job, so the food is fit to eat when she's done."

"I understand and I'll do my best," agreed Johan.

The door was closed without a thank-you.

Johan thought over the happenings of the day as he walked home. As he approached his friend Jacob's house, he decided to stop and ask for his help.

"Ho, Jacob," he called from the yard gate.

"Coming," shouted Jacob, striding out to join his friend. "How did your first day go at your new job?"

"I think it went well, and I believe I'll enjoy the work. But I have a question for you. Mynheer Voosterman wants some lady to work for him this summer—someone who is a hard worker, dependable, and knows how to do a good job at canning and preserving fruits and vegetables. Do you know of anyone looking for such a job?"

"Hmm," said Jacob, while squinting his eyes and scratching his head. "You know, my uncle was here just today and he said his daughter, Margaret, would like to have a summer job. I suppose I should walk the five miles over there tonight and find out."

"Sounds fine. I'll stop by in the morning then. Thanks for your help." With a wave of his hand, Johan hurried toward home.

chapter five

The Singing Gardener

The next morning Johan stopped at Jacob's gate. "Ho, Jacob. What's the news? Did you find someone?"

"I think so," shouted Jacob, his head appearing at the door. "My uncle and cousin plan to stop in and talk with Mynheer Voosterman tomorrow morning. You can give him the news."

"All right! Thanks, Jacob." With a wave of his hand, he hurried on.

He gave the news to his master, and then spent most of the day weeding the garden. *Those beans are hanging full and in a week they'll be ready to pick—and it looks like there will be a bumper crop of tomatoes,* observed Johan.

Later, while trimming the rosebushes, he considered a poem by Isaac Watts, which he had memorized and set to his own tune. Soon the inspiring words of "When I Survey the Wondrous Cross" were floating across the gardens.

When that song was finished, he sang "Jesus, Lover of My Soul." The master of the house heard the singing and came to an upstairs window, where his sick, God-fearing wife, Mary, lay in her bed. She, too, was intently listening. The kitchen servants came out onto the porch and the servant who cared for the carriage and horses stuck his head around the corner of the barn and cupped his hand behind his ear. When they returned to their work, they had something new to think about and their faces were less careworn. They were beginning to thoroughly enjoy their singing gardener.

Several days later the master's wife took a turn for the worse. Rychie, her husband, hovered close by her bed.

"Rychie," came Mary's weak voice, "please ask our gardener to come to my room and sing, 'Jesus, Lover of My Soul.'"

"I'm sorry, Mary, but it just wouldn't be proper to allow him into this room. We must remember he's only a poor servant." But after seeing his wife's disappointment, he added grudgingly, "I guess I could go down and ask him to stand close to the house and sing. Would that please you, Mary?"

"Yes, thank you, Rychie," gasped Mary, with a faint smile.

Mynheer Voosterman found Johan in the tool shed sharpening the tools. He found it embarrassing and humiliating to ask a favor of a mere servant. He cleared his throat loudly and said gruffly, "My wife wants you to sing 'Jesus, Lover of My Soul'. Stand close to the house over there." He pointed toward the open upstairs window. Then he stalked back to his wife, not waiting for Johan's reply.

As Johan quickly brushed the dirt from his hands, he breathed a quick prayer to God and walked rapidly to the appointed place. In sweet and tender tones, he sang the lovely words.

"Jesus, lover of my soul/Let me to Thy bosom fly . . ."

The sun was setting when Johan walked past the front of the mansion on his way home. He noticed the black crape hanging on the door. It could mean only one thing. Bowing his head, he prayed from the depths of his heart, *Thank you, Lord, for using me to comfort that sick woman in her final hour of need. Be near those who are sorrowing.*

A few days later Johan was trimming the hedge along the driveway when he saw a slender young girl standing on the back porch with a bushel basket in her hand. She was looking about, rather uncertainly. Her simple dress was neat, and she had a beautiful face.

But, shrugged Johan, *beauty is only skin-deep. Time will tell what she's really like.*

He saw the cook come out on the porch and talk to the girl, while pointing out directions to the vegetable gardens. *Oh,* thought Johan, *that must be Jacob's cousin. She's got a big job on her hands. When I finish this hedge, I'll see if she needs some help.*

After hanging the hedge trimmer in the shed, he picked up another basket. While humming a tune, he approached the girl.

Johan cleared his throat. "Hello, you must be Jacob's cousin, Margaret. I'm Johan, the new gardener and a good friend of Jacob's. I believe, by the looks of those beanstalks, you have a big job. Want help filling your basket?"

Margaret glanced quickly at Johan, then returned to swiftly plucking beans from the overburdened stalks. "You guessed right. My name is Margaret, and yes, it does look like a big job. The beans are beautiful and there are more than I expected. I appreciate your kind offer, but I wouldn't want to hinder you from your work."

"I think I have time to help you and still get my own work done," Johan replied. He swiftly but carefully began pulling the beans from the stalks and putting them into the basket he carried. When his basket was half full, he emptied it into Margaret's basket, making it nearly full.

"Are you living in the big house this summer?" inquired Johan.

"Yes, I'll be living here during the week, but I'll be free to leave on Saturday at 4:30 and spend Sunday with Cousin Jacob's family. I wouldn't want to miss the worship service on Sunday. I'm glad God wants us to rest on His day." She continued working while she talked.

"Yes, a day of rest and worship is very important," Johan agreed, eyeing her basket. "Your basket is full. You can take it to the house and get started preparing the beans for canning. I'll finish picking and set them in the shade on the back porch when I'm finished. I think you can count on another bushel."

"That will be a great help. Thank you. I think some of the servants in the house will help me prepare them. With so much help, I should be done before too late this evening." She lifted the basket of beans and hurried toward the house.

While Johan's fingers were busy filling his basket, he was convinced about several things. *Besides being beautiful, she's no flirt, she's not lazy, and she considers a day of worship to be important. Very interesting!*

He placed the basket of beans on the porch, then strode to the shed and put two more baskets in the wheelbarrow and headed for the apple orchard. The early apples were ready to pick.

The ladies in the house listened while the strains of sweet music drifted in from the orchard.

When there was a lull between songs, Molly, the cook, said, "Mynheer Voosterman got a real bargain when he hired that singing gardener."

Margaret listened with interest to Molly's words, and the other servants nodded their heads in agreement.

chapter six

A New Song

The weeks went by swiftly, with Johan doing the morning milking at home, then working as gardener during the day and helping Hilda with the evening milking. He worked in his tulip fields before the morning milking and again after the evening milking. Life was full, but he was strong and enjoyed his work.

One evening after milking the last cow, Hilda turned to Johan and said, "When I go to get hot water, Dame Bowman likes to talk about you."

"Really? What does she say?"

"She said, 'That brother of yours gets the credit for my becoming a Christian. If he hadn't invited me to church and then come out when I hesitated outside the church doors and walked with me into the church and showed me where to sit, I never would have become a Christian. He must have seen me wiping tears during the service because he asked if I wanted to speak with the pastor. He took me to the pastor and stayed with me until the way of salvation was fully explained to me and I accepted it. It's such a relief to know that I'm ready to meet my Maker.' She said to give you a special 'thank-you' from her," said Hilda, admiration written on her face. "I'm glad to be your sister, Johan."

"Thanks, Hilda, for sharing that bit of encouragement. I feel unworthy of such praise, for it was the Lord's doings. Without Him, I can do nothing. God wants to use each of us as instruments in His hand. Hilda, you can tell Dame Bowman I rejoice that she is a Christian, but to give the praise to God, for He alone is worthy."

"I'll tell her, Johan, but you were a willing instrument in God's hand, and I'm glad."

While Johan and Margaret worked for Mynheer Voosterman, they observed each other's work habits and how both reacted with respect to their curt master, their fellow servants, family, and friends.

They looked forward to their Saturday evening walk to Jacob's home. As they walked, they explored each other's beliefs about God and the church.

One evening Margaret asked, "Johan, how do you know so many songs? Many of them I had never heard before."

Johan's face flushed. "You see, our family is poor and we all work hard to make a living, so I was never privileged to go to school and learn how to read and write. After my father's death, I needed to learn how to add and subtract money, so I could manage the business for our family. I'm very grateful that Grootvader helped me to memorize many Scriptures and poems. Since I love to sing, I began putting tunes to the many poems I learned. It's my way of worshiping God throughout the day."

"That's interesting! All the workers at the Voosterman mansion are encouraged by your singing," said Margaret.

"It's my desire to always be an encourager and bring praise to God," said Johan humbly.

"You mentioned about being poor. Well, my family has to work hard, too," admitted Margaret. "My parents even bought me a Bible and had high hopes of sending me to school, so I could read it to them, but money was scarce and it never happened. But they were diligent in helping me to memorize the Scriptures they knew, and for that I'm thankful."

As Johan walked on home, he began to wonder, *Is this the one God has chosen for me? We seem to be in agreement in things that are important.*

That night Johan prayed more earnestly, *Lord, is this the girl you have chosen to be my life companion? Please lead me each step of the way. As I look on her outward appearance, she's beautiful, but you, O Lord, can see her heart. I'm open, Lord, for you to open or close doors to our friendship.*

But God did not close any doors and their friendship flourished. Johan was convinced God's hand was leading them together.

When the summer work was finished for Margaret, her family came to take her home. They attended church with Jacob's family on that last Sunday.

After the service was over, Johan, with fast-beating heart, approached

Peter Boekman, Margaret's father. "Mynheer, would you allow me to come calling on your daughter, Margaret?"

With a look of understanding, the father said, "I've heard many good things about you, Johan. Yes, you may come calling. If for some reason Margaret thinks otherwise, I'll send you word within the week. Is that agreeable?"

"Certainly, and I thank you," said Johan. Relief washed through him as he quickly joined his friends outside the church.

The next week was a time of waiting. *Will Margaret's father send word that she is not in agreement? I must remember I want God's choice, not mine.* When the week passed with no word from Margaret's father, Johan breathed a sigh of relief.

The next six months went well for Johan and Margaret and they felt God was leading them to marriage. Johan shared with her the special talk he had with Grootvader, and they promised each other and God that they would be faithful to Him no matter what the future held.

It was decided that they would live in Grootvader's little cottage. Merry hours were spent together as Greta and Hilda helped Margaret with the cleaning. How that little house shone!

Several evenings before the wedding, Margaret said, "Johan, for our wedding gift, my parents plan to give us a beautiful trunk where we can store important papers and clothing. Do you think we can carry it five miles or will we need a cart to bring it to the cottage?"

"I believe we should get a cart," decided Johan. "I'm sure Jacob will let us use his donkey and cart. I'll ask him."

The snow glistened like millions of diamonds in the crisp February air as the Blankenburg family, dressed in their Sunday best, walked briskly toward Margaret's home. It was a day of anticipation and the whole family wanted to share in Johan's joy when he would take Margaret to be his bride. They were glad for Jacob's donkey and cart, which gave transportation for some food for the noonday meal.

Johan's brother Karl asked, "Is it all right for my two youngest children to ride? I'll be glad to drive the donkey. That way I can keep an eye on the little ones."

"Certainly, and thank you, brother," said Johan, handing over the reins. Karl's other two children looked up at Johan with shy admiration as they caught hold of his hands and walked along together.

The wedding took place in the forenoon at Margaret's home, with the preacher and both families attending, followed by a delicious meal together.

When they were done eating, they loaded the cart and it was time for the final good-byes. Annie, Margaret's mother, held her daughter a bit longer than usual. She didn't trust her voice, but love was very evident as they looked deep into one another's eyes.

Her father's voice was husky as he took his daughter's hand in both of his. "We'll miss you, Margaret. We wish you much happiness. We are content that you have a good husband." Then he embraced Johan. "God bless you, my son. We welcome you into our family."

"Thank you for your kindness. It will be good to have a father in my life again," said Johan, with feeling.

With many a backward wave, the family started on their way home.

After a period of silence and steady walking, Johan said in quiet tones for Margaret's ears only, "Margaret, I wish I weren't so poor, so we could afford to take a few days off and do something special."

"Don't worry about that, Johan," assured Margaret. "We have that sweet little cottage of your Grootvader's waiting for us. I'm looking forward to keeping house for you and caring for Grootmoeder's tulips. With God's help, we can be just as happy together as they were."

"You're right, of course, and I need to count my blessings instead of wishing for more. Thank you for looking on the bright side even though you married a poor man," said Johan. "God is so good to give me such a good wife."

"It is my desire to be a good wife and I want you to know that I feel rich, not in earthly treasures, but I have been given a husband who dearly loves the Lord, and who is rich in spiritual values. I believe Grootvader's prayers were answered in bringing us together. I feel honored to be your wife, Johan."

"Thank you, Margaret! You have set my mind at rest. May we always seek first the kingdom of God, and then He has promised to give us what we need."

Suddenly their attention was drawn to a sight on the canal, which ran parallel with the road. Several women had been harnessed to a draw boat and were pulling it to the next town.

"Those poor women!" exclaimed Margaret. "They are probably desperate for a few stivers so they can feed their hungry kinder. I feel so sorry for them."

"Yes, and I feel sorry for the hungry little ones, whose fathers are most likely spending their money on drink. I promise you, Margaret, I will never touch the vile stuff."

"Thank you, Johan. That means a lot to me."

Karl, while driving the donkey, suddenly shouted, "Look up the road!"

They all craned their necks to see, and then Johan exclaimed, "It's the whole group of young people from our church! How nice of them to come and join us on our happy day!" Johan and Margaret raised their arms and waved energetically.

When the young folks saw them waving, they broke into a run and soon joined the wedding guests.

"We were afraid you'd think we were intruding, but when you waved, we knew we were welcome," explained Jacob. "We wanted to share in your happy day by walking along with you to your home. Here is a bag of gifts for your kitchen, Margaret. I'll jog up there and put them in the cart and give my little donkey the honor of transporting them."

"That was very thoughtful and we thank you for the gifts," said Johan, looking at the group surrounding them, while Margaret nodded her head, eyes shining.

Laughing and talking, the happy group turned the last two miles of their trip into a joyous occasion. Many neighbors came out on their porches and gave them a smile and a cheery greeting.

When they were nearly home, Johan's mother approached Johan and Margaret and quietly said, "Feel free to offer them a bite to eat. I would be happy to share the little cakes which were made yesterday, and we have plenty of cold milk and cheese to serve with the cake. You may use our house, since your house is too small for a group this size."

"Thanks, Mother. You are so thoughtful and kind," said Margaret, squeezing her mother-in-law's hand.

They stopped at Johan and Margaret's cottage and unloaded the trunk and the bag of gifts. Then with an empty cart they traveled on to Mother's house. The tired donkey was given a drink and tied to the hitching post, with a nosebag of grain attached under his chin.

Johan invited the group to stop in for games and refreshments and they gladly accepted. But when it was chore time, the group dispersed—all except Jacob, who offered to take Johan's place in helping Hilda with the evening milking.

"You're a true friend, Jacob, and I'll accept your offer," said Johan, smiling first at Jacob and then at Margaret. *What joy! How wonderful to walk arm in arm with my precious bride up the tulip-lined path to our own little cottage!*

chapter seven

Susie Is Encouraged

While Johan and Margaret were walking over to his mother's house to help with the evening milking, Johan said, "Mynheer Voosterman asked if you would be willing to do the summer canning again. He said I could help you so you wouldn't need to work late in the evening. But I've been noticing that you were a bit pale lately, so I didn't promise him that you would. I like having you right here in our home, so don't feel that you must accept the job."

"Johan, I was hoping to tell you this sooner, but I wanted to be sure. I think I'm with child, Johan. That is probably why I might have looked pale at times."

"Oh, Margaret, I'm so pleased about the baby and I'm so relieved." Johan exhaled a big sigh.

"Relieved? Why do you feel relieved?" questioned Margaret.

"Well, when I saw your pale face each morning and you didn't eat much, I thought you were terribly homesick and were regretting you had married me, but instead we're going to have a precious little one to teach and train in the ways of the Lord. Oh, I feel like shouting! God is so good to us. Of course, I'll tell Mynheer Voosterman you will not be coming to work this summer." Johan gave Margaret's hand an extra squeeze.

"Yes, I think that is best, because I will need to be canning and drying food for our own use and making baby clothes. It's all very exciting and I'm sure I'll soon be feeling better."

The happy months flew past while Johan and Margaret worked together and prepared for the little one to come. Summer was nearly over and the shelves in their little pantry held many jars of fruit and vegetables. The little bag of coins, kept in their trunk, was slowly gaining weight with their savings.

Supper was over, but Johan and Margaret remained at the table, just enjoying their time together. Johan had something special on his mind. "Margaret, I've noticed that you and Susie Granforbs enjoy talking together quite often after church. Her husband, Karl, spoke to me last Sunday. They are planning to sail for America on Friday. He says Susie is a good friend to you and they would like to have us go with them to the docks in Rotterdam and see them off on their journey. Would you like to do that?"

"They're going to America? Why would they do a thing like that?" asked Margaret, her eyes wide in surprise.

"Supposedly it is easier to make a living there, so they've decided to go. Then, too, Karl has cousins there who will help them out. What do you say, shall we tell them we'll go with them to the docks? If you don't feel up to it, that's fine. I'll understand, Margaret."

"Yes, that's fine, Johan. I'd love to be with Susie when she leaves. Just think, we may never see them again. That will be a special time for all of us. I feel honored that they want us to be with them."

"All right then! I'm glad you feel up to going. If Mynheer Voosterman will give me permission to have two days off, I'll stop by Karl's house on my way home tomorrow evening and tell him we have agreed to go with them to the docks. It will be good to enjoy something different for a change. Would you like to spend Saturday and Sunday with your parents?"

"Oh, that would be extra special. Do you think it would be possible, Johan, to show my mother the quilt and baby clothes I've made?" asked Margaret, her face lighting up with anticipation.

"I think that could be worked out. We can take our trunk, since that is where we store our clothes and quilt and the things you've made for the baby. I'm sure Karl would let us put it on the oxcart with their luggage. Karl's brother, Hans, is driving their parents' oxen to take their things. I'll need to send word for your parents to meet us at the docks on Saturday morning with their donkey and cart. Maybe they will let us use it to transport our trunk home again. They only live a couple miles from the docks, so that should work, don't you think?"

"Oh, I hope so, Johan. It will be so good to see my family again, and you're so kind." Margaret went about with a light step as she cleared the table and washed the dishes. She had a continual smile as thoughts of good things to come went through her mind.

Throughout the next day, Margaret wondered anxiously, *Will Mynheer Voosterman agree to let Johan have two days off?* When evening came, Margaret met her husband at the door.

"The plans are all made, Margaret," said Johan with a big smile. "Mynheer Voosterman wasn't too happy about it, but he finally said if I was willing to work an hour extra each day till then, I could go. Karl and Susie are very pleased about it too."

After Karl and Susie Granforbs gave tearful good-byes to their family and friends, their oxen were soon plodding up the road and stopped at Johan's cottage. Johan and Margaret were waiting beside the road with their trunk. Johan's mother and sisters got there just in time to see them off. Johan swung the trunk onto the cart and then turned to give a good-bye to his mother and sisters.

Hilda gave the trunk a look of concern. "Why are you taking your trunk? You are coming back, aren't you?"

"Yes, we plan to be back, Hilda. You see, it's like this: Margaret made some things she wanted to show her mother; that's the reason for taking the trunk. Don't you worry, Hilda. Keep those dogs in line and don't spoil them with too much attention while I'm gone," teased Johan, with a chuckle.

"Oh, Johan, you know they thrive on attention," said Hilda, giving her brother a playful punch on his arm.

After a last farewell, they started on their way.

"We can't tell you how happy we are to have you come with us," said Karl. "We didn't give you a wedding gift, so we've decided to pay for your sleeping quarters at the lodging house on the docks. We'll eat our last supper together there."

Margaret saw Susie's lips quivering and thought, *Poor Susie, it must be hard for her to leave her family and friends. She'll likely never see them again. I wonder what it will be like in America?*

Margaret reached out and clasped Susie's hand as they walked toward Rotterdam. Neither one felt like talking; tears were too near the surface.

When they arrived at the docks, Johan asked, "Do you girls feel rested since your last hour's ride? Would you like to take a walk along the wharf and see the sights?"

"I'd like that," Margaret decided. "We don't want to miss anything, do we, Susie?" Susie agreed.

"I'd like that, too," said Karl, "but first I'd better put our luggage on the ship. We'll be sleeping there tonight."

"You're right! Here, let me help," offered Johan, reaching for one of the containers.

"No, that won't be necessary, Johan," objected Karl. He gave a shrill whistle through his teeth and motioned for a stevedore*. After explaining the situation to the proprietor in the lodging house, they carried Johan and Margaret's trunk to a safe corner within. Then Johan walked to the ship with Margaret and Susie, while the stevedores stowed Karl and Susie's few possessions into the hold.

The ship's captain came swaggering along and stopped in front of Johan, looking him over. "Captain Boswell speaking!" He pointed proudly to his chest. "Want to come on board and have a look around? I can tell by the look in your eye you're hankerin' to learn a bit about ships. Bring your lady friends up the gangplank and look around. My *Minerva* is a right good ship. We've been friends for many a year."

"Would you like to go aboard, Margaret?" asked Johan eagerly.

"Oh, please, not yet!" interjected Susie, grasping Margaret's arm. "Please stay with me, Margaret. I'm not ready to go on board yet."

"Why don't you go ahead with the captain, Johan. Susie and I will stay right here and watch all the excitement on the wharf," replied Margaret.

Johan had noticed some shady-looking characters, so he stepped forward and shook the captain's hand and said, "I thank you, Captain Boswell, for your kind offer, but I don't like to leave my wife and her friend alone. Karl and Susie Granforbs will be sailing with you. Please take special care of our good friends as they sail to America."

"They'll get the best care possible," promised the captain. "Maybe when your friends come on board for the night, you can come up for a visit then. Think it over. Be glad to show you around." He wheeled around, hurried across the wharf, and marched up the gangplank of the *Minerva*. Before he disappeared into the captain's cabin, he turned and gave them a friendly wave.

"Please forgive me, Johan," implored Susie, "for spoiling your chance to look around inside the ship. I'm a big baby, I know."

"Don't worry. If we really want to look around, we can go with you and Karl when you turn in for the night. I wasn't about to leave you two here alone with those rough-looking characters over there," said Johan, nodding toward the building close by.

The girls looked and shuddered.

Joy lit Susie's face as her husband came down the gangplank. "Oh, there comes Karl." She gave a relieved sigh and the worry wrinkles smoothed

*Stevedore: one hired to load and unload ships.

away.

After everything was stowed away, Karl and his brother, Hans, gripped each other's hand. Finally Karl said, his voice husky with emotion, "Thank you, brother, for bringing us to the docks. I'll miss you greatly. Just wish you were going with us."

"Maybe I'll come later. I'm very glad we have cousins in America who will help you and Susie when you need it. I'd like to stay here with you tonight, but Father said he would need the oxen in the morning. God bless you, my brother, and keep you safe." They pulled out their handkerchiefs and blew their noses, then with another hearty handclasp, the brothers parted. The two couples watched the oxcart slowly move down the road. Hans gave one last wave before disappearing.

Margaret and Susie were silently wiping tears as they watched the difficult parting.

Karl gave them a wobbly smile. "I believe we're ready for our walk now. You girls stay close behind Johan and me. We don't want to lose you in all the hustle and bustle here on the wharf. A brisk walk and breathing in some good salt air will do us all good, and give us a good appetite."

Margaret and Susie looped their arms together and tried to stay within a safe distance of their husbands.

"Margaret," confessed Susie, "time and again I wanted to share with you at church about our going to America. I wasn't trying to keep it a secret from you, but I feared I'd cry if we discussed it there, and everyone would stare. I've always been shy, so I don't make friends easily. I felt so blessed when you began talking to me at church."

"My dear Susie," murmured Margaret, squeezing her arm, "I loved you the first time we met. I did sense there was something bothering you the last while, but I knew you would share with me when the time was right."

"Oh, Margaret, I don't know what I will do in America, if something should happen to Karl," Susie confessed. "Everyone over there will be strangers; maybe we won't even be able to speak their language. I wish I could be brave. I-I think I could be brave if you and Johan were going with us to America."

"Try to remember, Susie, the Lord is with you," Margaret comforted. "He will help you with every problem. There's a Scripture in Psalm 34 that goes like this: 'The angel of the Lord encampeth round about them that fear him, and delivereth them.' Isn't that a wonderful promise? You can fully trust Him, because He's the same yesterday, today, and forever."

"Thank you, Margaret, for that wonderful encouragement. I admire your faith in God and for all the Scriptures you have memorized."

"Susie, I have wonderful, godly parents. They helped me memorize many Scriptures. Through their lives and the Scriptures, I learned to trust God. I thank God if I have been able to encourage you."

Margaret glanced over her shoulder at the sound of hurrying footsteps on the boardwalk. "Oh, Susie, let's walk a bit faster. Our husbands are getting ahead and they told us to try to keep close to them."

Their husbands turned when they heard them puffing up behind them.

Johan said, "I guess we were walking too fast. Why don't you walk in front; that way we'll stay together?"

At the end of the boardwalk, they joined hands and faced the ocean. With the sea breeze ruffling their hair, they listened to the water as it lapped against the shore. It seemed so peaceful. Suddenly Johan's rich tenor voice reverently and softly rang out.

God moves in a mysterious way,/His wonders to perform;/He plants His footsteps in the sea/And rides upon the storm.

Ye fearful saints, (he looked at Karl and Susie) *fresh courage take;/The clouds ye so much dread/Are big with mercy and shall break/In blessings on your head.*

Susie and Margaret were both wiping tears while Johan continued the song.

Judge not the Lord by feeble sense,/But trust Him for His grace;/Behind a frowning providence/He hides a smiling face.

Blind unbelief is sure to err,/And scan His work in vain;/God is His own interpreter,/And He will make it plain.

"Thank you, Johan," said Karl, his voice trembling. "Now will you lead us in prayer?"

With a nod, Johan began, "Our precious Heavenly Father, we thank you that your ways and thoughts are perfect. You do move in mysterious ways your wonders to perform. Help us all to learn, more perfectly, to trust you completely. We know you will go with Karl and Susie and keep them in your tender care, as You guide them through the many adjustments in the new world. We fully entrust them into your hands. We pray this through the precious name of Jesus, our Redeemer and Lord. Amen."

No one spoke as they listened to the lapping water.

Finally Susie said softly, "Thank you so much. I feel new strength in my weary soul. With God's help, we'll make it."

"Good girl!" encouraged Karl, giving Susie a big hug. "The Lord will surely see us through. Now, I'm hungry! Let's head for the lodging house."

chapter eight

Welcome Aboard!

In the lodging house, they sat down at a long table laden with heaping platters of plump sausages, dishes of sauerkraut, cheese, and potato salad. For dessert there were slices of gingerbread and pure water from the city of Utrecht, flavored with an orange. Everyone knew that pure water was scarce in Holland.

"Just think, Susie, we didn't lift a finger to prepare this delicious meal," said Margaret. "We're dining like rich people tonight."

"You're right, the food is delicious," spoke up Johan quickly, "but it's not a bit better than our wives can fix."

"You're right about that," agreed Karl, smiling as their wives' faces flushed with pleasure.

Captain Boswell came hustling through the lodging house door, stopped, stood on tiptoe, and searched the crowd. He made a beeline for Karl and Johan's table, pulled up a chair, sat down, and leaned forward eagerly. "I've been looking all over for you folks."

The proprietor saw the captain and hollered angrily, "Go away, Captain. Quit bothering my guests. I know you all too well. At least two of these folks are staying the night at my place. Now be on your way!" He pointed toward the door, while balancing a platter of sausages on the palm of his hand.

"Tut, tut, my friend, don't be so hasty. These folks have a right to make up their own minds," insisted the captain.

The proprietor growled, shrugged his shoulders, and hurried to the kitchen.

Captain Boswell leaned forward, saying, "How would you and your wife like to spend a night, free of charge, on my ship with your friends before they sail away? I'll make sure there is an empty bunk for you two, right next to your friends."

"Oh, please do," urged Susie, clasping her hands. "We may never see you again."

"The lady's right," agreed the captain with a smile. "What do you say? Do you want a once-in-a-lifetime experience? My ship won't sail till tomorrow."

With pleading eyes, Susie waited for Johan's answer.

"Are you willing, Margaret?" asked Johan.

"I'm willing, if you are," agreed Margaret.

"Oh, that's wonderful," cried Susie.

"That's great, just great!" exclaimed the captain. "I'll send two stevedores over to help you carry your things. I'll be waiting for you beside my sturdy *Minerva*."

Smiling with satisfaction, the captain swaggered toward the door. The proprietor shook his fist at him, but the captain gave a hearty laugh and was gone.

Captain Boswell was waiting for them. "Welcome on board my seaworthy *Minerva!*" He eyed their beautiful trunk with interest. "I'll show you to your sleeping quarters, but first I want you to meet this special lad by my side."

Captain Boswell placed his big hand on the head of a smiling ten-year-old. "This industrious lad has come quite a distance to sell his mother's baked goods. My sailors sent him to me and I bought the remainder of his goods. He needs a place to stay the night, so I offered him free lodging in my cabin. Pretty exciting, isn't it, lad? He goes by the name of Tommy." He playfully ruffled the boy's hair.

"Sure is exciting! I'll have some tale to tell Mother and my friends when I get home," said the boy, looking the ship over with bright eyes.

The captain chuckled and said, "Well, come along, lad. Let's show these folks where they will be sleeping."

The captain and Tommy led the way. Johan's first misgivings came when they were led down the walkway to the dark, stuffy hold below. *So this is where Karl and Susie will stay until they get to America. Poor Susie has that scared look in her eyes again. Lord, give her strength. Help us to be a strength to them.*

The interior of the hold was dimly lit from natural light coming through the open hatch, plus a few fish-oil lamps attached to the bulkheads. As their eyes adjusted to the dimness, the captain pointed out their sleeping quarters, which were partitioned off with rough pine boards. There was only three feet of space between the upper and the lower bunks. The beds were extra long and made of the same rough pine, but they were barely wide enough for two adults to sleep comfortably side by side. Each bunk had a straw-filled tick for a mattress.

The captain grabbed an upright support of the bed and shook it roughly. "These beds are mighty sturdy," he said proudly. "They won't collapse when the first storm hits. No siree, the *Minerva* is very dependable."

Johan saw Susie tremble at the mention of storms.

The captain motioned to the far side of the ship. "You'll find some old canvas discards from our old sails. Feel free to hang pieces up on the open side of your bed. It gives some nice privacy to families, as well as separating bachelors and spinsters. This hold is plenty big enough for all; it's 83 feet long, 24 feet wide, and 10 feet deep. Her length from rudder to stern is 120 feet. There's plenty of room, and we try to take good care of our passengers."

Tommy was eagerly looking about. He walked over to one of the buckets, stationed here and there throughout the hold, and raised the lid. He wrinkled his nose as he let out a gusty "Whee!" and slammed the lid back on.

"Well, now Tommy, you've discovered the 'necessary'. It's a must in every ship's hold," said the captain, doubling over with laughter.

"Then, too," he continued, "there's always a few people with weak stomachs, who can't stand the galloping of my frisky *Minerva*, and then those buckets are called on for double duty. It's easy for you to see we're fixed for every emergency. Now, you folks make yourselves at home. I hope you'll enjoy your night with us." He started to stride away and then said over his shoulder to the lad, "Tommy, you may as well stay and get acquainted with these good folks, but come to my cabin when you're ready to turn in for the night."

"All right, I'll come later," agreed Tommy. As the captain's footsteps faded away, the boy walked over to Margaret and said, "I'm sorry this isn't nicer. The captain's cabin is much nicer. I'd be glad to sleep here and let you sleep there, but I guess that wouldn't be right. You make me think of my mother."

"Thank you for the compliment, Tommy," said Margaret, laying her hand on his shoulder. "I'm sure you're very special to your mother and father. Won't they be worried if you don't come home tonight?"

"No, she's not expecting me home tonight, and my father died when I was only a year old. You see, I had to walk most all day yesterday so I could get to the docks and sell her baked goods to the sailors. I try to take good care of Mother, since I'm the man in our house now, but maybe not for long." Tommy lowered his voice to a loud whisper. "Because, you see, our preacher lost his wife and he's been visiting Mother regularly. I think a father would be nice to have and he seems nice."

"Son, I understand," said Johan, laying his hand on Tommy's other shoulder. "I also lost my father. He died from a fall while working on the dikes, but I wasn't so young. The loss of a father is difficult, I know. You're a good boy to help your mother so well. May God bless you with a good father, if it's His will."

Tommy's face broke into a big smile as he looked admiringly at Johan. "So you know God too. My mother is always talking about God. She says she never would have made it if she hadn't known Him. We often pray together."

"Since you won't be home with her tonight, would you like to pray with Karl and Susie and us before we retire for the night?" asked Johan.

"I'd like that very much," agreed Tommy. Johan and Margaret gently held each of his hands, as Karl and Susie crowded close.

Johan looked around at the 200 or more passengers. Many stopped what they were doing and were looking their way and listening intently. "If any of you folks want to join in our prayer, just step in closer," Johan invited, loud enough for many to hear.

Several dozen edged closer, while others continued to give their attention, but stayed where they were. Several rough characters growled under their breath and turned their backs.

"Let us pray," said Johan, bowing his head. "Our precious Lord, these folks are about to sail across this vast ocean and begin a new life in a new country. Be with them, Lord, and help them to trust you and call upon you in every time of need. You tell us in your Word that you notice when a little sparrow falls to the ground, so we know that you know everything that happens to each and every one of us here in this ship's hold. May you help the passengers to be a blessing to each other—striving to make this trip a time to remember with joy. Bless us now and give us each a good night's sleep. In Jesus' precious name we pray. Amen."

A chorus of "amens" rumbled down through the hold.

"I suppose I'd better go up to the captain's cabin now," said Tommy. "Thank you for being so kind to me. I'll tell my mother, and she'll enjoy hearing about you."

"Now there's a brave soul," commented Susie, watching Tommy disappear from sight.

"Yes, he's brave, and his mother has taught him about God. I'd love to have a little boy like him," murmured Margaret, as she wondered, *What will our own little one be like?*

Johan opened Margaret's trunk and helped her remove sheets she had stored there, plus the beautiful quilt she had made. The beds had straw ticks, but there were no covers. After the bed was prepared, Johan took his knife and made some holes in one of the old pieces of sail canvas and looped it onto the nails that were permanent fixtures above the open side of their bed. "There now, that will give us a bit of privacy," he said, satisfied that he had done his best. "I think it would be best to lock your trunk for the night, Margaret. If you could give me a piece of yarn, I'll use it to hang the key around my neck during the night. I don't like the looks of some of those fellows on the other side of this hold."

"Where can we safely store the trunk for the night?" asked Margaret.

"I'm sorry, Margaret, but it looks like we're expected to put all our possessions on the bed with us. I noticed one fellow across the way has his walking plow in the bed with him." He smiled. "Not a very warm bedfellow—that plow."

"Maybe if you hold up the canvas, Margaret, I can duck under and place the trunk at the foot of our bed, against the partition between Karls and us. I'm glad these beds are extra long. I'm sure we can live through one night of this if the rest of these people can survive for several months. Without God's help, it would be pretty hard though."

When they were all prepared for bed, they knocked on the wall between Karls and them. "Good night, dear friends," Johan said in low tones. "We'll see you in the morning."

"Good night," chorused Karl and Susie together.

Then Susie added, "I'm so thankful we are here close together. I can't tell you how much this means to me. It's a memory I'll always remember with pleasure."

"And this is an experience I'll never forget either. I'm glad we can be here with you and Karl," assured Margaret.

It was impossible to sleep for some time. Several little children cried loudly, fearing the strange surroundings, so Johan and Margaret spent some time talking over the pleasures of the day and how they would spend the weekend with her parents. Finally the last squalling youngster quieted down, and soon they heard someone snoring. Johan and Margaret dropped off to sleep with the gentle lapping of the waves against the hull of the ship.

chapter nine

Tricked!

Leaving Johan and Margaret in the hold, Tommy hurried to the captain's cabin. As he walked through the door, he stopped short in surprise. There were four more boys besides the captain occupying the cabin—two were crowded into the bunk that Tommy thought he would occupy and two more boys were curled up in blankets on the floor, sleeping soundly. The captain looked up from his writing at the table and motioned for Tommy to quietly come to him. Tommy carefully closed the door and walked over to the captain.

"These lads," whispered the captain, nodding at the four boys, "also needed a place to sleep. They must have been very tired out, because after I gave them a cup of tea, they promptly went to sleep. I saved a cup of tea for you too, Tommy. Sorry about those two boys using your cot, but here is a nice warm blanket you can roll up in and you'll be able to have a good night's sleep. Here's your tea, lad. I've kept it warm for you." He handed the warm cup to Tommy.

"Thank you, Captain," said Tommy, eagerly grasping the cup and taking a swallow. Tommy's forehead wrinkled. *This tea has a strange flavor. I wonder—do seafaring men drink a different brand of tea? The captain seems to be watching me closely, so I suppose I'd better drink it. I don't want to hurt his feelings.* The tea was soon swallowed, except for some thick, whitish sludge in the bottom. He handed the cup back to the captain.

"Find a spot and roll up in this nice blanket. You're sure to have a good sleep," instructed the captain, pointing to a vacant corner.

Tommy, rolled in his blanket, was soon fast asleep.

Tommy would have been surprised if he could have seen the satisfied smile on the captain's greedy face as he looked over his five husky prizes, and thought of the strong young couple sleeping in the hold. He picked up Tommy's cup, noticed the sludge in the bottom, and frowned—deep in thought. *That boy will take some close watching. Why didn't I think about stirring his tea? I'll get one of the sailors to keep a close watch when I need to be gone from the cabin. The other four will sleep all day tomorrow and when they start to stir, they'll still be very groggy and easy to handle. But that last one. . .* He studied Tommy.

An hour later, the captain stepped out of the cabin, found one of his toughest sailors, who could speak the Dutch language, and gave him orders to keep watch on the door to his cabin. The sailor agreed with a snort, knowing full well what the captain's orders meant.

At midnight, when the tide was going out and there was a good wind, the captain gave his men orders to work quietly while they pulled the anchor and set the sails. The wind filled the sails and the frisky *Minerva* moved secretly and quickly from the shore.

When dawn was breaking, the captain heaved a sigh of relief—there was no land in sight anywhere.

Down in the hold, Johan stretched and was suddenly conscious of his strange surroundings. *Thank you, dear Lord, for giving me this priceless gift beside me. I'm glad I waited on your timing for the right wife.* His prayer was cut short as the *Minerva* heaved upward over the crest of a wave. It awakened Margaret.

She smiled at Johan, then murmured, "Well, we made it through the night, Johan. You weren't too cramped, I hope. Did you sleep well?"

"Yes, praise God, we made it through the night. No, I wasn't too cramped and slept well. But why is this ship bouncing around so much? Must be we're having a storm outside. Why don't we get dressed, then go up on deck to see what's going on?"

Speaking softly and moving quietly, so as not to awaken Karl and Susie, Johan and Margaret were soon on their way to the deck.

Johan was the first to look out over the railing. His knees got weak and he groaned, "No, it can't be!"

"What's wrong, Johan?" cried Margaret, joining her husband and looking around with unbelieving eyes at the endless sea. "Why are we out on the ocean? Did the captain forget about us?"

At first Johan was speechless with shock, but finally he exploded. "That captain! What does he think he's doing? He knew we were on board!"

Her voice quivering, Margaret voiced the unthinkable. "Do you think he tricked us? He seemed so nice."

"I don't know," Johan replied. "But one thing's sure—I'm going to have a talk with him. Maybe there's been some mistake. Let's go!"

Johan led the way as they headed for the captain's cabin. Knocking briskly on the door, they waited for the captain to open. After hearing some shuffling sounds inside, they heard the captain's gruff voice saying, "Come in!"

Pushing the door open, Johan and Margaret started in surprise at all the boys sleeping on the floor and on the bunk. The captain was seated at his desk, a half smile on his face.

Before the captain had a chance to speak, the words rolled from Johan's mouth. "We'd like to know what's going on. Why are we out in the middle of the ocean?"

The captain's half smile disappeared as he rose to face them. "The reason we're out in the middle of the ocean is because we're going to America," he said tersely. "There is no turning back. You're going with us."

"You mean you deliberately tricked us?"

"I guess you might call it that," the captain replied grudgingly. "Now, please, I'm busy right now. We can talk later."

But Johan wasn't done yet. "How could you, Captain? You know it's wrong. The Bible says, 'Be not deceived, God is not mocked. Whatsoever a man soweth, that shall he also reap.'"

The captain took a step forward as he gave them a withering look. "Trying to preach to me, huh? Well, I'm not interested. Get out!"

As they headed toward the hold, Margaret clung to Johan's arm. "What will we do?" she sobbed.

"I don't know," Johan replied. "I guess there's not much we can do but go to America. Maybe there'll be a way to come back again."

Just as they were about to enter the hold, running footsteps drew their attention. A young lad dashed across the deck, then stopped and stared wildly in all directions. He grabbed the guardrail and threw his leg across the ship's railing. Margaret gasped and clutched Johan's arm. "Look at that boy—he's going to jump overboard! Oh, do something, Johan. Hurry!"

Just as Johan was ready to spring forward, the brawny arm of a sailor reached out and knocked the boy off the railing and rolled him roughly onto the deck.

"That'll teach you not to try to get away," growled the hardened sailor.

"Why are you treating me like that?" sobbed the boy. "The captain was kind and I'm sure he wouldn't approve. Anyhow, I'm a good swimmer and my mother needs me. She's depending on me." He again sprang toward the railing.

The sailor clamped his fingers down hard on the boy's arm, while he tried to bite and fight his way loose.

When the rough sailor began to cruelly kick the boy, Johan rushed forward and jumped between the two. "Here, here!" he shouted, grunting as the sailor's kick glanced off his own shin. "Why, Tommy, is that you?" he gasped, pulling Tommy's shaking body close against his side. "Are you hurt, my boy?"

"Yes," sobbed Tommy. "He kicked me and-and he won't let me swim to shore. My-my mother needs me; I must go right away. Please help me, Johan."

Margaret came to her husband's side as Johan dropped to his knees and gathered Tommy gently into his arms. "Listen, Tommy," Johan comforted, his voice quavering with emotion, "it is easy to see that the captain has pulled a mean trick on you and us alike. We all trusted him, but he has betrayed our trust. We must trust our Heavenly Father to carry us through this hard time."

"But, Johan, I have to go home to my mother," insisted Tommy, gulping back the sobs.

"I understand your feelings, Tommy," murmured Johan, picking up the boy and standing him on a box close by, "but let's look around and make a wise decision."

Tommy, standing on the box, was head and shoulders above Johan. He brushed away the tears and looked all around.

"Do you see any land, Tommy?"

"No, no land in sight," gulped Tommy.

"Do you think it is wise to swim? You and I are both good swimmers, I'm sure, but we'd never make it—would we?"

"No, I-I-I guess not," sobbed Tommy. "Oh, Johan, my mother needs me."

Margaret stood beside her husband and said softly, "Listen, Tommy, we're hurting together, but you can come down in the hold with us and we'll take care of you. You would surely die if you jumped into the ocean, so let's trust God to help us. All right?"

"All right," sighed Tommy, his shoulders drooping. "I'm glad you and Johan are here."

Johan noticed the sailor watching them closely. "Will it be all right if we take this lad down in the hold with us, sir?" he asked.

"Sure thing!" snarled the sailor. "Good riddance."

Ignoring his smarting shin, Johan picked up Tommy in his one arm, while helping Margaret keep her balance in the swaying ship with his other arm.

"I think I can walk, Johan," said Tommy, struggling to get down. "I don't want to act like a baby, even if I do hurt."

"If you're sure, Tommy, but tell me if it's too much," said Johan, lowering him to the deck, while keeping a hold on his hand.

They carefully made their way down the gangway into the hold. It was hard to see in the sudden dimness. They were almost to their sleeping quarters when they realized there was someone occupying their quarters. The canvas was moving about vigorously as someone struggled within.

Johan snatched the canvas aside and came face to face with one of the questionable characters he had noticed the evening before. The man jumped guiltily and slipped a knife into his pocket. He had moved Margaret's trunk over to the edge of the bed and was working on the lock. "'Scuse me. I musta got in the wrong quarters," he mumbled. Slipping swiftly out the other end of the canvas, he walked rapidly away.

"You're right about that, my friend," said Johan.

At the word "friend", the man whirled around and stared, then swung around and went on his way, muttering under his breath.

"I wonder," murmured Johan. "I've heard that the authorities sometimes ship criminals over to America. We must keep a closer watch over our things, Margaret. It will hardly be safe for both of us to go up on deck at the same time after this."

"Yes, it will," objected Tommy, when he noticed the worried look on Margaret's face. "I want to help. When you two want to go up on deck, I'll watch over your things."

"You're a good boy, Tommy," said Margaret, placing a kiss on his cheek, while tears trembled in her own eyes. "I know we can trust you to keep a sharp lookout for us. You see, God is sending us both the help we need. We need each other."

"Yes, but what about my mother? What's going to happen to her?" asked Tommy, blinking back the tears.

"Listen, son, we'll talk about this later. We all have many things to figure out. Right now I see Karl and Susie are preparing for the day." Johan knocked his knuckles on the partition between them and called, "Time to get up."

"We're nearly ready," Karl called.

"We'll be with you in a little bit, but what makes this ship leap about so?" asked Susie.

"Because we're all on our way to America, whether we like it or not," Johan informed her.

Karl's brawny arm suddenly flipped their privacy canvas aside. He stood there with Susie, a look of disbelief on their faces. When Susie saw Margaret's effort to keep from crying, she knew it was true. She rushed over and the women threw their arms around each other, weeping on each other's shoulders.

"Oh," groaned Susie, "how can I be so happy and sad at the same time? I can't tell you how happy I am that you're going with us, but this is a terrible shock to you, and for your families back home. Aren't you glad you brought your trunk on board last night?"

"Yes, I'm thankful that the Lord gave wisdom to Johan to bring our things with us, but, oh, this is such a shock." She gulped back a sob. "And Tommy here was tricked by the captain in the same way we were. We've promised to look out for each other, so he'll be staying with us." She glanced at Tommy, who was holding his side. "I'm sorry, Tommy. I know by the way that sailor kicked you that you're bound to be in pain."

"I'll set this trunk out on the floor, so you can use it for a chair, Margaret," said Johan, "and we'll let Tommy rest in our bed."

Quickly the trunk was swung out for the women to sit on and Johan helped Tommy to snuggle into their bed. "Thank you, Johan. Lying down helps my side to feel better, but my head is thumping terribly."

"Did the captain give you anything to drink before you went to sleep last night?" asked Johan.

"Yes, he did, but it tasted funny and there was some white stuff in the bottom so I didn't drink all of it. There were four other boys up there sleeping soundly when I walked in. Three of us had to sleep on the floor. Sleeping on the floor didn't bother me, but being tricked does," said Tommy, clenching his fists.

"I know how you feel, Tommy, but we'll never be truly happy again until we're willing to forgive that captain for what he did. Margaret and I are having a hard time forgiving him too. It was a really mean trick he played. But remember this, Tommy: God has a reason for allowing us to go through this experience. We're God's children and He'll see us through. He's trying to make it easier for us by giving us each other. We're glad we have you and I hope you're glad to have us."

"I'm mighty glad for you and Margaret. Will you pray with me, Johan? I don't feel like getting out of bed. Do you suppose God will mind?" implored Tommy.

"No, Tommy, I'm sure God will understand that you're hurting too much to kneel."

With as much privacy as possible, Johan asked Margaret, Karl and Susie to join him in prayer.

"Our kind Father, we've had a terrible shock this morning, but we know it was no shock to you. We can see your hand in it already. You gave us wisdom to bring our things on board, so we have a change of clothing at least. You also know about Tommy being here with us. Last night you gave us the privilege of learning to know and love Tommy before this happened. You knew we would need each other. Help us to continue to trust you, dear Father.

"Right now, the three of us are having a hard time forgiving the captain for tricking us, but we know what your Word says. You won't forgive us if we are unwilling to forgive others. We need your help, Father. Please give us a forgiving heart. Especially help Tommy, Lord, because he's having a hard struggle with it. Be with his mother and help her through this hard time and help that kind preacher man to take her to himself for a wife. Lord, we thank you for Tommy; he's a special gift to us from you.

"Then, our families at home—how they will grieve! But, Lord, I know you will be their comfort." After a pause to gain control, he went on. "May this experience only help to draw them closer to you, dear Father.

"Help us to show love to the man who was trying to open Margaret's trunk. Give him a chance to know you.

"Lord, you've told us to give you thanks in all things, but we need your help to be as thankful as we ought to be just now. We know if we submit our wills to you, you will bring much good out of this. We'll be looking to you, dear Father, to give us much wisdom as to what we should do when we get to America. We trust you, Father. We know you have our plans all made; we just need your will made plain to us. Father, we'll be waiting on you to lead us each step of the way. In Jesus' name we pray. Amen."

They arose from their knees, wiped their eyes, and blew their noses. Turning to the others, Johan said, "May God give us the grace to lay this burden on Him. Oh, it's hard! My whole being cries out against this injustice. And yet I know that if we truly trust Him, He will help us bear our burdens. May we allow the Lord to give us strength to quit dwelling on the past, and put our focus on what He would have us do with our future."

"I feel a little better now," mumbled Tommy, "but I am still so tired."

"Just stay there and relax," encouraged Johan. "Maybe you can sleep some more. That would be good for you."

Margaret leaned over and gave him a gentle kiss on his cheek and whispered, "Sweet dreams, Tommy." Even as they watched, Tommy drifted off into dreamland.

"I believe he's still feeling the effects of that drugged tea," said Johan. "Poor boy. This is a tough experience for one so young." They stood a moment longer and looked with compassion on the face of the young lad sleeping on their bed. They shed tears for the boy's mother, who would grieve the loss of her brave lad. It was evident that she had been faithful in teaching her boy about God. God was laying on them a great responsibility of continuing the mother's teaching.

chapter ten

Midnight Departure

Margaret's parents hurried their donkey along toward the docks. They were anxious to see their children and also wanted to be there in time to see the big ship sail out to sea. But when they arrived, there was no ship in sight. They looked up and down the wharf, but there was no sign of Johan and Margaret anywhere. Finally they entered the lodging house and searched the dining hall. Where could they be?

The tavern owner came over and inquired, "What's the problem? Can I help you?"

"Oh, Mynheer, we promised to meet a young couple, our daughter and her husband, this morning. We don't see them anywhere," cried Annie, Margaret's mother, forgetting her usual shyness around strangers. "They were here to see another couple sail for America. The ship was to sail later this morning."

"Yes, I heard the ship captain say his ship would not leave until sometime today, but I've learned that captain cannot be trusted." The proprietor frowned, deeply concerned. "I think he was trying to persuade them to sleep on his ship last night, and I personally saw the ship leave at midnight. I was still up caring for a very sick woman, one of my customers."

"Oh, no!" exclaimed Peter, Margaret's father, while closing his eyes and clapping his hand to his forehead. "Do you think they trusted the captain and slept on his ship?"

"I'm sorry to tell you, but if they're not here, they probably did just that. They ate supper here last night and I was starting over to warn them not to trust that captain, but I was interrupted when a sick woman was brought in. I had to take care of her needs, and I completely forgot about the two couples. Take it from me, I know that captain well; he can't be trusted. He's out to fill his ship with passengers, using any method he can. I'm sorry, folks, but I believe both couples are likely on their way to America."

Annie turned pale as she staggered across the dining hall and collapsed on a bench.

Her husband dropped beside her and groaned, "Our dear daughter! How can we tell Johan's family? We were looking forward to a happy weekend, but it's turning into a nightmare. May the Lord help us."

The proprietor hurried away and returned with two cups of steaming coffee. "I'm very sorry, folks. I know this is a terrible shock. Here, drink this hot coffee; you might feel better."

After taking a sip of the hot liquid, Peter looked up with tears swimming in his eyes and asked, "Mynheer, why would a captain want to fill his ship with people who don't have money to pay their fare?"

The proprietor hesitated and then said, "I hate to tell you this, but when they get to America, he will sell them for the cost of their passage as indentured servants. Adults must serve their master for a term of anywhere from five to seven years, but young children are made to serve much longer. Quite likely that captain also has some kidnapped children in his ship, as well. I wouldn't want to be in his shoes when he meets his Maker. No, siree!"

"Oh," moaned the mother, "what shall we do?"

"Lady," the proprietor continued, "there's nothing you can do, but as my wife would say, 'If you're a praying woman, you'd be helping them if you prayed for them.' I'm sure they'll need it. Breakfast will soon be ready, but I have my doubts if you'll feel like eating, so I packed this lunch for you." He placed the lunch into Peter's hands. "You're bound to be hungry before you get home."

"Thank you; you're very kind. How much do I owe you for the lunch?" asked Peter.

"There's no charge this time. It's just a little token to show my sympathy," said the proprietor.

"We appreciate your kindness, Mynheer," said Peter, as he and his wife walked away with drooping shoulders.

Peter looked at his wife. "Annie, do you feel able to make the trip to give the news to Johan's family? They must be told."

"I'll try, Peter, but I find it difficult to believe," sobbed Annie, once more searching the wharf for some sign of Johan and Margaret.

"I know, Annie," Peter agreed. "As soon as we get out of town, we'll stop and pray. God is the only one who can help us."

At that early hour, there was very little traffic on the road. On the outskirts of town they entered a grove of trees. Here they fell to their knees and sobbed out their grief.

Finally Peter prayed, "Lord, our hearts are too heavy to know how to pray, but hear our cry and help those poor children of ours. They must be going through a terrible shock about now. Help them to be strong and, Lord, I beg of you, don't let them be sold to separate masters. We're so thankful that Johan is a godly man and will take good care of Margaret, if at all possible. And above all, you are all-powerful and very able to care for them both. We pray this through Jesus, our blessed Redeemer. Amen!"

"Amen!" echoed Annie, wiping her tears.

The closer they came to the home of Johan's mother, the more Peter and Annie dreaded the task of telling them the sad news. As they drove the donkey and cart into their lane, Johan's mother and sisters hurried out into the yard to welcome them in. Even Jacob was there.

Everyone was deathly quiet as they watched the tears coursing down Peter and Annie's cheeks. Something was terribly wrong.

When Johan's mother was able to speak, she spoke with quivering lips. "Please, do come in. We want to know all."

After caring for the donkey, they slowly walked into the house and the sad news was told.

Johan's mother said brokenly, "Let us have a period of silent prayer for Johan and Margaret. We're all in shock, and I suppose you, as well as I, feel the need of being in communion with our Lord. Our children also need our prayers; this has been a shocking experience for them as well."

After a time of silent prayer, the "Amen" was said.

Johan's mother was very pale as she said, "Children, this experience makes me think of Job in the Bible. The Lord gave us Johan and Margaret and He has a right to take them away. Blessed be the name of the Lord. I know that Johan never expected to sail to America, but God has allowed it to happen for a purpose. I think it will do us good to think of the possible blessings involved in this terrible disappointment." She cleared her throat, and then continued. "I know they'll be a blessing to Karl and Susie. Susie was all broken up over leaving Holland. Now, can you think of something, Hilda?"

"Maybe some of the big ship load of passengers will also need them," Hilda suggested, "especially if the captain kidnapped some children. It seems that Johan and Margaret always know how to comfort others."

Jacob was next. "It's a blessing that they decided to take the trunk with their clothing and valuables with them. Greta said Margaret had made some baby clothes and they planned to show them to you folks." He nodded toward Margaret's parents. "So they do have their clothes—even some for the baby."

Greta took her turn. "I'm glad that Johan was willing to teach Hilda how to handle the dogs and to run the milk route so well. It's just like God was preparing us for this day." Her voice trembled. "How I'll miss my dear brother and his precious wife." Greta's head dropped into her hands in silent grief.

"Yes, I believe God was preparing us all, Johan included," agreed the mother. "Do you remember how God used Grootvader, the day before he died, to help prepare Johan by telling him about the hard things he and Grootmoeder suffered because they loved God more than their lives? The days to come will be hard for all of us, but God will comfort our hearts as He did when your father and Grootvader and Grootmoeder were taken from us." She paused to gain control. "But what can we do about Johan's gardener job for Mynheer Voosterman? He'll need to know so he can get another gardener. Do any of you have any suggestions?"

"Do you think he would let me have the gardener job?" asked Jacob. "I've always enjoyed that kind of work and it would give me the feeling of helping Johan."

"Why don't you go over and talk to him. He'll want a gardener, that's for sure. If he knows the day you'll be coming, he might be able to get the old gardener to come and show you what's expected," suggested the mother.

"I would like to add a blessing we experienced because of this terrible disappointment," said Peter, his voice trembling. "We feel blessed to have a family like you to share our sorrow with. It was good for us to hear you mention the various blessings. I know now why Johan is such a godly man—he has a godly mother. Thank you for setting such a good example."

"May God be praised. He alone is worthy," murmured the mother.

"Yes, praise God," murmured Annie shyly.

The grieving family watched Peter and Annie drive away.

"Poor things! Margaret is their only child," said Greta. "This has been a hard day for them."

"It's been hard for all of us," sighed the good mother. She turned to

Jacob and said, "Since you and Greta are planning to marry, maybe you would like to live in Grootvader's cottage. It would mean a lot to Hilda and me to have you close by."

"Yes, that would seem like the right thing to do. We'll all work together, and with God's help, we'll make it." Jacob struggled to hold back the tears. "That doesn't mean that I won't be missing Johan. Since childhood, he has been my closest friend."

chapter eleven

Pete the Unbeatable

After Johan and Margaret saw that Tommy was sleeping, they slipped from behind the privacy canvas and found Karl and Susie in earnest conversation, sitting on the trunk. Karl got up and motioned for Margaret to take his place. The men found a couple wooden boxes, moved them close to their wives, and sat down.

"Karl," Johan began, "we're wondering what happens to people who haven't paid their fare. I'm sure the captain doesn't expect to give us free passage to America. How can we find out? Do you have any idea?"

"I think you should approach the captain and bluntly ask him what happens to people who haven't paid their fare. He tricked you and was dishonest last night, but I believe when he thinks there is money involved, he'll be willing to talk business," advised Karl.

"I believe you're right, Karl," Johan replied, glancing at Margaret. "Actually, we did talk to him this morning and it didn't go too well. I have a feeling maybe I spoke a bit too rashly. Anyway, he wasn't very cooperative. Now, before talking to him again, we'd like to spend some time thinking and praying about how to approach him. Maybe by tomorrow we can do it."

"By the way," Johan continued, his voice falling to barely more than a whisper, "did you know that while we were gone this morning, a rough-looking man crept into our sleeping quarters, pulled Margaret's trunk out to the front of the bed, and was trying to pick the lock with his knife?"

"No! We must have been sleeping," gasped Karl, while Susie looked pale and shaken.

"We caught him in the act. He jumped with guilt, stuck his knife into his pocket, and slipped away," explained Johan. "I was relieved that he left so quickly, but still, it was pretty unsettling."

"I'm glad you shared this," Karl said. "We'll try to look out for one another's possessions from now on, Johan. I think…" There was a disturbance as four boisterous sailors, with what looked like bags thrown over their shoulders, came tromping down the gangway, blotting out the feeble light coming through the hatch.

Margaret gasped, "They're not carrying bags; they're carrying unconscious boys. Johan, what are they going to do with them?"

From the encounter of the morning, Johan recognized one of the sailors as he stopped in front of the two couples and nodded with his head toward the top bunk. "Anybody occupyin' the top bunk?"

"Yes, some of our family will be using it tonight, sir," answered Johan.

"What about the next top bunk?" he asked, nodding toward Karl and Susie's quarters.

"No one will be using that bunk," assured Karl.

"All right! Up you go, you little landlubbers. When you open your sleepy eyes, you'll have a big surprise coming." With a grunt, two of the sailors carelessly pitched their burdens, plus two blankets, on the top bunk. "There now, they can get 'emselves untangled when they wake up. Here's another blanket for the one you brought down this mornin'." The sailor threw another blanket at Johan, who pitched it up on the top bunk. They swaggered up the walkway, laughing boisterously.

The other sailors tumbled the remaining two boys into the upper bunk above the rough man who had tried to pick the lock on Margaret's trunk.

"Those poor boys," mourned Margaret. "I feel so sorry for them—especially those two over there with that evil man."

"I know," Johan agreed. "It could double their problems. We'll have to do what we can to make this trip as enjoyable for them as possible. If I were a rich man, I'd adopt all five of them, but we know that would be impossible. I know God will show us what to do for them while we're together. And above all, we can pray for them.

"Karl," he said, rising and walking toward the boys' bunk, "would you help me untangle these boys so they can rest better? They look mighty uncomfortable to me."

That done, the two men stepped back, then glanced at each other. Each knew what the other was thinking—*What about the other two boys in the bunk above that unfriendly, evil-looking man?*

"Do we dare do it?" Johan finally asked. "Surely if we're careful he won't get too upset."

"We can try," agreed Karl. "That's what I'd want someone to do for me if I were thrown up there in a heap on that top bunk."

"You men be very careful," cautioned Susie.

"God go with you. We'll pray as you go," encouraged Margaret.

"We'll be careful," said Johan, his hand on his wife's shoulder.

Swaying unsteadily, the men slowly walked across the brine-soaked planking in the heaving ship's hold. Since the evil man didn't bother to put up a privacy canvas, he saw them coming. As they approached, he sprang from his bunk. He stood with fists propped on his hips, legs braced far apart, and an ugly scowl on his face. His belligerent voice carried through the hold. "If you Dutch lads are spoiling for a fight, I'm good and ready. Just want you to know, I've made a name for myself—Pete the Unbeatable."

Heads turned, and a small group of bored men began to head their way. Hearing the outburst, Margaret and Susie clutched each other's hands and prayed more earnestly.

"Friend," said Johan kindly, "we come in peace."

"Friend!" Pete spat out the word. "It's a lie! No one has ever called me friend or ever wanted to be my friend. State your business and be quick about it." He took a step forward, an oath rumbling under his breath.

"Pete," said Johan, "we noticed the sailors pitched two lads in the bunk above you. They landed in an uncomfortable heap and we'd like to lay them out in a more restful posture and cover them with their blankets."

"Why should you care for strangers, I'd like to know?" growled Pete.

"Our kind Heavenly Father teaches us through the Bible to treat others just like we'd like others to treat us. If we were those boys, we'd be glad if someone cared enough to make us more comfortable," explained Johan.

"Heavenly Father? You mean God? Ain't no God and that's sure, or he'd never let happen what's happened to me," argued Pete.

"We're truly sorry that you've had a difficult time in life. We just wanted to do something to let these boys know that someone cares about them. It's going to be bad enough when they wake up and find out they've been kidnapped."

"Kidnapped, huh? At least someone will likely miss 'em. Now me, nobody will be sorry I'm put on this ship. They even wanted to get rid of me in the prison where I came from. Couldn't stand the sight of me and some of my buddies. Shoved us into this hold like cattle and they plan to sell us to some farmer when we get to America. They'll sell us for indentured servants for likely seven years and then maybe we'll be free. I'll run off. That's what! I ain't workin' for any ole farmer." Suddenly he looked like a broken man; his arms sagged. "Help yourself to the lads, I guess." He flopped his big frame onto his bunk, rolled over, and turned his face to the wall.

"I'm really sorry, Pete. Please remember, as long as we're on this ship, you do have some friends. We care what happens to you," said Johan, with deep feeling.

"Bah!! Don't believe a word of it," grunted Pete, with an angry flip of his shoulder. "Just get your job done and leave me alone. I'm not interested in your lies."

Karl and Johan hurriedly untangled the two lads and covered them with the blankets. "Poor little lads. I wish we could make their lot easier," murmured Johan.

"Get out of here," roared Pete, "before I break your bones."

"We're going, my friend," said Johan, as he and Karl walked away.

Several of the men standing by caught Johan by the sleeve and said, "Mynheer, from hearing your prayer last night and your talk with Pete just now, we think you must be a servant of God. Are we right?"

"Yes, my friend Karl and I are servants of God. Why do you ask?" inquired Johan.

"We're wondering, since this is the Lord's Day, if you would be willing to have some sort of service for us? It would mean a lot to us all."

"Sure," agreed Johan, "I would be happy to do that, but I want you to know that we are not ordained ministers."

Just then they heard a sailor shouting, "Chow time!"

"It sounds like it's time to eat right now, but after that, if the interested ones would gather as close as they possibly can to our quarters, we'll have a short service of some kind. Please pray for me," requested Johan humbly.

The men smiled and nodded in agreement.

As the passengers surged up the gangway to get their food, the privacy canvas was suddenly pushed aside and Tommy came out rubbing his eyes. "What's all the commotion about?"

"Hello, Tommy. It's suppertime. Are you feeling better?" asked Margaret.

"My side is still sore, but my head doesn't thump as much." Tommy made a brave attempt to smile.

"Johan, you and Margaret and Tommy go up and get your food first," offered Karl. "We'll go later. We can wait and watch over things here. You'll need a bit of time to prepare for the meeting anyway."

"You're very thoughtful," agreed Johan, with a grateful smile. He and

Margaret and Tommy walked over and got in the chow line, taking deep breaths of the fresh salt air as they came up out of the smelly hold. When it was their turn, each one was handed a wooden bowl of barley soup, a wooden spoon, and some oat bread. Repeatedly the following instructions were given to the passengers through a bullhorn, "Take good care of your wooden bowls. There will be no replacements if the bowls are lost. Since it's too much work for the cook to prepare food each day for 200 people, you'll be expected to cook your own food after this meal. The women can take turns cooking over little fires in a number of sandboxes on the deck. Each full-freight passenger (adult) will receive one Scotch pint of sweet water per day for drinking. Children will receive less. You can wash your clothes in seawater. Each week every full-freight passenger will receive three pounds of salt beef, four pounds of bread, and four pounds of oatmeal. Again, the children will receive smaller portions. You may pick up your rations for this week at any time."

"I'm glad you know how to cook, Margaret," Johan said, smiling down at her.

"I suppose we'll make do," Margaret replied rather forlornly, "but I've never cooked with those kind of rations. And what will we use for a cooking pot?"

"Maybe Susie has an extra one. We'll ask. If she doesn't, we'll ask the captain," promised Johan.

After finishing their barley soup and oat bread, they gathered their rations together and headed back to the hold below.

After breathing fresh air for awhile, the stagnant smell of brine–soaked wood, urine, and vomit was almost overpowering. "Oh, this is terrible!" Margaret groaned. "I'm not sure I can handle it."

After sitting down, Johan informed Karl and Susie of all they had learned while above on deck.

"I have an extra cooking pot for you, Margaret," assured Susie.

"That means we're ready to set up housekeeping, I guess," said Margaret, making a brave attempt to smile.

"Try not to let this tough experience get you down, Margaret," Johan encouraged after Karl and Susie had gone on deck to eat. "I know it's going to be hard, but we'll just have to trust God to give us strength to live one day at a time. I'm reminded of a Bible verse I learned from Grootvader. 'All things work together for good to them that love God.' "

"I'm sorry," said Margaret, with tears springing into her eyes. "I do want to trust God. It's just that it's so. . . so hard to accept."

"Thanks, Margaret, I appreciate you so much," Johan said with feeling, giving his wife a quick hug. "We're really going to need each other in the days to come."

Turning around, Johan glanced at Tommy, who was sitting on the bunk behind them. "Why don't I help you into the top bunk? We're going to have a little church service in a few minutes, and up there you can lie down if you want to and still see and hear all that's going on."

"And now," Johan continued after Tommy was settled in, "what shall I say to encourage these people when we ourselves are the ones needing encouragement?"

"I don't know," Margaret responded. "I guess just speak to them from your heart. Maybe we can be encouraged too."

Feeling a great need of God's guidance, Johan and Margaret knelt behind the privacy canvas by their bunk and prayed that God would give Johan words of encouragement for the people who would soon be gathering.

chapter twelve

Where Two or More Are Gathered

From the top bunk, Tommy had a good view of everything that was going on, plus he could see all who came and went on the gangway that led to the deck above. A group of people were beginning to walk toward Johan and Karl's quarters. *I wonder,* thought Tommy, *who the preacher will be.* He blinked back the tears as he thought of the nice preacher man who came to see his widowed mother. He closed his eyes and breathed a prayer. *Please, Lord, help that preacher to take good care of my dear mother. Help her not to cry too much because I'm gone and because she doesn't know where I am.* He opened his eyes in time to see Johan moving toward the middle of the floor while facing the group of people. *Well, I might have known,* he mused. *I believe Johan is going to be the speaker.*

Tommy could clearly hear Johan as he began to speak.

"Good evening, friends," welcomed Johan. "I think it would be nice if we could get acquainted with each other this evening. After we do a bit of singing and reciting of Scripture, we'll take turns introducing ourselves. The father of each family may come forward and give your family name, why you're sailing to America, and anything else you might want to tell us. Before we sing, how many have heard the poem, 'When I Survey the Wondrous Cross' by Isacc Watts?"

Tommy saw several hands go up.

"It looks like several of you have heard of it. That's good!" encouraged

Johan. "I enjoy singing, so I made up a tune to go with it. I'll sing it first, then we'll all sing it together."

Johan's rich tenor carried to the farthest corner of the hold. Even those who hadn't bothered to gather with the group gave him rapt attention. The song was sung with such love and reverence that people bowed their heads and worshiped. Tommy's love for God and Johan grew as he listened. His attention was drawn to some legs coming down the gangway. When the head appeared, Tommy saw it was Captain Boswell. Struggling to control his feelings, Tommy's hands clenched as he stared at the man. *Deceiver! What's he doing here?*

The captain stood quietly and listened to the complete song, then went back upstairs with a smug, self-satisfied smile.

After the song was finished, Johan began, "My friends, I've never had the privilege of going to school and learning to read or write, but my grootvader helped me memorize a number of poems and many Scriptures. So tonight I'd like to quote some verses in Luke 23:33-47. This passage from God's Word tells about a few things that happened on the day that Jesus, the Son of God, willingly gave His life for you and me by being nailed to the cross. The song we just sang also told about that day. Jesus was sinless, but He was crucified between two thieves as though He were the worst of the lot."

Tommy noticed the mean-looking man on the opposite side of the ship, who had been lying on his bunk with his back to Johan, suddenly flip over at the mention of the word "thieves". The man glared angrily at Johan.

Johan began to recite God's Word slowly and with deep meaning.

"'And when they were come to the place, which is called Calvary, there they crucified him, and the malefactors, one on the right hand, and the other on the left.

"'Then said Jesus, Father, forgive them; for they know not what they do. And they parted his raiment, and cast lots. . .'"

When he finished, all was quiet as the people pondered the words that were spoken.

After a brief pause, Johan said, "My friends, have you considered how loving our Lord is? While He was dying and in terrible agony, He took time to help a repentant thief. The soul of the one thief went to hell, while the other went with Jesus to paradise, which means heaven. Salvation is for anyone who will call to Him for help."

Tommy heard a sneer as the mean-looking man flipped over and faced the wall.

After another hymn, the worship service ended with a prayer.

Facing the group, Johan smiled and said, "Now we'll have the introductions I was talking about. I'll start with myself. My name is Johan Blankenburg and my wife is Margaret. We are from Holland. We never intended to go to America, but we were tricked and kidnapped, like several others on this ship. We got up this morning and there was no land in sight. We are still in shock, but now we have a decision to make. Will we choose to forgive and make the best of the situation or will we become bitter and unforgiving? We need your prayers that we can trust God as we face an uncertain future." His voice faltered.

The hearts of the people were strangely drawn to Johan and Margaret after they knew how they had been tricked, but had chosen forgiveness. One after the other they introduced themselves and explained why they were going to America. A few planned to start a business, but most of the people were poor and would be sold as indentured servants, in order to pay the captain for their passage to America. They were hoping for a better life in America after their indenture was completed. They thanked Johan for having the service and hoped there could be at least one each week.

As the people wandered back to their own quarters, Johan and Margaret returned to their bunk and said, "Good night, Tommy."

"Good night," Tommy answered. "Did you know the captain came down and listened to you sing the first song? Also, the man across the way acted angry when you talked about thieves. I had a good place to see everything."

"It sounds like you saw some things we didn't." Johan chuckled. "I suppose the other four boys will be waking up sometime tomorrow. The sailors brought them down here while you were sleeping and put two above Karl and Susie's bunk and the other two are above the mean-looking man that you mentioned across the way."

"I feel sorry for the boys when they wake up," said Tommy, his voice trembling. "It's going to be a terrible shock, I know. You'll try to help them, won't you, Johan?"

"Yes, we'll do what we can, and you can help too. Now say your prayers and go to sleep, my boy."

Shortly after, Tommy's even breathing told them he was asleep.

Johan and Margaret sat together on their trunk and talked in low tones.

"From what I've been hearing from the other passengers," Johan began, "I'm guessing the captain is planning to sell us as indentured servants. Let's pray that God would work it out so we can stay together as a married couple. I can't bear to think that we might be separated. I don't believe the Lord brought us together only to have us torn apart. Let's trust the Lord to show us how to work through this problem, Margaret."

"Yes, Johan, we must trust Him." Margaret choked back a sob. "I'm glad we don't need to go through this alone. That would really be scary. When I think how our parents must be suffering and how we'll miss them, I think I can't bear it." Margaret covered her face, overwhelmed with grief.

"A cry will do you good, Margaret," Johan said, blinking away his own tears. "Together, with God, we'll make it. And let's not forget Tommy. He's both a blessing and a responsibility. We must be strong for his sake."

"That's right," Margaret agreed. "And somehow, when we get to America, we must try to keep him with us."

"We'll pray for guidance and do our best," assured Johan. "Now I'd like to get that piece of canvas over there and see if I can somehow fasten the trunk to the partiton between Karls and us. If there should be a storm, we don't want that trunk to be pitched on top of us while we're sleeping."

"Good idea, Johan. We need to guard against accidents as well as theft. There are things in the trunk that I'd hate to do without—for instance, the medicines my mother made from herbs."

When the trunk was made secure, they settled in for the night. Alone at last, Johan and Margaret clung to each other as they gave vent to their emotions.

"What a day!" Johan exclaimed, drawing in a shaky breath. "Just think, I may never see my mother again—nor my sisters and my brother. And Jacob, my boyhood chum—how can I bear the loss?"

"And my mother and father and. . ." Margaret couldn't finish as sobs shook her body.

"No, it's not going to be easy," Johan continued, "but with God we'll make it. Actually I feel better about it already."

Finally, the healing tears were wiped away, and they were able to sleep peacefully after committing their all to God.

In the early morning hours of their second day at sea, Johan and Margaret were awakened by a terrible moaning.

"Johan, do you think Tommy is seasick?" asked Margaret.

"I don't think so, but I'll check." Johan slipped out of bed and checked the top bunk. "It's not Tommy, Margaret. He's sound asleep." Johan snuggled back into bed with a contented sigh.

Suddenly there was a knock on the partition between them and Karl and Susie. "Are you awake, Johan?" came Karl's quiet voice.

"Yes, Karl, I'm awake. Is there a problem?" asked Johan.

"The boys up above us are in a bad way, and my Susie is seasick. I hate to bother you, but I need help."

"I'll be right there," Johan replied.

"Shall I help, Johan?" asked Margaret.

"Wait a little and I'll let you know if you're needed. You need your rest, Margaret. I don't want you to get sick."

Johan found two miserable boys in the bunk above Karl and Susie. They desperately needed to use one of the stained, covered buckets, but every time they raised their aching heads, they dropped back with a groan. They were suffering the side effects of the captain's drugged tea. Johan lifted both boys, one at a time, from their bunk, helped them use the bucket, then placed them gently back in their bunk and covered them with their blankets.

"Where are we?" whimpered the boys.

"Listen, boys, the best thing for you to do right now is try to rest. You'll feel better after awhile, then we'll have a talk and I'll try to answer your questions. I'm sorry your heads hurt so badly, but you will get better," promised Johan.

The boys sighed and were soon fast asleep again.

Johan was heading for his own bunk when he heard Pete's rough hollering at the two boys above him. *Oh, no, those boys need help too.* With a heart full of pity, Johan went over and repeated the performance. The boys were weeping and groaning from pain and also from Pete's harsh words. After Johan spoke a few comforting words, the boys heaved a sigh and dropped into a deep sleep.

"Why don't you tend to your own business?" Pete growled.

"Helping others who are suffering is my business," Johan answered gently before returning to his bunk.

chapter thirteen

What Now, Captain?

Cooking their first meal the next morning was not easy for the women in the galloping *Minerva,* but hungry stomachs must be fed. While the women stooped over the cooking pots and stirred the porridge with one hand, they braced themselves by clutching the railing with the other. The cooking pots were hung over small fires built in sandboxes at various places on the deck. While they ate, they enjoyed getting better acquainted with one another—chattering about happenings in their past and speculating about the future. Some had heard that ferocious people called Indians were sometimes seen in America. This caused the women to cast anxious glances at their husbands and children.

Susie was still seasick, so Johan and Margaret cooked for both families, while Karl watched over their belongings. They cooked only one hot meal each day, so cold leftovers were their normal evening fare. Chips of salt beef were cooked with the oatmeal, which helped to season it. They guarded the drinking water carefully, which was scarce. Johan and Margaret heard much grumbling as the people wished for more variety in their food.

"I know it would be nice to have more variety in our diet—especially for you, Margaret—but let's try to be content and thankful that we have food," encouraged Johan.

"Yes, if we have food and raiment, the Bible tells us to be content," agreed Margaret, "even if we have to wash the dishes with sand! Maybe if we are cheerful and refuse to grumble, it might help the others have a better attitude."

"Margaret, since our housekeeping chores are finished, I think I will go up and talk with the captain. Maybe you could try to encourage Susie while I'm gone."

"Good idea," agreed Margaret. "And I'll be praying for you while you talk with the captain."

"Thank you, Margaret. I'll need it." He turned to Karl. "I would rest easier if you would stay here with our wives, Karl. Feel free to take a nap on our bed if you wish while they talk. I know you didn't get a lot of sleep last night." At Karl's relieved nod, Johan turned to Tommy. "I think I'll take you with me. What do you say, son?"

"Yes, I'd like that!" Tommy exclaimed. "I'd like to hear what the captain has to say for himself." He eased himself down from the top bunk to the floor planking, moving gingerly to avoid irritating his hurt side where the sailor had kicked him.

As Margaret watched her men go up the gangway, she turned to Karl and said, "It's your turn to take a rest in our bed while I sit here beside Susie and get her caught up on the news."

"Thank you, Margaret. I appreciate that," said Karl, slipping out of his shoes and stretching out on their bed. "Call me if you need me."

As Margaret drew the canvas aside, Susie looked up with a wan smile and said, "It's so good to have you sitting here beside me. I wish this boat would quit rocking."

"There's not a chance of that happening, Susie, so let's try to get our minds on something else. Right now, Johan and Tommy went up on deck in the hopes of talking with the captain. They're hoping to find him in a reasonable mood and want to find out what options we have when we arrive in America. Will you help me pray for them, Susie?"

"I'll try," agreed Susie.

After praying together, Margaret told Susie what it was like to go up on deck to cook their food. She described the women she had met and discussed their conversations. She avoided any mention of Indians.

Susie lifted her head. "You know, I believe I'm beginning to feel better and a wee bit hungry."

"That's good news, Susie. We have some leftover food for you." Margaret hurried to bring it to her and Susie managed to eat a few bites as Margaret continued talking. Then they quoted Scripture together.

Johan and Tommy made their way up to the deck. Holding on to the railing, they watched a porpoise swimming beside the ship. Had they looked behind them, they would have seen the captain intently watching them before ducking quickly into his cabin. They watched the sailors at work, and then, spotting the sailor who had kicked Tommy, they walked over and asked, "Sir, where can we find Captain Boswell?"

"In his cabin yonder. But tread softly and don't get him riled up," he ordered rudely. "Hear? When he's riled up, we all have to pay."

"Thank you, sir," Johan said offering a smile.

As they walked toward the cabin, Tommy looked up at Johan and asked, "Are you scared?"

"Not really. God is with us, Tommy. We can trust Him," encouraged Johan as he knocked on the cabin door.

"Who's there?" called the captain.

"Johan Blankenburg and Tommy."

"I'm a busy man, but I can give you a few minutes," the captain replied, opening the door. "Come in and have a seat there on the cot, but no preaching!"

"Thank you," Johan said, "but we won't be staying long, so we'll remain standing." Johan cleared his throat and asked, "First of all, I'd like to say I'm sorry for the way I talked to you yesterday morning. We were upset, and I talked too rashly. I hope you can forgive me."

The captain listened quietly, and Johan noticed the half smile was back on his face. When he didn't reply, Johan went on. "We really would like to know why you tricked us the way you did. Actually, you kidnapped us. What are your reasons for doing this?"

"Well, it's like this," the captain replied after a moment's pause. "When I saw you—a fine young couple and an energetic lad—I knew you would know how to get ahead in America and I wanted to give you that chance. Mark my word, the day will come when you will feel like thanking me. And also, every captain likes to make a trip with a well-loaded ship—to make his trip worthwhile, you know." By now the captain was smiling broadly.

"There are a few things we need to know, Captain. How much money will you charge for our passage to America? We want to know our options."

"So you want to talk business. I charge twenty-two pounds and seven six-pence for every full-freight passenger. We furnish your food, lodging, and transportation. Tommy's passage is fifteen pounds even."

"And what happens if we can't pay our passage?" inquired Johan.

The captain's smile disappeared and he looked the other way. "Well, there are many eager farmers in America just waiting for good strong workers. They will gladly pay your fare, but you will need to sign a contract, promising to work five to seven years for that farmer. The farmer will furnish you with room, board, and clothes. When you finish your term, he will not send you away empty-handed, but will provide you with land and supplies so you can get started on your own. They call it 'freedom dues'. Sounds like a good deal, don't you think?"

"Does that mean the poor families down there in the hold will be split apart and sold to different farmers?" Johan looked keenly at the captain.

"Yes, at times that happens," admitted the captain, still refusing to make eye contact.

"And what language do they speak in America? Surely they don't all speak Dutch."

"You're right there," agreed the captain. "There are many languages, but if need be, you're young enough to learn a new language. The children learn especially fast. Language won't be a problem for long, so you've nothing to worry about."

"And what about the young boys you kidnapped?" Johan continued. "Who cooks their meals and sees to their other needs? I took care of them early this morning, but we don't have enough rations for both them and us."

"Tut, tut," the captain protested. "Let's not call it kidnapping. I was only giving them a better chance to get ahead in this world. I'll give you enough rations for the boys and a cooking pot to use. And if one of your women would be willing to cook for them, I'll give you a little bonus—an extra child's ration of salt beef per week. If I made it for an adult, maybe someone would need to go without before this trip is over. If we have a good wind and no storms, we should make it in two and a half months, but sometimes it takes three. Then the food and water gets scarce. I'm not trying to be stingy, just using good judgment. Is it a deal?"

"We'll do it," agreed Johan, "because we care about those boys."

"Good! Now before you go back to the hold, I'll go with you to get those rations for the other four boys, plus the extra ration for doing the cooking. There's one more thing we need to discuss, Johan. I noticed you brought on board a very nice trunk. It's hardly safe there in the hold, so I will be glad to keep it under lock and key here in my cabin." The captain's smile was back on his face.

"I thank you, Captain Boswell, but we have our clothes, as well as bed clothes and baby clothes in there. I'm sure we'll want to keep it close by where it is handy," explained Johan.

"I'm just warning you," insisted the captain. "There may be trouble if you don't accept my offer. You'd be wise to change your mind."

"If we change our minds we'll let you know. Now, if we can get the promised rations, we'll return to our family in the hold," said Johan.

Later, while Tommy was helping Johan carry the food rations to the hold, he looked up and asked, "You won't let the captain take care of your trunk, will you, Johan? He can't be trusted."

"No, Tommy. I think we can watch after the trunk, don't you?"

"I'm sure of it." Tommy stretched to his full height.

chapter fourteen

Caught!

Deeply concerned, Johan and Margaret talked and prayed much about the future. One thing sure, they didn't have the funds to pay for their passage.

"Margaret," asked Johan hesitantly as they discussed their options, "I hate to even ask you as I know you'll be busy with our new baby, but do you think you would be willing to be indentured as a seamstress? That quilt you made was beautiful—and the baby clothes."

"That's an idea, Johan," Margaret replied. "I just hope the Lord blesses us with a contented baby. Yes, I'm willing to offer my services as a seamstress. That job would work better than some, while caring for a little one. But that's another thing to think about—we need a buyer who will be willing to accept a tiny baby in the house. Some might object. And then there's Tommy to think about."

"Tommy," Johan asked the next day, "would you mind joining us as we discuss some things that have been going through our minds?"

"Sure, I was wondering what you were thinking," said Tommy, scrambling down from his bunk above.

Johan beckoned for Tommy to sit between them on the bunk.

"Tommy, would you be willing to do farm work for five to seven years?" asked Johan. "I guess they often want children to work longer, but we hope that won't be necessary."

"Sure, I don't mind work, but I don't want to be separated from you. I just want us to stay together," pleaded Tommy.

"That's what we want too, Tommy, but God alone can bring that to pass, because we don't have enough money to pay for our passage. It will be a miracle if a buyer can be found who will need us all and who can afford us. But our God is a miracle-working God, and nothing's too hard for Him. He has ways for working things out—ways we would never imagine. Then too, we have no land, house, or furniture, so I suppose being indentured will take care of our immediate needs. It will give us time to learn their ways of farming."

"I'm just so glad you will try to keep me with you," said Tommy. "I would hate to be sold off by myself somewhere. Maybe after our years of service are over, I can help you farm your own place. I'd like that, Johan."

"You're a good lad, Tommy, and I hope the day comes when we can take you up on your offer." Johan paused and then said, "Tommy, I won't insist, but Margaret and I would be happy if you felt free to call us ma and pa. Or is it too soon after being torn away from your mother?"

"No, I would be happy to call you ma and pa," agreed Tommy. "It makes me feel like I'm really part of your family."

"Good! Now, back to where we left off. I know our plan is a big order for our Heavenly Father," continued Johan, "but He is all-powerful, so let's pray daily that He will send the right farmer along, who will accept us all."

Tommy looked very grave. "I'll be praying a lot, that's for sure."

The next several days were taken up with caring for and learning to know the four new boys in their care. The two above Karl and Susie's bunk, Kendrick and Abe, responded with grateful hearts for the love and care shown to them, but the two above Pete's bunk were withdrawn and sullen. They constantly cast fearful glances at Pete, who kept a close watch on them. *I wonder what Pete has said or done to make them so fearful,* Johan thought. *May God show me what to do to help them.*

Susie was feeling stronger and was able to cook enough food for them and the two boys above them. Johan and Margaret cooked for their family, plus the two boys above Pete. The boys looked longingly at the feeble daylight that filtered down the gangway, but it was obvious their fear of Pete was great.

When Johan brought them their dish of food the next day, he said, "You boys will be sick if you don't get out and get some sunshine and fresh air. I'll be glad to go with you if you'd like to go up on deck for a while. How about it?"

"Well," the boys hesitated, "we would, but. . ."

"Leave those boys alone," roared Pete, leaping from his bunk and facing Johan with a snarl. "They'd likely fall overboard if they went up there. Their food is your job, but I'll see to the rest. Now mind your own business."

"Calm down, Pete," Johan pleaded as he stepped backwards. "We'll stay out of your way." Then, as he looked into Pete's smoldering eyes, he continued quietly, "We're praying for you too, Pete. We care about you."

Pete sprang forward with upraised hand, but Johan nimbly sidestepped the onslaught and walked swiftly back to his quarters, his thoughts in a turmoil.

The next morning, Karl told Johan to go along with Margaret and Tommy to do their family cooking while he and Susie kept their eye on things. Then they would do their own cooking later.

After they were gone, Karl and Susie busied themselves cleaning up around their bunk and making up their bed. While Susie was sweeping with a stub of a broom, the ship gave a sudden heave over a big swell, throwing Susie off balance. She fell, hitting her head on a supporting post, knocking her unconscious. Karl sprang to help his wife and gently carried her over and laid her on their bunk. He felt her head; a huge knot was beginning to swell. In his concern for his wife, he didn't notice the commotion in Johan's quarters.

Day after day, Pete had been watching Johan's quarters like an eagle. When he saw Susie fall and Karl giving his full attention to her, he grabbed the two boys roughly from the top bunk and said, "It's time to act; remember it's your job to take care of those boys who sleep in the top bunk and I'll grab the trunk and rush it to the captain. Get a move on. We've got to be quick about it." He shoved the boys roughly ahead of him. He whipped out his knife, thrust aside the privacy canvas, and lunged across Johan's bed, cutting and slashing the canvas that secured Margaret's trunk to the partition. Quickly freeing the trunk, he pulled it to the front of the bunk, swung it onto his shoulder, and headed for the gangway. He barely glanced at his boy slaves, who were sitting astride Kendrick and Abe with their hands clamped tightly over their mouths. Nor did Pete notice the group of men who had gathered to see what the commotion was all about. It was obvious to them that Pete was stealing from their good friend, Johan, so two of the strongest men sprinted after him up the gangway.

Grabbing one handle of the trunk, the newcomer said, "That's too heavy for you, Pete! Let me give you a lift with that trunk."

The other man threw his arms around Pete's neck, and then clasped his hands tightly together. He gave a mighty jerk backwards, bringing Pete and the trunk crashing down on the gangway. Another man sprinted forward, snatched up the trunk, and returned it to Johan's bunk.

When Johan and Margaret started down the gangway, the three men were still in a tangled heap. Johan, with Margaret following, hurried past with the covered kettle of steaming hot food and set it down at their bunk.

"What's going on?" exclaimed Johan. "Look, the boys are all in that top bunk, fighting!"

"It looks like someone was after our trunk again," replied Margaret. "See? It's loose!"

"How about it, Klaus and Ben?" Johan asked after he pulled the boys apart. "Do you know who was trying to steal our trunk?"

They dropped their heads, casting wary glances at Pete, who was groaning and clutching his painful hand, still unable to stand.

Finally Klaus hissed, "Ask Pete; he made us do it."

"I thought as much. He's been making you afraid and miserable. Here, boys. Margaret has your porridge ready."

The boys accepted the food and gave Margaret sheepish smiles.

"Boys, we're here to help you," comforted Margaret. "I'm sorry he is making it hard for you."

"I-I'm sorry about being involved with your trunk," confessed Klaus.

"Me too," said Ben, studying his bare toes.

"We'll forgive you, boys," said Johan and Margaret together.

Karl brushed the privacy canvas back from their bed and said quietly, "Johan and Margaret, could you come here? Susie lost her balance when the ship went over a big swell, and banged her head into a supporting post. She has an ugly knot on her head. She was unconscious for a while and… Hey, what's going on here? Why is Pete lying over there groaning in pain?"

"Evidently, while you were caring for your wife, Pete decided the time was right to steal Margaret's trunk," Johan explained. "But it appears that we have some friends in this hold who understood what he was doing and brought the trunk back to our bed, so things didn't go as Pete had planned. Actually, I feel sorry for the man."

"If you men want to check on Pete, I'll see to Susie," offered Margaret. "And don't forget, Johan, I brought some things to help with various hurts and sicknesses. If Pete has a need, I'll be glad to help him in any way I can."

"That's what I call real forgiveness, my dear," said Johan. "You check on Susie while Karl and I go over and see where Pete is hurt. We'll let you know if you're needed."

Margaret flipped the canvas curtain aside. "How is your head feeling by now, Susie? I'm sorry about your accident."

"I feel bad that we didn't do a good job in seeing to your trunk," said Susie.

"Let's not worry about that, because our trunk is back on our bed. Even though there are some important things in our trunk, your life is more precious than anyone's trunk. Karl did right to see to you," encouraged Margaret.

"I think I'll try sitting up. Maybe I'll be able to go up on deck and cook our food." Susie struggled to a sitting position, but sank back with a groan. "I'm so dizzy," she gasped. "I hope I'm not seasick again."

"I don't think so, Susie. Likely you're dizzy from that bump on your head. We'll take care of your cooking today. Will you be all right if I go and do that right now?"

"Yes, I'll be fine if I stay quiet. I'm sorry for the extra work I'm making for you," mourned Susie.

As Margaret measured out some rations into a cooking pot, she glanced up and smiled; the boys were in friendly conversation—any ill will forgotten.

"Klaus and Ben, would you boys like to go up on the deck with me?" asked Margaret. "Johan doesn't like for me to go up there alone, and I see he and Karl are busy helping Pete."

"We'd be happy to go with you," chorused the boys as they eagerly looked at the sunlight streaming down the gangway.

"Here, let me carry the kettle for you," offered Ben, and Margaret willingly handed it over.

"Abe, will you go over and tell Tommy I need him?" asked Margaret, pointing at the men.

Abe ran, eager to do her bidding, and Tommy was soon at her side.

"Tommy, do you think you could sit here and guard my trunk until Johan can fix it back like it was? There's your bowl of porridge on that box. You can eat while you're on guard duty. All right?"

"You can trust me to look out for your trunk, Ma," agreed Tommy, with a nod and firmly pressed lips.

"If he should need help, Kendrick and I are willing to help him," assured Abe.

"Thank you, boys," said Margaret with a smile. Then she and the other two boys climbed the gangway to the deck above, gratefully breathing in the bracing salt breeze.

As Johan and Karl walked toward Pete, they found him lying there alone, groaning and clutching his left hand. Pity welled up in Johan's heart. *Poor Pete! No one has ever loved him. No wonder he doesn't know how to show love to others. Lord, help me to show your kind of love to him.*

"Oh," groaned Pete, when he noticed the two men approaching, "not you again! I suppose you're just coming over to laugh at my misery."

"No, Pete, this is no laughing matter," replied Johan. "We can see that you're hurting something awful." He dropped to one knee beside the hurting man. "We'd like to help you get back to your bunk, but first tell us where you're hurting. We don't want to make matters worse by moving you."

Pete closed his eyes and gritted his teeth to keep from screaming with pain. It was obvious to Johan that a battle was raging in his heart. He needed help, but he didn't want help from the man he had tried to rob.

Finally Pete opened his eyes and held out his left hand, while his whole body shook with pain. Three of the fingers were twisted at odd angles and blood was dripping from some cuts on his hand and arm.

"It looks like you have some broken fingers, Pete, or maybe they're pulled out of joint. The trunk must have landed on your hand when you and it crashed to the floor. I'm really sorry you have this misery. I think Margaret might know how to help your hand. Her mother taught her some things about helping hurting people. Are you hurting anywhere else?"

He groaned while pointing with his good hand to his right ankle.

"Yes, it's very swollen," Johan agreed after taking a look. "If it isn't broken, it's at least badly sprained." Johan looked around at a number of men who had gathered to watch. "Would someone get some of the old canvas over there? We need to get Pete onto a large piece and pull him as gently as we can over to his bunk. If we work together, we should be able to do that."

The men were willing enough to help, since Johan was taking the lead. A short time later, Pete was groaning pitifully while he lay on his own straw tick in his bunk.

"Pete, try to be patient until Margaret comes. Rest assured, we'll come back as soon as possible."

After thanking the men who had helped, Karl and Johan went back toward their own quarters. As they passed the pile of old canvas, Johan selected some strong pieces to secure their trunk to the partition again. He smiled as he noticed the three boys, with serious faces, standing guard in front of the trunk.

"Thank you, boys. You've done a good job," he praised.

The boys stepped aside and smiled shyly.

"Now, I want to tie this trunk fast to the partition again. We don't want it tumbling on top of Margaret and me if a storm should come up in the night. Where is Margaret, boys?"

"She's up on deck with Klaus and Ben, cooking our supper," said Abe. "Susie isn't able to be up because she's dizzy since she got that bump on her head."

"Well," grunted Johan, as he hefted the trunk back into position and secured it to the upright partition, "one thing is sure; God gave me the best wife in the world."

chapter fifteen

New Life for Pete

When Margaret and the two boys came back with the steaming food, she dipped it out for Karl and Susie and the boys. Karl sat on the side of the bed and fed Susie, so she wouldn't need to raise her head. Then Margaret turned to Johan and asked, "How is Pete?"

"He's hurting terribly. His left hand has some broken fingers or maybe they're out of joint. There are also cuts and bruises on his arm and hand, and his right foot and ankle are badly swollen. Do you think we can help him, Margaret? I don't want you to do more than you feel able to do."

"Yes, I think we can help him. Maybe Karl would let us borrow his candle lantern and we could see to thoroughly check out his injuries."

With Karl's ready loan, they approached Pete's bunk. Grudgingly, Pete allowed them to check out his injuries.

"I think I can help you, Pete," offered Margaret. "Are you willing to stand a bit more pain until we can get those fingers straightened out? It won't be easy."

"I'll take it," growled Pete through clenched teeth.

"That's good, because your fingers will need to be straightened before they can get better. First we need to get some supplies out of our trunk. We'll be right back," promised Margaret.

Soon Johan and Margaret returned with the necessary things. With some vinegar, they disinfected the cut on his arm, applied salve, and wrapped it up.

Next Margaret selected a couple wooden splints and some strips of cloth. "Now this is the hard part, Pete. Just try to relax while we pull and straighten these broken fingers. We'll try to be as careful as we can. Johan, will you pull and straighten his forefinger and I'll do the same to the next two fingers. Then I'll put this cloth-covered splint between two fingers and bind them together. We'll need to do the same with the next two fingers, and then we'll put a thin piece of wood on the top and bottom of his four fingers and then bind them all together. His thumb seems to be all right."

Pulling quickly, Johan and Margaret straightened three of Pete's fingers. He gave a mighty yell, then groaned loudly, and squeezed his eyes shut.

"Poor man, I'm sorry you need to feel all this pain," said Margaret, her voice full of pity.

When they finished binding up the fingers, they proceeded to use a coarse, strong bandage to bind his foot and ankle. "I think it's only sprained," decided Margaret as she secured the end of the bandage by tying a slipknot.

Still groaning, Pete slowly opened his eyes and asked, "Are you finished?"

"Yes," said Johan, "we just finished wrapping you up, but Margaret wants to give you some herb medicine that is good for pain. If it helps, maybe you can get some rest. Are you hungry?"

"Not hungry. Too much pain," groaned Pete.

After Margaret gave him the medicine, he mumbled something and turned his face to the wall, but not before Johan saw a tear sliding down his cheek.

"Listen, Pete," said Johan, laying a comforting hand on his shoulder, "if you need help to use the bucket, just wave your good hand and I'll help you. We'll be checking on you from time to time. All right?"

Pete gave a sound somewhere between a grunt and a sob.

"The poor man," Johan empathized, as he and Margaret returned to their quarters. "He is so overcome; he doesn't know how to respond to kindness. It might be the first kindness he has ever experienced."

With several days of bed rest, Susie was again able to cook her family's food. Johan and Margaret were now cooking food for their family of five plus Pete. Pete's foot and hand were becoming less painful, but he had developed a deep chest cough. They tried different remedies, but nothing seemed to help.

One evening Pete was having difficulty breathing. "Johan. . . Margaret. . ." he gasped, "come close; I need to tell you something." He stopped until a spasm of coughing was over. His voice was weak, but he continued. "The captain told me if I would agree to bring your trunk to him, he would set me free when we got to America. I agreed, but as you know, our scheme did not work out. I want you to know that I'm sorry. Your kindness has made me so wretched. Why are you kind when I've been so mean to you?"

"Pete," said Johan, gently drawing his good hand into his, "we love you, because God first loved us. The Bible says that while we were yet sinners, Christ died for us. It's true that we have been kind to you, but we haven't come close to dying for you, like Jesus Christ did. He died for you and me and Margaret—yes, for the whole world. All who are willing to confess their sins and believe in Him as their Saviour and Lord can be saved and go to heaven when they die."

"You mean there might be a chance for someone as evil as me?" asked Pete, a spark of hope lighting up his face.

"Yes, there's hope for you, because Jesus said, 'Whosoever will, may come.' That means the invitation is for all people. You must choose, Pete. No one is forced into accepting the invitation, but Jesus' arms are stretched out to you in a welcome and He says, 'Come unto me, all ye that labor and are heavy laden, and I will give you rest.'"

"'Heavy laden' describes me, Johan. I want to be saved. Will you help me?"

"Sure, Pete. I'll be glad to help you. You've already said you are a sinner."

"There's no doubt about that," admitted Pete, with a weary sigh.

"I think, Pete, you're too weak to get down on your knees, but God can hear you just as well lying down. Margaret and I will kneel beside your bunk while you pray and freely confess all the sins that you can remember. Then you need to ask Him to forgive and cleanse you from all those sins. He's promised to forgive us if we confess our sins. Thank Him for making it possible for you to be saved. Tell Him that you want Him to be your Master, and that you will do anything He tells you to do."

Johan and Margaret cringed as Pete slowly confessed his many sins, but they praised God as Pete begged for forgiveness. They knew God was looking down; He was hearing, and forgiving, and there was great rejoicing among the angels in heaven.

"Oh, thank you, Lord, for forgiveness," sighed Pete, as peace flooded his soul. "I'm not worthy of your love. I want to be obedient to you, Lord. Just tell me what you want me to do next and I'll do it." Another spasm of coughing shook his body. Then, struggling for breath, he said, "Johan, I know what God wants me to do first. Please call Klaus and Ben to me. God wants me to ask their forgiveness for the way I treated them and the evil influence I have been to them."

Johan turned and saw the five boys looking intently their way. He raised his voice just enough to be heard and said, "Klaus and Ben, come here, please."

The boys came with lagging feet, fear plainly written on their faces.

Johan and Margaret went partway to meet them and quietly told them enough to quiet their fears. They were soon standing together beside Pete's bunk.

"Boys, the Lord has just forgiven my sins and saved my soul, but I need to tell you that I'm sorry for the way I treated you and got you involved in trying to steal Johan and Margaret's trunk. I was very unkind to you in many other ways too. Can you forgive me?" Pete's voice was weak and barely more than a whisper.

Too surprised to talk, the boys could only nod their heads.

"Thank you, boys. And thank you, Johan, for helping me. I feel like a great load has been taken from me. Maybe I can rest now."

"You're welcome, Pete. You try to sleep now and maybe you'll feel better in the morning, my friend," said Johan.

"Friend!" exclaimed Pete. "I never had a friend in all my life, but now I have you and Margaret and, best of all, I have Jesus. It's wonderful to have friends. I never knew how nice it was."

"Let me tell you a secret, Pete. The more you have Jesus as your best friend, and the more you yield your will to His will, the more you will become kind and gentle like Jesus. And then naturally you will have many friends, because almost everyone responds to kindness. Well, we'll go now so you can get some rest. We hope you have a good night."

Johan gave Pete a gentle pat on his shoulder as they left.

As Johan and Margaret headed back over the heaving floor to their quarters, they could hear the strident tones of a young boy arguing with his mother. There was a slap and then more angry cries.

"It seems the children on this boat are becoming more irritable by the day," Margaret observed. "I wish there was something we could do to make their voyage more pleasant. Their bickering is hard on their parents."

"I think all children enjoy listening to a story. How about it, Margaret, would you happen to know a story that would interest the children?" asked Johan.

"Yes, I do! There's a story I dearly loved to hear as a child. My mother was a wonderful storyteller, and there was one story I especially liked. I heard her tell it many times."

"Would you feel up to telling that story tomorrow? I could walk down through the hold this evening and tell the mothers to bring their children tomorrow after dinner and someone will tell them a good story. Maybe it would stop some of the quarreling if they knew they had something to look forward to."

"I'm not sure how good a storyteller I am," Margaret worried. "My mother was the one who always told the stories and I did the listening."

"You'll do fine, I'm sure," Johan encouraged her. "After we eat our supper, I'll walk down through the hold and give them the good news."

chapter sixteen

The Hero of Haarlem

The next afternoon, Margaret's eyes glowed with excitement as she watched the mothers bringing their children. *Oh, I wonder if I can tell this story well enough to hold their attention. With God's help, I'll do my best.*

Margaret noticed her trunk had been moved out to the middle of the open space between their bunk and Pete's. "Thank you, Johan, for moving my trunk out here, so I will have a place to sit. There must be forty or more children coming our way. Please pray for me, Johan."

"I'll pray, of course, but I'm sure you'll do just fine." Johan's eyes twinkled. "I think I'm looking forward to the story just as much as the children!" he teased.

Susie carried a wooden crate over and sat among the children. It helped to give Margaret confidence just to see Susie's smiling face.

Margaret settled herself on the trunk and cleared her throat. "Boys and girls, I'm glad you have come to hear my story. Some parts of this story are made up, but it shows how courageous the Holland people are. It was told to me many times by my dear mother, who lives in Holland." The thought of her mother caused her to pause. Gaining control of her emotions, she continued. "How many of you boys are eight years old?"

Ten boys held up their hands, eyes sparkling with excitement.

"Well," continued Margaret, "the title of our story is 'The Hero of Haarlem.' It's a story about a boy who was eight years old and I want you to remember that you don't need to be very old to be a hero. This boy lived in Haarlem, one of the main cities in Holland. I don't know the boy's name, so we'll call him Hans. Hans was sunny-haired and had a gentle disposition.

"Hans' father was a sluicer. How many of you know what a sluicer is?" asked Margaret. Several hands were raised. Margaret continued, "For those of you who don't know, a sluicer is a man who opens and closes the sluices. The sluices are large oak gates that are placed every so often across the entrances of the canals. These gates are raised and lowered to control the amount of water that flows into the canals. This job is very important, because if the gatekeeper is careless about his job, the land of Holland would be flooded. A large portion of Holland is lower than the level of the sea, and the waters are kept from flooding the land only by building strong dikes, or barriers, and by these sluices, which are often strained to the utmost by the rising tides. Even the little children in Holland know that everyone must watch constantly to keep the rivers and ocean in their place, but especially so for the sluicer. If he should neglect his duty, it could bring ruin and death to all.

"One lovely autumn afternoon, Hans asked his parents, 'May I take some of mother's good cakes to blind Jansen? He gets very lonely and I wonder if he always has enough to eat.'

"His parents looked at their boy with concern. His father asked, 'Do you realize that is a long walk, Hans? Blind Jansen lives on the other side of the dike, out in the country.'

"'Yes,' insisted Hans, 'but I've been there with you and mother many times and I know my way perfectly well. Blind Jansen will be so happy for my visit.'

"'Well, if you think you can go straight to blind Jansen and not stop and play with boys along the way, you may go,' consented his father.

"His mother prepared a packet of cakes and Hans started on his errand with a light heart.

"Jansen, his blind friend, was very happy to have Hans come for a visit. After spending an hour with his friend, Hans started for home.

"While he trudged along by the canal, humming a childish song, he noticed how the autumn rains had made the water rise. Hans thought, *I'm glad those old gates that father takes care of are strong, because if they gave way, we would all be drowned and these pretty fields would be flooded.* With these thoughts going through his mind, Hans leaned over and picked some pretty blue flowers beside the path. He snatched a feathery seed ball and threw it into the air, watching it float away, and now and then a frightened rabbit hopped across the path and went speeding through the tall grass. Hans smiled as he recalled the joy of his blind friend he had just visited. Hans liked the way the blind man had listened closely when he had something to say.

"Suddenly Hans looked around in dismay. The sun was setting and the long shadows on the grass had vanished. He was in a lonely ravine, where even the blue flowers had turned to gray. It was growing dark. He was still some distance from home, so he quickened his footsteps. With his heart beating in his throat, he recalled nursery tales of children returning in the night through dreary forests. Just as Hans was bracing himself for a fast run, he was startled by the sound of trickling water. Where was it coming from? He looked up and his eyes filled with fear. There was a small hole in the dike. A tiny stream of water was flowing from the hole."

All the children and mothers were leaning forward, listening intently.

Margaret continued, "Any child in Holland will shudder at the very thought of a leak in the dike! Instantly, Hans understood the danger. If the water is allowed to trickle through, that little hole will soon be a large one and a terrible flood will cover the land.

"Quick as a flash, Hans saw his duty. He threw away his flowers and clambered up the steep dike until he reached the hole. He thrust his chubby finger into the hole and the water stopped! *Ah,* he thought, with a chuckle of boyish delight, *the angry waters must stay back now! Haarlem shall not be drowned while I am here!*

"All went well at first, but the night was falling rapidly. The night air turned chilly, and little Hans began to tremble with cold and dread.

"He shouted, then screamed, 'Come here! Come here!' But no one came. First his tired little finger became numb with the cold, then his hand, then his arm, and finally his whole body. He was miserable.

"He shouted again, 'Will no one come? Mother! Mother!'

"But alas, his mother had already locked the doors and decided that Hans must get a good scolding for staying the night with blind Jansen without her permission. Hans tried to make a shrill whistling sound, thinking it would attract attention, but his teeth chattered, making it impossible. Then Hans called to God for help. Suddenly he realized that God wanted him to do this job, even if it meant staying all night.

"The midnight moon looked down on Hans, a small boy sitting on a stone, with bowed head. He was not asleep, for now and then one restless hand reached out and rubbed the other arm that seemed fastened to the dike. Often he turned his pale, tearful face quickly at a real or imagined sound.

"It is hard to imagine how long and fearful that night was to little Hans. He thought of his warm bed at home and of his brothers and sisters. He thought of his parents and sighed as he considered the long, dreary night. Was it worth all this suffering? Yes, it was worth it, for if he drew his finger away, the angry waters would rush forth and never stop until they had swept over the land. *No, I must not give up*, he thought. *If I live, I will hold it here until daylight. But I'm not sure that I will live, for I'm so cold. Why is there such a buzzing in my head? And it feels like little knives pricking and piercing me from head to foot. I'm so stiff that I'm not sure I could draw my finger away even if I wanted to.*

"Finally daybreak came. A minister, walking along the top of the dike, was returning from the bedside of a sick church member. Thinking he heard groans, he bent over and looked far down the side of the dike. Could it be? Why, it looked like a child writhing in terrible agony.

"'My dear boy,' the minister shouted, 'what are you doing down there?'

"'I am holding back the water, so it can't run out,' was the simple answer of the hero. 'Tell them to come quick.'

"Of course the workmen did come quickly and relieved the suffering hero. They carried him home to his loving family. The workmen repaired the dike and the city was saved."

Margaret smiled at her audience as they sighed with relief that the little sufferer was rescued and the dike was repaired. Then she said, "How many of you would like to be a hero?"

Many hands went up.

"But are you willing to suffer?" Margaret asked quietly. "It seems that all heroes are brave and must suffer in one way or another. Now, how many want to be a hero?"

There were still a good number of hands waving above their heads.

Then Margaret asked, "Do you think it takes a hero to be cheerful while making this long and tiresome voyage to America?"

After some thought, a number of heads began to nod.

"Yes, it's not easy to be cooped up in this hold, with nothing much to do. It's not easy to keep from hitting and quarreling when our brother or sister aggravates us. It will make it easier if you remember that your brothers or sisters are also bored. If you want to be a hero, try to keep cheerful and think of some kind thing you can do for them. One thing you can do is to tell this story to those who weren't invited to our little meeting. If we all work together and try to be brave, we can help each other have a happy voyage, instead of a boring and grumpy one. Shall we try to be heroes?"

Every hand went up.

"That's fine. Now, I want to do my share, so once a week I will try to tell you another story. Do you think that will help you to be a hero?"

Nodding, the children clapped their hands and the mothers also smiled and nodded their heads.

"Thank you for coming. You may come every week on Friday after your noon meal."

The mothers and children crowded around Margaret and told her how much they had enjoyed the story and that they would be back next week.

After the group went back to their quarters, a slender young girl with glossy dark hair and troubled brown eyes remained. She hesitated and then slowly approached Margaret.

Margaret gave the pretty girl a welcoming smile. "Sit down," she invited, indicating the space beside her on the trunk.

The girl's tense face relaxed into a smile as she accepted the invitation.

"Please, I need a friend," begged the girl. "I've been watching you and your husband. It seems you're always helping someone, so I've been longing to get acquainted with you. I thought maybe you would listen to some of my problems. I think we're nearly the same age. I'm eighteen."

"Why, yes, we're very close to the same age," Margaret replied. "I just turned 20 a few weeks ago and my husband, Johan, is nearly 23. What's your name?" asked Margaret.

"My name is Elizabeth Hanley. I came from England, but I'm on my way to America. I'm so glad I learned the Dutch language in the girls' school I attended and am able to understand you."

"That's wonderful, but you're not traveling alone, are you?" inquired Margaret, viewing the girl with concern.

"Yes, I am, and I'm very lonely. I've been wondering if I've done the right thing. Oh, I know I can't change my mind, for this ship is headed for America and not England. There's no turning back now." Elizabeth gave a weary sigh.

"Would you like to tell me why you are sailing for America?" asked Margaret.

"I was hoping you would want to hear my story," Elizabeth confided, "for I feel I must share with someone and I thought you might have some advice for me."

"I have time to listen, so go ahead," encouraged Margaret.

"My parents are wealthy," she began, "and sent me to a private girls' school to get a good education. When I was nearly finished, I received a letter from my father. The letter said, 'You will soon be at home for good, and since girls your age should be thinking of a home of their own, and also a good husband who is able to provide well for them, I have promised your hand in marriage to a brother of my best friend. He is older than you, but he will make an excellent husband. So prepare your mind for this event.' When I read the letter, I rebelled. I knew it is a common practice for parents in England to choose a husband for their daughter, but I did not want a husband which someone else had chosen for me, especially an older man I had never met. I've always been rather strong-willed, so I went to nearby Liverpool, where many ships depart for America. There I met the captain of this ship. I told the captain I had no money, but I was sure I could find work in America and pay him later for my passage. He agreed and seemed happy to take me on as a passenger. I'm having second thoughts about my decision, because some of the prisoners in this hold are far too friendly to me. I'm beginning to feel unsafe. What shall I do?" Elizabeth's voice quavered with emotion.

"You poor girl. I understand your fears," said Margaret, putting her arm about the girl. "Would it help if you spent most of your days with us? You could also join us when we go on deck and we could do our cooking together. Would you like that?"

"Oh, yes, thank you; that would be wonderful," said Elizabeth. But then she sighed heavily. "Then there's another problem. From what I hear, those who can't pay for their passage are sold as indentured servants to pay the cost. I feel the captain tricked me, for he didn't say anything about me being sold to pay my passage. I thought he agreed that I would get my own job and pay him the passage money. I don't want to be sold as a slave. I need help." The tears which had threatened earlier now burst forth, and Elizabeth sobbed uncontrollably.

"You poor girl," repeated Margaret, putting her arm around her shoulder. "Are you a child of God? Do you know how to pray to Him?"

"I've never been taught about God or how to pray," Elizabeth confessed. "But I would like to learn to know Him. Maybe He can help me with my problem. Please help me to know Him."

chapter seventeen

Epidemic!

Margaret motioned for Johan to join her and together they explained the way of salvation to Elizabeth. She asked many questions, and then finally she said, "I know I'm a sinner. I've been a very willful girl and I need a Saviour. I want Him to be Lord and Master of my life, for I can see what a mess I've made while following my own willful ways."

After she had confessed her sins, and thanked the Lord for taking her into the family of God, she implored God to order her life and tell her what He would have her to do.

After her prayer, she said, "Does this make us sisters, Margaret?"

"Yes, it does," Margaret replied, "and there's real security in having a Father who is all-powerful, and in being part of His family. Remember this, if you put your complete trust in God and submit your life wholly to Him, He will not allow anything to happen to you but those things which will bring about His perfect will for your life. If you experience trials, God intends them to make you more Christ-like. Are you willing to trust Him, Elizabeth?" asked Margaret.

"Yes, I will trust Him," promised Elizabeth. "I have so much to learn about God's will for my life, but I want to learn."

"One of the first things you need to learn is a verse from God's Word. It goes like this: 'The angel of the Lord encampeth round about them that fear him, and delivereth them.' That has often been my comfort."

"That's a wonderful verse. Will you help me memorize it, Margaret?" implored Elizabeth.

They repeated the verse until Elizabeth had it memorized.

After Elizabeth returned to her quarters, Johan turned to Margaret. "Aren't you glad you told a story to the children? I kept my eye on you the whole time and I could tell it was a blessing to them and their mothers. And now the Lord has given you an added blessing—the privilege of helping another soul find rest in our wonderful Saviour. Tell me, how did the storytelling go for you? Was it too stressful?"

"The children and the mothers loved the story, Johan, and I was surprised at how much I enjoyed telling it to them. I hope it's all right that I promised to tell them more stories—after their dinner each Friday." She searched Johan's smiling face and knew his answer.

"I'm pleased that you are allowing God to use you. It will be a bright spot in their dreary week."

"And your Sunday services the past few weeks have also been a bright spot for all the passengers to enjoy," reminded Margaret. "I've been wondering, Johan, do you think a time of singing on Wednesday would be asking too much? I miss the beautiful songs you used to sing in Holland. Your songs were such a blessing to the sick mother upstairs and to all the servants who worked for Mynheer Voosterman. Maybe your songs will help others just like they helped us." Thoughts of home brought tears to Margaret's eyes.

"I think that's a good idea, Margaret. I admit I have missed the freedom to sing whenever I felt like it."

"Your singing is what caused me to trust you when we first became acquainted," confessed Margaret.

Each evening, Karl and Susie, with their two boys, and Johan and Margaret and their three boys had been meeting beside Pete's bunk for a time of spiritual encouragement. Now Elizabeth joined their group. It was a blessed time of growing in the Lord. Many questions were asked and answered. Many Scriptures were quoted.

Margaret's parents had given her a Bible for a gift, hoping that one day they would be able to send her to school. That day had never come. But when Margaret realized Elizabeth could read, she pulled her Bible from their trunk and encouraged her to read from it.

That evening when they met together, Elizabeth exclaimed, "Margaret, your Bible is a wonderful book! The story of creation and the flood and the part about Jesus' life is amazing. I hope it won't be too long after I get to America that I can afford to buy a Bible of my own. I love it."

"Elizabeth, you may come to our quarters every day and read as much as you like," invited Margaret. "The light is a bit stronger there, because we're close to the open hatch and the gangway where we go up on deck. But Elizabeth, I'm curious. How did you learn to speak and read Dutch?"

"The teachers in the school where I attended saw that I had the ability to easily learn different languages, so they encouraged me to learn all I could. Dutch and German seemed to be the easier ones for me to learn. I'm so glad I applied myself, because now I can read this precious book," said Elizabeth, joy shining from her face.

"You know, Elizabeth," said Johan, "I believe, even while you were learning the Dutch language and didn't yet know Him as your Saviour, God was preparing you for this day, when you could learn to know Him personally."

The five boys were quietly talking in a huddle. Then Tommy looked at Elizabeth. "Elizabeth, we were wondering if you would read the Bible out loud to us?"

"Why, yes," Elizabeth replied, her eyes shining. "I'll be glad to do that." As Elizabeth started reading the precious Word, everyone listened intently—the boys, Pete, Johan and Margaret, and Karl and Susie.

"This is wonderful!" Johan exclaimed when Elizabeth was done reading. "Having God's Word will help us all to be strengthened in our faith. Now let's bow our heads and reverently sing our thanksgiving to God for the gift of salvation." The strains of sweet music floated down through the hold, and men, women, and children stopped to listen.

When their worship time was over, they bade each other good night and retired to their own quarters. Tommy came to Johan and said, "Kendrick and Abe said they started with chills just when we were walking back to our quarters. Do you suppose they're getting sick?"

"Oh, I hope not," said Margaret. Concerned, she called the boys to her.

The boys came, trying to put on brave smiles.

She placed her hand on their foreheads and nodded her head. "You both have a fever. Have you been playing with anyone who wasn't feeling well?"

"Some of the boys back in the hold said they were just getting over the measles," confessed Abe, suddenly clapping his hand over his mouth while his stomach convulsed.

Johan rushed Abe to one of the necessary buckets and supported him while he lost his supper. They gave him a sip of water and placed him in his bunk, and a very sick Kendrick was placed in beside him.

"Here, boys, take this pan into bed with you," offered Susie. "You can use that if either of you needs to throw up. Since you're in the top bunk, you'd never make it to the bucket in time."

"Listen, boys, just call me if you need someone during the night," offered Karl.

"My head aches terrible," moaned Abe.

"Mine too," groaned Kendrick, pressing his fingers tightly against both sides of his forehead.

Margaret dipped two cloths into a bucket of seawater, then squeezed them out and said, "Place these on your heads; maybe that will help. I'd give you some of my mother's herb medicine for pain, but I don't think you could keep it down just now. Try to be brave."

"Boys, let's ask the Lord to be with you during the night." Johan placed a gentle hand on each of the boys as he prayed. He could feel their tense bodies relax.

After the boys were settled, Johan said, "I had the measles when I was a lad, but what about you, Tommy? Have you ever had the measles? And you, Margaret? Measles can be very serious."

"I've had them and I was awful sick," answered Tommy

"Me too. I had them when I was around eight or nine," said Margaret. "I'll never forget how my mother pulled the blinds and we lived in a darkened room. It seemed like a long time, but I suppose it was no more than a week. Since there is no bright sunlight down here in the hold, the boys' eyes will be protected."

"Susie and I had the measles when we were youngsters," Karl said. "Do you suppose this might start an epidemic? We're all so close together and there is so little fresh air."

Throughout the night, Kendrick and Abe were two very sick boys. Karl did all he could for them. The next morning, Johan took care of the boys, and insisted that Karl and Susie use his and Margaret's bunk to get some much-needed rest. Margaret, Tommy, and Elizabeth went up on deck to do the cooking.

After eating their food, Margaret relieved Johan from his care of the boys. Their fevers were raging, so cool, wet cloths were continually applied to their heads. Kendrick's speech was muddled and incoherent. Margaret was deeply concerned.

She quietly recited Psalm twenty-three, hoping it would bring comfort to the boys. "Poor boys," she murmured. "Not to be with their mother and father at such a time must be very hard.

"Lord," she prayed, "help us to do our best for them."

It was Saturday afternoon when Johan came back from a visit with Pete. "How are the two boys?" he asked.

"They're very sick boys. I wish we could do more," Margaret said. "I'm worried, Johan."

"We're doing all we can, Margaret. We'll keep praying. God will do what's best for the boys. Let's trust Him. At least Pete's health has been improving every day. It looks like the Lord needed to bring Pete down low before he would come to Him. It's a joy to watch him growing in his walk with God and to see how kind he is to the two boys above his bunk. Today a few coarse words slipped out of his mouth and he felt terrible afterwards. He begged the Lord for forgiveness. Truly our God is great, to be able to make a new man out of someone like Pete. Can you imagine what he wants to do at the service tomorrow?"

"No; what?" asked Margaret.

"He wants to speak to the people. He said he promised God that if his health improved enough, he would like to give his testimony and also thank those who stopped him when he was stealing our trunk. Talk about a changed man; Pete is a good example." Johan shook his head in wonderment.

chapter eighteen

Burial at Sea

Sunday arrived, and Pete and Johan were prepared when the people began to arrive for the church service. Margaret and Elizabeth stayed with the two sick boys, but they were close enough to hear what was being said. Margaret's trunk was brought over for Pete to sit on. He still found it difficult to stand for long periods of time, because of his sprained ankle.

Johan stood up to greet the ones who came. "Welcome, my friends, to another Lord's Day service. We're beginning to feel more like family, instead of the strangers that we were five weeks ago. Because of this, I think I should inform you of a recent development. Two of the boys in our hold have come down with the measles. They're very sick, with extremely high fevers. You'll want to warn your children to stay clear of our quarters unless they've already had the disease. Let's do all we can to keep this from being a serious epidemic. Margaret and I, as well as Karl and Susie, have had the disease, so we want you to feel free to call on us for help. Let's bow our heads in prayer and ask our Heavenly Father to watch over us all. After that, I would like to recite some Scripture from John 14; it will strengthen our hearts."

When the prayer and Scripture recitation was finished, they sang several songs. Many people were able to join in the singing. Johan smiled and breathed a silent prayer of thanks as he watched Tommy singing with all his might.

After the song, Johan said, "We have someone here who has asked to say a few words." He turned to Pete and said, "Go ahead, Pete."

"Thanks for letting me tell you what God did for me," Pete began. "I was once known as 'Pete the Unbeatable'. I no longer claim that title, but I have a Friend who has every right to claim it. Yes, Johan is my friend, but he is not 'unbeatable'. My best Friend is Jesus. Since I gave my heart to Him, I don't curse anymore. Now I praise and bless my God and those around me. I once hated all people, but now I love them. I treated the two boys terribly, but now we're good friends. When we were shoved roughly into this hold like cattle, I didn't have a friend—had never known what it was like to have a friend. I was bitter. Now the bitterness is all taken away; instead, there is wonderful peace in here." Pete laid his hand over his heart. "Nearly four weeks ago I was injured. I tried to steal this very trunk I'm sitting on." He stopped to pat the trunk. "It belonged to Johan and Margaret, so some of you decided to put a stop to my theft. When I was halfway up the gangway, one man tried to jerk it off my shoulder, while another clasped his arms around my neck and gave a mighty jerk backward. Well, we came down with a mighty clatter. I lay there groaning, unable to get to my bunk. No one wanted to help a mean man like me. But Johan and Karl saw me and had mercy. Yes, the very one I tried to steal from came to help." Pete's voice broke. "With the help of some of you men, I was placed in my bunk. Johan got his wife to help fix me up and gave me some herb medicine for pain. I was miserable in more ways than one. I had never experienced such love.

"You know, folks, it's probably easy to love those who love you, but no one can love their enemies and return good for evil unless they have God's love in their heart. These dear friends continued to take care of me and feed me. After that I got pneumonia, and I thought I was about to die. My Lord, the Unbeatable One, brought me to death's door and there with Johan's help I met my Saviour and Lord, and I've been rejoicing ever since. I want to say 'thank you' to those who refused to let me steal this trunk. I would have thanked you in person if I had known who you were, but I told the Lord that as soon as I was well enough, I would speak for Him and let others know what He has done for me. What He's done for me, He can also do for you. Just ask Johan; he'll help you. God has taken away my hard heart and made it like clay in His hands. Praise His Holy Name!" Pete nodded at Johan.

"Yes, let's praise Him, for He alone is worthy," said Johan. "May He get glory from your testimony. Pete is a shining example of what our Lord can do for anyone who willingly comes to Him. Like Pete said, I'll be glad to help anyone who desires the same blessing." After singing a song of praise, the people went to their own quarters.

Johan's warning to the parents was heeded, but it was too late. A measles epidemic broke out soon after their Sunday service. Twenty-seven children were struck with the disease. They did everything they could to alleviate their suffering. Many caring people lost sleep, and were willing to give of their time to relieve the parents and their sick children. In spite of their efforts, three children died—two of them were Kendrick and Abe. The other was a little girl.

"Oh, Johan," sobbed Margaret, "do you think we could have done more? Why didn't God answer our prayers and let them live? They were too young to die."

"Don't grieve so, Margaret," comforted Johan. "Our God knows best. He never makes a mistake. Maybe those boys would have been sold to an evil master in America. I know they were spiritually ignorant, but they were eager to learn of God's ways and they loved Jesus. We know God is just, so I believe they are now safe in His arms, which is far better for them."

"It does help to think that way and I'm sure you're right. But, Johan, we can't even give them a decent burial. It seems so awful to just drop them into the ocean," Margaret shuddered.

"I know, Margaret. I don't like the thought either, but we can't avoid it. With God's help, we can be brave."

Johan turned to Karl, saying, "Let's prepare them for burial."

They wrapped the dead bodies in pieces of old canvas and carried them up on deck. The body of the little girl was also prepared and laid beside the boys. The father of the little girl asked Johan to say a few words before the bodies were buried in a watery grave.

Susie came to Margaret and said, "Margaret, I don't think I can stand to watch the burial. I'll stay here to watch over our possessions and you may go to be with Johan if you want to."

"I understand, Susie. I don't look forward to watching it either, but my husband needs Tommy and me by his side. Those boys were precious to all of us." Suddenly, they threw their arms around each other and shed healing tears.

Margaret turned at the sound of footsteps on the gangway; Johan was heading their way.

"Margaret, do you feel able to come to the funeral? I won't insist if you feel it is more than you can bear."

"Tommy and I want to be with you, Johan. I know this is not easy for you either."

"God bless you, Margaret. This means more to me than I can tell. May God give you special strength." Johan placed his hand on her shoulder.

"There's a group of people waiting for the service to begin." He looked with compassion at Tommy, who was standing sadly by his side. "Come, Tommy, I know this is hard for you, too, but let's go up on deck. God will help us all."

When Johan's family appeared on deck, the group of people parted, making a path for them to walk to the front where the three small, canvas-wrapped bodies lay. The father and mother of the little girl were sobbing, while others stood by trying to comfort them.

Johan looked beyond the group and saw the captain standing outside his cabin door, observing Johan and the grieving crowd.

Johan stood a moment with bowed head. *Lord, I need your help. I dread lowering these children into their watery graves, but this service must begin.* Looking up, he cleared his throat, "My dear friends, this is a very sad day and our hearts go out in sympathy to the parents of this sweet little girl. These two young lads have no parents present to grieve their death, but they had become very dear to us—just like our son, Tommy." Johan placed his arm around Tommy, whose shoulders were shaking with sobs. "Tommy, Klaus, and Ben had become very close friends to Kendrick and Abe, so these two boys will be greatly missed by us all."

Johan stopped to gain better control. "I take comfort from the fact that these three children are safe in the arms of Jesus. They will never meet with any more hardships in this life. God has a plan for each person's life, and these three children have completed God's plan for their lives. I would like to remind each of us that there is a day coming when we will all stand before God. John, one of Jesus' disciples, was privileged to see a wonderful vision. Of this vision he wrote; 'And I saw a great white throne, and him that sat on it, from whose face the earth and the heaven fled away; and there was found no place for them. And I saw the dead, small and great, stand before God; and the books were opened: and another book was opened, which is the book of life: and the dead were judged out of those things which were written in the books, according to their works. And the sea gave up the dead which were in it; and death and hell delivered up the dead which were in them: and they were judged every man according to their works.' Then the last verse goes like this, 'And whosoever was not found written in the book of life was cast into the lake of fire.'"

Johan cleared his throat again, and continued, "I wanted especially to quote these words, 'And the sea gave up the dead which were in it.' Dear friends, we are about to bury these dear children in the sea, but God's Word says the day is coming when the sea will give up all who are buried at sea. Whether we are buried at sea or in an earthen grave, there's a day coming when we will all stand before the great white throne and God will open the books, in which all our deeds are recorded and we will be judged by the things we have done. Then God will open the Book of Life and anyone whose name is not found written in that book will be cast into hell—the lake of fire. Today is still a day of mercy. God is standing with outstretched arms to all people; He doesn't want anyone to be lost. But if His wonderful plan of salvation is rejected, then He has no other choice but to cast the sinner into eternal hell. When we are cleansed from our sins, God writes our names in the Book of Life, and we will have no fear when we stand before that great white throne to be judged by our Maker. These three little bodies remind us that we will all face death someday. Let us bow our heads in silent prayer."

As heads were reverently bowed, sobs broke the stillness.

Finally, Johan said, "Amen." When he raised his head, he noticed the captain had edged up closer to the group.

"Captain Boswell, would you let us borrow two long cords to lower these bodies into the water?" asked Johan.

"Well, we don't generally lower them down with cords. It's easier to just . . ." He hesitated and then continued. "Oh, well, I suppose we can round up some cords." He motioned to two of the sailors.

Johan handed one long cord to Karl and after finding the center, each man wrapped his cord once around the body of one of the dead boys. Grasping both ends of their cords, the men lifted the body and swung it over the railing. Hand over hand, they slowly and gently lowered the body. When it touched the water, the men released one end of the cord and pulled the other, rolling the body out into the water. They repeated the same procedure for the other two children.

When the last one had been lowered, Johan said, "Remember, friends, this is not the end for these children. Someday, the sea will give up the dead which are in it. That's a promise from God, who cannot lie."

Margaret moved over and gently placed her arms about the grieving mother. "I am so sorry. I know you're hurting terribly. I want you to know that we are hurting with you."

When her tears had subsided, the grieving mother sighed. "That was so good to weep with someone who understands." She looked at Johan. "Thank you for gently lowering our little girl into the water and for reminding us of the hope we can have through our Lord Jesus Christ. I think it would have been more than I could have borne if her body had been carelessly thrown into the water. Your gentleness was a balm to my bleeding heart. May God bless you."

"Yes, I too want to thank you for your kindness and your comforting words," said the grieving father. "We know this day was not easy for you either, and we want you to know we appreciate what you have done."

"You are welcome for anything I've done. It was only possible by the help of the Lord. May God get glory from this time of suffering in our lives." Johan's voice faltered with emotion.

Johan noticed that he and Karl were still holding the dripping cords in their hands. "Here, Karl, if you want to get back to Susie, I'll take these cords back to the captain," he offered, reaching for the cord in Karl's hand.

"Thank you, I appreciate that. I'm sure Susie is getting anxious." Karl took a gulp of fresh air before heading down the gangway into the smelly hold.

chapter nineteen

Unseen Hands

After Karl left to join Susie, Elizabeth squeezed Margaret's hand to get her attention.

"Did you want something, Elizabeth?"

"I've been wondering if it is too soon for me to make a request?" Elizabeth hesitated, and then continued. "I would feel much safer if I could move into the bunk above Karl and Susie. Do you think they would mind?"

"Why, no, Elizabeth. I'm sure they wouldn't mind. That's a wonderful idea. We would be glad if that empty bunk would be occupied and especially by you. I agree, it would be a safer arrangement for you to be closer to us." Turning to Tommy, she said, "Tommy, will you help Elizabeth exchange the straw ticks on the two bunks and give her a hand with moving her things to the top bunk above Karl and Susie? We'll be down shortly."

As Johan and Margaret watched them walk away together, Johan said, "'And we know that all things work together for good to them who love God, to them who are the called according to his purpose.'"

Margaret gave a relaxed sigh and said, "Yes, God is so good."

"Well, we better take these cords back to the captain and then get down into the hold and help Elizabeth get organized," said Johan, looping the long cords together in his hand.

They walked toward the captain, who was standing outside his cabin as though waiting for them. Johan handed over the two cords and said, "Thank you, Captain, for the use of your cords."

"You're welcome, I reckon. But I never saw the likes, nor heard such words as you spoke. Do you really believe all that you said—you know, about standing before God to be judged?" The captain's voice was serious.

"I believe every word, Captain, and much more," Johan firmly replied. "Our God is a God of love, but He is also just. We will all reap what we sow. If we sow to the flesh, we'll reap to the flesh and if we sow to the Spirit, we'll reap to the Spirit. We all must be born again if we want our names written in the Book of Life."

"This is all very interesting and new to me. I'd like to talk longer, but the sailors have informed me that a real storm seems to be approaching." He cast an uneasy eye at the fast-darkening sky. "You'd be wise to empty all buckets that sit close to your quarters and stay lying in your bunks while riding out the storm. It's safer, you know. Those who venture upon the deck are sometimes washed overboard into the foaming sea. There's also a chance for broken bones caused by bad falls during a storm."

"Thanks for the warning, Captain. We'll hurry and give notice to those in the hold. I'll be looking forward to talking with you later. We'll pray that God gives you wisdom to bring us all safely through the storm."

Johan walked the full length of the hold, giving out the captain's warning to the passengers. Immediately the men grabbed the buckets and hurried up on deck to empty them. When Johan returned, he saw Karl needed his help to place Elizabeth's baggage on the top bunk. After all was stowed above, they used old canvas to tie it tightly to the side of the ship, and hung up a privacy canvas to guard her from any prying eyes.

"There you are, Elizabeth," said Johan with a smile. "I believe we've done the best we can, considering what we have to work with."

"Thank you, Johan. I'll feel so much safer now," said Elizabeth, with a pleased smile. "I wish there was something I could do to show my appreciation."

"You're certainly welcome, Elizabeth. There is one thing you might do, if you don't mind. I can feel the sea getting rough; would you mind occupying the same bunk with Tommy—just during the storm? Since he is only a young lad, I'm concerned that he'll get pitched out onto the floor and maybe receive a broken bone. Be sure to keep the guardrail in place, along the front of the bunk."

"I'll be glad to. It will be less frightening for me to have someone near, since I've never been in a storm on the sea." Elizabeth looked agonizingly toward the hatch, where the daylight had turned alarmingly dark.

Turning to Margaret, Johan said, "I think I'll go and see if Pete, Klaus, and Ben want to come over here for prayer. I don't think it's safe for you to walk over there, the way this boat is beginning to pitch about. Please don't try to walk anywhere without my help. I won't be gone long."

Holding tight to the upright pieces of the bed, while the boat pitched about, Susie and Elizabeth slowly eased toward Margaret and seated themselves beside her.

Tommy, holding tightly to the bed, tried to be brave while watching Johan's uneven steps as he slowly lurched his way over to Pete's quarters.

"I'm scared," admitted Susie, pushing her shaking body against Margaret.

"Same here," replied Margaret. "But we must remember our lives are in God's hands, and His hands are always trustworthy. Let's remember the verse that I helped Elizabeth memorize. Maybe if we say it together we can somewhat forget about the storm. Will you help us say it, Tommy?"

Slowly they all began reciting the verse. "The angel of the Lord encampeth round about them that fear him, and delivereth them."

"What a promise!" Margaret said. "May God give us the grace to truly believe it."

"Look, there comes Johan and he's coming alone," said Tommy.

They held their breaths as they watched Johan slowly covering the short distance between them, sometimes stopping and throwing out his arms for balance as the ship rose and fell.

Finally he stood before his wife and friends. "Well, I made it safely, but Pete doesn't think he and the boys are going to try to come over and I don't blame them. Pete invited Claus and Ben to share his bunk, so he could protect them if need be. We had a short prayer together and committed ourselves into the care of our great God. Let's also pray together and then retire. Bed is the safest place for us to be in a time like this."

After a short, fervent prayer, they crawled into bed.

They were barely settled when there was a blinding flash of lightning through the hatch, followed by a loud blast of thunder. The wind increased to a fearful howl and a huge ocean wave hurled itself over the deck, causing a mighty splash of water to come showering through the hatch. Almost immediately, sailors slammed the hatch door down with a bang and fastened it firmly, leaving the passengers in total darkness. Even the few fish-oil lamps were extinguished to guard against fire.

The storm raged with a vengeance. Johan and his friends held on wherever they could grab something dependable. The wind howled and the ship repeatedly raced up steep mountainous waves, then dropped with a crash into the trough of the next wave.

Please, dear Father, keep this ship from breaking apart. Give the captain wisdom, and do protect our unborn child, prayed Johan, while guarding

Margaret as best he could from the sudden ups and downs of the ship. At times their bed lurched straight up, causing them to stand nearly upright. Then, seconds later, they were standing on their heads as the ship lunged down again.

They could hear the loose baggage slamming and slithering across the planking as the ship climbed steeply, then pitched into sudden nosedives. Children were screaming in fear, while men and women cried out to God to spare their lives and forgive their sins.

The waves finally became great swells, and the ship no longer took sudden dives. Johan knocked on the partition and started reciting the twenty-third Psalm in a strong voice. Karl and Susie, along with Elizabeth and Tommy, joined in with thankful hearts.

When the hatch was opened, they knew the storm was over, and they all settled down to a peaceful night of rest.

The next morning a large group of passengers got together to praise and thank God for keeping them safe during the storm. Several had bad bumps and bruises, but there were no broken bones.

"Now that was a storm to remember!" exclaimed Pete, shaking his head. "It will be a wonderful story to tell, proving what a great and powerful God we serve."

"You're right about that, my friend," shouted one of the men in the group.

Pete's face lit up with a delighted smile at the word "friend".

Fires were built for the women to cook their porridge for the day. It was wonderful to be up on deck and to breathe the fresh sea air, for many had been seasick during the night and were unable to get to the buckets, making the smell in the hold almost unbearable.

Johan and Tommy were standing together at the rail, looking out across the vast expanse of ocean, and breathing deeply of the pure air. Suddenly they were aware of another presence; the captain had joined them at the rail.

After a lengthy pause, the captain cleared his throat and said in a subdued tone, "Thank you for praying last night, Johan."

"And I want to thank you for your good work at the helm," praised Johan.

"I've been through many storms," the captain continued. "I've often tied my body to the helm to keep from being pitched into the sea, and I did the same last night, but I've never had an experience like last night."

"What do you mean?" asked Johan, as he and Tommy swung around, their eyes riveted on the captain.

"There was one time during the storm," explained the captain, "when I thought all was lost. I was in despair, but then suddenly, I felt unseen hands being placed over my hands, guiding my every move. Without those hands we wouldn't be here to talk about it. Johan, I believe the hands of your God were guiding mine. Again I want to thank you for your prayers." The captain blew his nose.

"By the way," he added, "I'd like for you and your wife to come to my cabin tomorrow afternoon. There are things I'd like to discuss with you. I would also like for you to bring Elizabeth, Pete, and the three young lads with you when you come. I made some promises to God last night during the storm and I plan to carry them out." Captain Boswell's lips were firmly set.

chapter twenty

God Gives Direction

When Johan's group went over to Pete's quarters that evening for their regular Scripture and prayer time, Johan said, "With the exception of Karl and Susie, the captain wants to see the rest of us in his cabin tomorrow afternoon. He had some serious thoughts after witnessing the funeral yesterday. Then while we were up on the deck this morning, he told us he made some promises to God during that terrible storm last night, and plans to carry them out."

"That's wonderful news!" exclaimed Pete. "If God could change me, He can surely change the captain, too. Makes a person wonder what he wants with all of us though, doesn't it?"

"Yes, it does," agreed Johan. "He told Tommy and me about a strange experience he had during the storm last night."

"What was it?" several of the group asked together.

"He said there was one time during the storm when he thought all was lost, but suddenly it seemed that another pair of hands was placed over his and guided him. If those hands hadn't helped him, he said none of us would be here to talk about it." Johan's voice shook.

Pete exclaimed, "What a powerful God we serve!"

"Amen!" agreed Karl and Johan.

The next afternoon, Karl and Susie offered to watch over everyone's possessions and to be in prayer for the seven people while they talked with the captain in his cabin.

What does the captain want? they all wondered as they slowly walked up the gangway.

In answer to their knock, the captain opened the door and invited them in. He moved his chair over for Pete to use and insisted that the other three adults should sit on his cot. Then he motioned for the three boys to sit on a folded blanket nearby.

"But you don't have a place to sit," objected Johan. "I don't like to sit while you stand."

"Don't worry, Johan. It gives me pleasure to have it so." He leaned against the table and nervously cleared his throat. "I don't know how to say what I need to say, so I guess I'll just blurt it out. I'm sorry for the way I tricked you, Johan and Margaret, and also, you three boys. And besides tricking you, I tried to get Pete to steal your trunk, Johan. I hope you can forgive me. I've asked the Lord to forgive me and I believe He has."

"We have already forgiven you, Captain," said Johan. "The Bible says if we don't forgive others for what they do to us, neither will our Heavenly Father forgive us."

"I've never met anyone like you and your wife, Johan," said the captain. Next he turned to Pete. "I need to tell you, Pete, it was wrong of me to ask you to steal their trunk. I made a promise to you which I never intended to keep. I'm thankful the plan fell through, but you were hurt through it all and later you nearly died. I'm sorry, Pete. Can you forgive me?"

"Gladly!" Pete said with no hesitancy. "You see, I was a terrible sinner and it took this experience to bring me low enough to come to the end of myself and to ask the Lord for mercy. Now He has forgiven me and made a new man out of me. For the first time in my life, I enjoy life and have good friends."

As the captain listened to Pete's testimony, his mouth dropped. "Indeed, you are a new man, Pete! You're nothing like the ranting, raving, cursing man that the authorities forced into the hold of my ship. I thought I had never seen any man with a face so full of hate, but now your face is shining. You've given me courage, Pete; if the good Lord can change a fellow like you into something worthwhile, maybe there's hope for me."

"There sure is!" agreed Pete.

The captain turned to Elizabeth and shamefully admitted, "Elizabeth, I deceived you when I allowed you to board my ship. I had every intention of making some big money by selling you as an indentured servant. I am sorry."

"I, too, have forgiven you, Captain," said Elizabeth.

"I can't tell you what it means to hear all of you say you will forgive me." His voice quivered. "Johan probably told you about the strange but wonderful experience I had during that terrible storm. That convinced me there is an almighty God, and since then He has been convicting me of my sins, which are many." He bowed his head and shook it sadly. "It's impossible to speak to everyone I've wronged, but as the Lord gives me opportunity, I promised Him I'd do what I could."

"We're glad for you, Captain," Johan said. "Living for God is the happiest life you could choose."

"I'm sure you're right, Johan. You've proved it by your life. Now, there's one more thing," continued the captain. "I want to do something special to show how sorry I am for what I've done. I'd like to say I'll take you all back home again, but it's really not that easy. The owners of this ship keep careful record of everything. They'll know how much food we used and will see you upon arrival. They'll be demanding payment for every passenger aboard. So smuggling you back would be impossible. I've thought long and hard about this, but I don't see any way I could do it. But I want to do everything in my power to help you. I'm wondering, is there something special I could do for you when you get to America? Don't answer now. I just want you to think about it and if you think of something, feel free to come to me and we'll talk it over. I'll have to dismiss you now, as my men are waiting on me."

They all gave the captain a heartfelt "thank-you" and quietly left the cabin. As they walked down the gangway, Johan asked, "This isn't a dream, is it?"

Elizabeth chuckled and said, "If it's a dream, we all had the same dream."

They burst out laughing, which eased away much of the tension. Karl and Susie looked up expectantly when they returned and listened eagerly to the news of what had taken place in the captain's cabin.

"That's good news for sure!" exclaimed Karl. "Sounds like the captain is ready to help you in any way he can."

"Oh, how wonderful!" exclaimed Susie, giving Margaret a quick hug. "Prayer really does change things, doesn't it, Margaret? Your future may not be too bad, if the captain is willing to help."

"Yes," agreed Margaret, "we're really excited about the captain's change of heart. Our God is great and able to work out the details of our lives. Oh, for faith to trust Him fully!"

"That's right, Margaret!" exclaimed Johan. "Tonight, let's each one pray and ask the Lord to show us what each individual should request of the captain, then tomorrow we can discuss it together."

"That sounds like a good plan to me," agreed Pete.

Their prayer time together was a time of praise and thanksgiving.

While Elizabeth read another portion from Margaret's Bible, they all leaned forward, eagerly drinking in God's Word, then they went quietly and prayerfully to their own quarters.

While preparing for bed, Johan said, "Margaret, I believe the Lord has opened the way for us to lay our plans and wishes before the captain."

"Yes," agreed Margaret. "And there is one other request I'd like to make."

"What's that?" inquired Johan anxiously.

"Well, I thought since Elizabeth can write, maybe she would be willing to write letters for us and the captain would agree to take them back to our families when he returns to Holland. Surely he could do that much."

"That's a wonderful idea, Margaret. I know our families would be delighted to hear from us and would be relieved if they knew where we are, and maybe. . ." His voice dropped to a whisper as he pressed his cheek against hers. "Just maybe, our baby will be born by then and we can tell them the good news and tell them his name."

Margaret chuckled. "Did you say 'his' name? It could be a girl, you know."

"I know," Johan replied with a laugh. "Regardless whether it's a boy or a girl, I'm eagerly looking forward to this baby."

"Me too," murmured Margaret. "By the way, do you have any idea how long it will be before we arrive in America?"

"From what I could hear, I think they are planning to arrive in less than two weeks, if all goes well. Why?" asked Johan.

"Because I believe the baby will come soon after our arrival. I hope that doesn't complicate things. Do you think it will?"

Johan heard the concern in her voice. "We'll just have to turn it over to God. He is able; don't you agree?"

"Yes," agreed Margaret, "I know He is, and I do want to trust Him. It's just that I find it so easy to dwell on my problems."

The next day, the little group gathered at Johan and Margaret's quarters. After a time of earnest prayer, Johan said, "I wish it were possible for one master to buy us all, but that is not likely to happen. Margaret and I have decided to request that Tommy can stay with us. We hope the captain will try to make that happen. Tommy is willing to work alongside me, and Margaret is a wonderful seamstress. Klaus and Ben, we're concerned about you too, and would hate to see you sold to a harsh master. What are your thoughts?"

"I don't want to be separated from Ben and," Klaus hesitated, then continued with a trembling voice, "and Pete." Ben vigorously nodded his head in agreement.

"Really, boys? You mean you would really like to stay with me?" Pete's voice was filled with emotion. "Last night after I had prayed, the Lord impressed me with a thought and it wouldn't go away. I believe the Lord wants me to ask the captain to find a buyer who will buy all three of us and one who will agree to the boys being set free at the same time when I'm released. I'd even work an extra year or two if the master would agree to it. These lads are special to me."

"Oh, Pete, do you really mean it?" shouted Klaus. "That's wonderful! That's exactly what we were hoping for. Thank you! Oh, thank you!"

"Yes, Pete, you've become like a father to us," said Ben, wearing a happy smile.

"This is great!" exclaimed Johan. "I didn't want everyone to be scattered about. But what about you, Elizabeth? Has the Lord given you any special directions?"

"Yes, I think He has. I was feeling terribly scared last night when I began to pray, but suddenly a thought came to my mind that brought peace to my heart. I'm going to request that my master be the owner of a Bible, and that I be allowed to read from it daily when my work is done. The Bible must be in a language I can read, of course. I've become so attached to Margaret's Bible, I feel I can't live without it. Then, too, I believe a master who has a Bible would be more apt to treat me right."

Johan's eyes were shining. "I can't tell you how happy this makes me. I believe each of you has been led of the Lord. Such joy must be expressed! Let's sing a song!"

As their voices rang with praise, some others in the hold joined in.

"Praise God from whom all blessings flow,/Praise Him, all creatures here below/Praise Him above, ye heav'nly hosts/Praise Father, Son, and Holy Ghost."

Karl spoke, his voice hoarse with emotion. "I find this experience so encouraging to Susie and me. Truly we have a powerful God, who through the Holy Spirit will direct our lives if we but let Him. It's so exciting to hear each of you tell how He has directed your thoughts while you prayed for guidance. I want this to be a lesson to us that we might remember to seek His guidance daily for our lives."

"This has been a wonderful lesson for all of us," agreed Johan. "If the going gets tough in the future, let's remember this time together and go to God in prayer. He is faithful." He turned and looked at Margaret. "Would you like to share the suggestion you made last night, Margaret? I'm quite excited about it."

"Yes, if only the captain and Elizabeth will agree to it!" exclaimed Margaret, turning to Elizabeth.

"Me? Please tell me. What can I do?" asked Elizabeth.

"If the captain promises to deliver some letters for us, would you consent to writing them for us, Elizabeth? I long for our families to know where we are. I know they would be so happy to know we're alive and where we are." Margaret looked earnestly into Elizabeth's face.

Tommy jumped up and planted himself squarely in front of Elizabeth. "You mean I could send a letter to my mother? Oh, Elizabeth, would you please do that?" He eagerly clasped Elizabeth's hand. "That preacher who was coming to see Mother can read and write. He could read it to her."

"Why yes, Tommy, if the captain agrees, I'll be glad to do that!" Elizabeth exclaimed. "I even have writing paper in my trunk."

"Yippee!" shouted Tommy as he whirled about and raced up the gangway out of the hold. Taking a great gulp of fresh air, he raced back to the group, his face flushed with excitement.

"Thank you, Elizabeth. That will be a real spirit lifter," said Margaret, smiling with pleasure at Tommy's antics.

"I'll be happy if I can do a little something to show my gratitude for all you've done for me," replied Elizabeth. "I don't like to think what would have happened to me if it hadn't been for your kindness."

"I'm glad for you folks, and I hope it all works out," said Pete. "As for my two lads and me, we don't have a soul who would care what has happened to us, but that doesn't keep us from rejoicing with you. I thank God that we do have some true friends right here and hopefully we can keep in touch with each other once we get settled in America."

"That's another thing we need to ask the captain, Pete. Thanks for thinking of it. It would be so nice if each of us knew where the others lived. Then if we get a day-pass, we might be able to visit one another if we don't live too far from each other."

"And don't forget us. We want you to keep in touch with us too," begged Susie.

The next day, the group approached the captain. He politely listened to their requests. "Well," he said, after writing them down, "you've asked some hard, almost impossible, things, but I am learning that God can do some impossible things. Each of you must earnestly pray and I'll do my best, with God's help, to give you your heart's desire. This is going to be exciting to see how God works out all these plans. Then about the letters—I'll be happy to mail them when I return to Holland and also England, where Elizabeth boarded my ship. Now, before you return to the hold, would you lead us in prayer, Johan?"

"Sure, I'll be glad to pray." Heads were bowed as Johan began, "Our dear Heavenly Father, we thank you for helping our captain so marvelously during the storm and we ask you to bless him for wanting to help us when we dock in America. We've presented our requests to him, and you heard him consent to do his best with your help, so now we will all lean upon you to work things out according to your will for our lives. We praise you because you've promised to help us in every time of need. In Jesus' name we pray. Amen."

After each one had given heartfelt thanks to the captain, they returned to the hold to take care of their daily duties. Their hearts were full of praise to their Heavenly Father. When evening came, the people gathered for their Wednesday meeting. By now the passengers thoroughly enjoyed this weekly singing. Johan had taught them many songs, and their voices rang out with enthusiasm. Even some of the hardened sailors joined the group when they were not busy with their work.

Johan and Margaret smiled at one another when they heard two sailors talking as they walked by. The one said, "There's never been a voyage like this one."

"You're right," the other one answered. "Maybe there is a God after all."

Margaret squeezed Johan's arm and murmured, "It's wonderful, Johan, to see what God can do through those who truly love Him."

"You're right, Margaret. God is able to do great things if we will submit our lives fully to Him."

chapter twenty-one

"Land, Ho!"

On Thursday, after they tidied up their sleeping quarters, Elizabeth sat near the gangway, where the light was best, and wrote a letter for Johan to his family, for Margaret to her parents, for Tommy to his mother, and last of all to her own parents. There was much excitement as they told Elizabeth what to write.

Tommy knelt at Elizabeth's side, watching each squiggly mark that she made. *Oh,* thought Tommy, *how I wish I could read and write like Elizabeth!*

After Elizabeth wrote the last letter, she said, "We'll not seal these letters yet, because we will want to add information as to where we will be living. That way, they can write back to us."

"Oh, Elizabeth, you mean I might get a letter from my mother?" Tommy nearly upset the ink in his excitement.

"Yes, I mean just that. It would be wonderful to know that they really got our letters and to read some personal news from home," agreed Elizabeth.

After dinner on Friday, the women and children gathered together for another of Margaret's stories. They were often taken from the Bible. This time she told about Daniel, who was faithful in prayer to his God, even though he knew he would be thrown into the lions' den. The children clung to every word! Their eyes got big and their mouths dropped open as she described Daniel being lowered into the den. They gave a big sigh when she said the angel of the Lord shut the lions' mouths so they could not bite Daniel. Their little hands clapped over their mouths to keep in the screams when later the wicked men and their families were lowered into the den and they had no God to protect them. When the story was finished, Margaret said, "I hope you'll always remember this story, boys and girls. It is very important to keep right on praying even when the people around you do not pray. Our Heavenly Father is all-powerful and can help you through every problem in this life if you are faithful to Him. This will probably be our last storytime together, as the captain says we will likely dock in America before next Friday. I have enjoyed this time together and I hope we will meet each other again when we are established on American soil. If you see me walking along the street or anywhere and I don't happen to see you, please come and speak to me. I'll do the same for you. It almost seems like we're part of a big family. If we never meet again on this earth, may we all meet some sweet day in heaven."

After the meeting, the mothers and children crowded around Margaret. They thanked her profusely for making their voyage much more pleasant. Some of the bolder children clambered up on one end of the trunk where Margaret was sitting and threw their arms around her neck and kissed her.

Johan, who was sitting close enough to hear, watched the display of love. He shook his head and marveled, *What a woman! What a wonderful mother she will make for our children! Thank you, Lord.*

The passengers on the *Minerva* were getting restless and tempers were short. Several times a day they climbed the gangway to the deck, shaded their eyes with their hands, and searched for land, only to return to the stinking hold, shaking their heads in discouragement. Food was getting scarce, and the drinking water, which was fresh when the voyage began, had begun to look like scummy swamp water, with pieces of green mold swimming on the surface. The ship's biscuits (hardtack) were now spoiled and infested with weevils.

Margaret had a thin piece of gauze in her trunk, with which she strained the water. She added a few drops of vinegar to make it drinkable.

The following Sunday when the people gathered for their last worship service, Johan said, "Dear friends, we will soon be docking in America. It will be new to all of us. The language may be new, also. I want to encourage you all to put your complete confidence and trust in our almighty God. He will help us. I feel God wants me to tell you some things that happened in my grootvader's life when he fled from Switzerland to Holland to save his life. For grootvader, Holland was a strange country, just like America will be to us."

The people sat spellbound as Johan recounted his grootvader's life story. After Johan completed the story, he said, "This story has given me courage to face the future and I hope it will do the same for you. Now I would like to recite some verses from the Bible. They are found in Hebrews 11:8-16. These verses tell about Abraham and how God asked him to leave his country and go to a strange country—one he had never seen. He stepped out with his faith in God, trusting Him to do what He had promised."

After the Scriptures were recited, they sang several songs and the service was dismissed.

On Wednesday, they enjoyed their last evening of singing. Many had learned the beautiful hymns and they sang with great fervor. This last meeting was interlaced with mixed feelings. They longed for the sight of land, but they dreaded the parting from these friends. In spite of the terrible storm and the three burials at sea, it had been a good voyage—one where they had been drawn closer to God.

Six days had passed since Margaret had told her last story to the children. Surely there should be some sign of land soon.

That very afternoon, a number of passengers were up on deck, with hands shading their eyes, intently searching for land. Suddenly someone screamed, "Seagulls!"

The passengers rushed down into the hold, shouting the good news.

"Seagulls! There are seagulls flying around the ship! That means we're getting close to land. Imagine solid ground to stand on for a change." The exciting news spread like wildfire as everyone raced to tell their families. Johan and Tommy, with many following, raced up on deck to see the birds and were just in time to hear a sailor shout from high in the rigging, "Land, ho! Land, ho!"

Racing back to the hold, Tommy shouted, "Land, ho! Land, ho!"

The announcement brought on a rumble of voices up and down the hold, praising God for a safe voyage.

Johan joined Margaret with a serious face. "I hope the next experiences these people face won't be heartrending."

"Why, what do you mean, Johan?"

"Well," Johan continued in a low voice, "most of these folks are poor people and will be sold as indentured servants. I'm afraid some families may be torn apart, never to see one another again."

"Oh, Johan, I hope you are wrong! That would be terrible," groaned Margaret.

That evening when their group met for Bible reading and prayer, they prayed earnestly that God would send the right masters to buy them and that the captain would be true to the promises he had made to them. They also prayed that the captain would have compassion on the passengers who had agreed to be sold when they boarded his ship.

When most of the people were bedding down for the night, a barefooted sailor, in dirty, ragged knee-britches, gathered tightly about his waist with a rope, swaggered down to the hold and nodded at Johan. "The captain wants to speak with you for a bit." Pivoting on his calloused heel, he disappeared up on the deck.

Tommy poked his head over the side of the top bunk and whispered, "Does that mean trouble? You want me to go with you, Pa?"

"No, son, let's just pray and trust God," encouraged Johan.

Johan quickly made his way to the captain's cabin. The captain ushered him in and shut the door.

"Johan, this next part, the selling of those who can't pay their fare, is going to be unpleasant business. They did agree to be sold as indentured servants. It never bothered me before, but things are different in here now." He laid his hand over his heart. "I dread the selling of family members—some of them will never see their families again. Johan, I'm sure you understand that something must be done with these people. I can't keep them on this ship indefinitely."

"Yes, I understand, and I'm glad it's a job that you're dreading. Because of your compassion, I believe you'll do the best you can for these poor people. We'll be praying for you, Captain."

"Thank you, Johan. I'll be glad for your prayers. I want you and your close friends to stay in the hold while the selling takes place, because it's a difficult time. Then, if a likely buyer comes along who seems right for you or your friends, I'll send someone to fetch you. How does that sound?"

"Sounds good to me. Thank you, Captain, for trying to spare us the agony of watching families being torn apart. When do you expect to dock and what is the name of the place where we're landing?"

"We'll be docking at Philadelphia, sometime in the early morning hours, and the buyers will swarm onto the ship as soon as I give the word. They'll be looking the people over. They are most interested in the stronger ones—the ones who are able to work hard in the fields. You tell Pete to stay out of sight, because he is noticeably strong," cautioned the captain.

"I'll tell him, Captain, and there's one other thing; my wife is nearly ready to give birth and Elizabeth would like to stay with her during the delivery. Would that be possible?"

"I can't promise, but it might work out that way, because buyers will be coming from quite a few miles away—maybe thirty to forty miles, so they will keep straggling in for several weeks. This ship will be docked for three or four weeks—unloading the cargo we brought over and reloading new cargo that merchants want to ship back to England. I hope your wife gets along well, Johan." He reached out and shook Johan's hand. "Thank you for all you've done to make this voyage one I'll never forget."

"You're very welcome, Captain. We, too, experienced many blessings from God on this trip. May God's hand continue to guide you in the days ahead."

Johan hurried back to his friends and told them how the captain was asking them to remain down in the hold until he called for them. "Also," explained Johan, "he wants to spare us from seeing the agony of those being separated from their families. The captain desires our prayers. Let's pray earnestly for these poor people being sold."

"Did he say when he expects to dock?" Concern was plain in Margaret's eyes.

"Yes, Margaret, the ship is expected to dock in the early morning hours, but it will stay in port for three or four weeks and we will stay on the ship until God sends along a buyer of His choice. The captain said it might work out for Elizabeth to stay with you for the birthing," comforted Johan.

"Good, I hope it works out," said Margaret, exchanging a hand-squeeze with Elizabeth.

"You know, Margaret, I would like to stay too," explained Susie, "and see you through this ordeal, but some of Karl's relatives will be meeting the boat to take us out to their farm soon after we arrive."

"I understand, Susie, but do remember to have Elizabeth write down where you'll be living, so we can try to see one another sometime," said Margaret.

After their evening meal of cold gruel, Margaret said, "Johan, please help me to open the trunk. I feel strongly that I should get out your best shirt, my Sunday dress, and maybe some baby clothes. It might help if I can prove my ability as a seamstress."

"That sounds like a good plan," agreed Johan, untying the trunk and pulling it forward.

Margaret pulled out her neatly folded dress and said with a catch in her voice, "My parents liked this one; it should do if they need proof of my abilities."

The next morning, October 29, 1767, they went up on deck to cook the morning meal, and just as the captain had said, the ship had already docked. The passengers stared longingly at the land, but the captain said, "Don't be in too much of a hurry to get your feet on land. The women and children will stay here, but the men will follow me over to Thomas Willing's office, where you must sign the required statements of loyalty and renunciation. Then we will all return to the ship. If you have paid your fare, you may go your way; if you couldn't pay your fare, you will wait here until a buyer comes along who agrees to buy your services."

"But, Captain, about that document we must sign—I can neither read nor write. How will I know what I'm signing?" asked Johan.

"Just so! It's the same with us," many voices murmured.

"Don't worry, folks. The document will be explained to you. You just tell them your name as well as the names of the persons in your family and they'll write it down. Then they will ask you to make an X beside your name. Now keep together and I'll lead the way to Thomas Willing's office."

Giving Tommy instructions to stay nearby, Johan gave Margaret's hand a parting squeeze, then moved into line with the other men.

"Oh, Margaret," wailed Susie, "I don't like to be parted from Karl. They will come back, won't they?"

"Yes, they will come back. Don't worry. Do you see anyone in the crowd on the shore who might be Karl's relatives?" asked Margaret, trying to get Susie's mind on something else.

Susie intently studied the crowd. "Karl said the couple was ten years older than we are and they have four small children. Oh, look, Margaret! There's a woman over there with four children. She's waving her handkerchief. That might be them!" she exclaimed, frantically returning the wave. "Oh, and look, there's a man following along beside the column of men and I believe he's talking to Karl."

"I believe you could be right, Susie. I hope you can soon leave that stinking hold and go where you can have a proper bath and something different to eat. I'm thankful for the food we had on this ship, but it will be nice to have a change of diet. If those are your relatives, be sure to have them come on deck and have Elizabeth write down where they live, so we can come to visit you sometime."

"Oh, I will. But right now I'd better go and see that everything is packed and ready to go. Please give my gruel a stir now and then so it doesn't burn." Susie hastened to the hold below.

Tommy stayed by Margaret's side as she finished cooking the gruel for the group of nine people. The cooking pots belonged to Susie, so Margaret knew she must finish as quickly as possible.

Margaret spoke to Tommy. "When your pa returns, maybe you could go with him to ask the captain for another cooking pot. Both of these belong to Susie, so we need to get them cleaned up and send them along with her. The captain knows we'll need a cooking pot as long as we are on this ship."

"Sure, I'll take care of that when Pa returns," assured Tommy.

When Johan, Karl, and Pete returned, they ate their last simple meal together with Karl and Susie.

"It's wonderful how my relatives got here soon after the ship docked. I'm glad for their sakes, because I'd feel bad if they had to wait for days and pay for food and lodging," explained Karl. "I want to say again, Johan, how nice it was to have you and Margaret with us on this voyage. I know it wasn't planned to be this way, but it was a Godsend to have you with us." Karl noticed some people approaching. "There comes my cousin—Sam Herting and his family. They are coming on board to help us carry our baggage."

"Elizabeth, don't forget. Write down where they live," repeated Margaret, her eyes sparkling with excitement.

"There's paper and pencil right here in my pocket," assured Elizabeth.

Margaret watched Johan and Tommy striding quickly to the captain's cabin and soon they returned with a well-used pot. Margaret quickly emptied the remains of the gruel into the new pot and handed Susie's pot to Tommy. "Please, see how quickly you can clean that for Susie, Tommy."

Tommy quickly scoured the pot with sand then handed it over to Susie.

When Margaret inquired about the Hertings' address, Sam said, "We don't have any mail delivered out our way. But we get into Philadelphia every three months and then we pick up our mail—if there is any. Just write down: Philadelphia, Pennsylvania Post Office—to be held until picked up. We live in Berks County, about 20 miles beyond Philadelphia. Just follow the main road to the left," he said, while pointing out the direction, "and it will lead you to our home where you would be most welcome."

"Oh, yes, do come," begged Susie, hugging Margaret with surprising strength.

"We'll do that whenever we can, Susie," Margaret replied. She watched with amusement as Tommy was getting acquainted with the Herting boys. He was obviously telling them about the terrible storm. He was gesturing wildly with his arms, swooping up and then down and smacking his hands together, as he described the great waves and how the boat groaned and creaked when it crashed down into the trough of the next wave coming up.

After many words of farewell and many a backward wave, Karl and Susie walked away with their relatives. The Herting boys called back to Tommy, "Sure hope we can meet again. We'd like to hear everything that happened on your voyage."

"We sure have lots to tell," shouted Tommy with a broad smile.

chapter twenty-two

The Captain Shows Mercy

A chilly November breeze whistled about their heads as Johan's group waved from the deck and watched the cart, pulled by two oxen, carrying the two women and the baggage belonging to Karl and Susie. The men and boys walked briskly beside the cart and periodically they would turn and wave at their friends on the ship.

The captain joined their group after the last paying passenger had left the ship and said, "Do you see that crowd of men looking this way? Those men are anxiously waiting to board this ship as soon as I give them the signal. They're eager to buy indentured servants to help with their farm work, such as cutting down trees and putting up buildings. You'd do well to go down into the hold and stay there until you are called. I gave orders to two sailors to bring four five-gallon buckets of fresh water and some extra pans. Just thought you might need such when your baby sees the break of day. Is there anything else you could use?"

"For myself, I wouldn't ask for a thing, but I know that Margaret, in her condition, must be very hungry for fresh fruit and vegetables—and a loaf of fresh bread would be nice." Johan smiled at the eagerness in Margaret's eyes.

"We'll see what we can do about that," the captain replied. "My crew will be bringing the water shortly." He reached for his bullhorn to call the buyers to come on board the ship.

"Oh, Johan, do you think there is a chance of getting some fresh food? It was kind of you to ask," murmured Margaret as they turned their steps toward the hold.

"I sincerely hope the captain can find something to improve your diet," encouraged Johan.

Just as the captain had promised, two sailors soon descended into the hold with four five-gallon buckets of fresh water.

"Thank you! We appreciate having fresh water," said Johan.

With a wave of their hands, the sailors hustled on to the back of the hold, flushing out all the remaining passengers and forcing them up on deck. As the people passed Johan's quarters, many of the mothers were fighting tears as they clutched their babies to their breasts or held tightly to their children's hands. The men were noticeably worried, but helpless to do anything about it. They were doing their best to be brave and to keep their family moving.

When the last family was gone, Johan said, "We are helpless, but God is not. Let us pray for the captain and these poor people. Margaret, you remain seated, but will all the rest of you fall on your knees and pray with me?"

There was a time of earnest prayer, as they beseeched God to have mercy on these poor people. They prayed that the captain would have compassion and yet get enough money to pay the required fare for his passengers.

The group was just rising from prayer when a screaming young mother came clattering down the gangway, clasping her five-year-old daughter in her arms. Her eyes were darting wildly about, looking for a hiding place. "Somebody help me, please. They can't take my Rosie from me. I won't let them. They will have to kill me first. I didn't know it would be like this." With a groan, she collapsed on the planking and pulled her daughter into her lap, while both mother and child shook with sobs.

Soon they heard the captain's strong voice calling. "Madam, please come on deck. I've made arrangements for one buyer to buy you both, but you'll need to work an extra year. How does that sound?"

"Oh, praise God," gasped the young mother. "I'll gladly work the extra year if we can just stay together." The mother and child struggled to their feet and slowly returned to the deck.

"Our God is so good," murmured Margaret with a sigh, her body weak with relief. "I'm so glad the captain was able to keep them together."

Johan softly sang their praise song, "Praise God from whom all blessings flow."

"Thank you, Johan," said Elizabeth when the song had ended. "I believe that song has helped to soothe all of our nerves." While the others nodded, she continued, "At times I, too, am tempted to worry about what will happen to me—who will buy me and so forth."

"Let us trust God, for He is the one who is powerful enough to help us," urged Johan.

"I know you're right and it helps so much when I remember to quote that verse that Margaret helped me to memorize. 'The angel of the Lord encampeth round about them that fear him and delivereth them.' That's a wonderful promise that I plan to cling to."

"That's good, Elizabeth. Our God can be trusted to keep His word," encouraged Margaret.

One by one the days went by, with more and more indentured servants being sold off to one master and then another.

Early each morning before the buyers were allowed on deck, Johan's group went up on deck to cook their gruel.

One morning the captain came on deck with a warm loaf of bread, plus three bags—apples, turnips, and potatoes.

"Oh," gasped Margaret, as the captain presented them to her, "are these for me?"

"All yours. Hope you enjoy them," said the captain with a hearty chuckle. "The sight of your sparkling eyes is pay enough."

"I'm sure nothing will ever taste so good to me. May God bless you richly, Captain Boswell, and I thank you with all my heart," said Margaret, trying to keep her eyes off the delicious food long enough to say a decent thank-you.

"You're very welcome, and I hope I brought enough that the rest of your group can enjoy a little of it, also. Before the buyers start coming on board, I think, if you hurry, you might have time to cook a few potatoes and turnips, with a bit of salt beef thrown in for seasoning. Come with me, Tommy, and I'll give you another cook pot and some peeling knives, so the women can get the food prepared," instructed the captain, quickly striding toward his cabin with Tommy at his heels.

"Here, Margaret," said Johan, helping her to sit on a rough bench, "sit right down here and sink your teeth into one of these apples. They smell wonderful!"

"You must eat one too, Johan."

"Later I'll be glad to accept your offer, but right now I'll help remove the peelings from these turnips," said Johan, reaching for a knife that

Tommy had brought.

"And I'll peel several potatoes," volunteered Elizabeth.

Tommy sat down beside Margaret and tried to ignore the apple, but Margaret pulled him close, holding her apple out and said, "Here, Tommy, take a bite and chew slowly so you can enjoy the rich flavor. If this is a taste of America, it's wonderful!" Then, looking at the rest of their group, she offered, "When Johan and Elizabeth are finished with their knives, we'll cut some apples in half and you may each have a piece. I couldn't enjoy these apples if I kept them to myself."

Soon they were all enjoying the tangy, crisp apples, a treat they would remember as long as they lived.

On the seventh day after they had docked at Philadelphia, all the people except Johan's group had been sold, so they were allowed to spend more time on the deck. They were enjoying the unusually nice weather when an elderly man with a white beard walked up the gangplank and approached the captain.

"Captain," asked the kindly man, "do you have a strong man who would be the makin's of a blacksmith? My name is Joel Bowman."

"Well now, Mister Bowman, I might, if we can strike the proper bargain," said the captain, motioning for Pete and his two boys to come over. The rest watched, wide-eyed, holding their breath.

"Pete, do you think you'd like to make things from steel, like shoes for horses and oxen and maybe learn how to put them on their feet?" asked the captain.

"I think I could do that if my two lads could come with me," said Pete, looking squarely into the kind eyes of the white-haired man. He then added, "I'd be willing to work an extra year or two if we three could be released from our contract on the same day."

The elderly man looked closely at the boys. "Are you boys willing workers? Would you be willing to pump the bellows and keep fuel on hand in the shop and maybe lead horses around and tie them at the hitching post? Also, my wife will need your help at times to carry water, split wood, and the wood box must be kept full. There's no tellin' what all she'll think up for you to do, but she's a mighty good cook and she's got a kind heart," bragged the man. His gentle smile caused his eyes to crinkle at the corners.

"Oh, sir, we'll be glad to work for you and your wife," said Klaus. Ben nodded vigorously.

"Well, then, I believe we might be ready to make a deal, Captain. How much are you asking for these three?"

"For Pete it'll cost you twenty-two pounds and seven six-pence and for these two young ones, Klaus and Ben, it will be ten pounds each. How does that sound? I generally charge fifteen pounds for young lads, but these three are some of the cream of the crop and they're special to me. Instead of the usual five years, would seven years sound like a good deal, since Pete offered to work a bit longer?" asked the captain with an encouraging smile.

"I believe they'll suit me just fine, Captain. Go ahead and write up the contract and we'll all sign it to make it legal, then I'll pay you in cash."

The three sighed with relief and exchanged satisfied smiles.

The captain sent a sailor to get the city mayor to be present when the signing took place. After the contract was signed, the captain passed it over to Elizabeth. "Since you can read and write, I want you to look this contract over and write down any information you may want, so you all can keep in touch with one another. The blacksmith shop is located right in this town on Walnut Street. You can't miss it."

Elizabeth studied the contract and jotted down a few figures, like their date of release and also the name and address of their master.

"Well, then, since our business is finished," said Master Joel, nodding at Pete and the boys, "just gather your things together and let us be going. My good wife will have a tasty dinner waiting for us."

"That sounds good to us, don't it, lads? About gathering our things together though, we don't own anything but the clothes we're wearing. But, Master Joel, could we have a few words with our friends before we leave?"

Master Joel nodded assent.

Pete, his face working with emotion, made his way toward his friends. Johan met him halfway and threw his arms around him. They stood quietly together, each trying to get control of his emotions.

Finally Johan said, "Pete, it's been a pleasure to have you as a friend."

"And you'll never know, Johan, what your friendship has meant to me. I never had a friend before. And better than that, you helped me to know the Friend that sticks closer than a brother." Pete brushed the moisture from his eyes. Klaus and Ben studied their toes, trying not to cry.

"Let's remember to pray for each other, so we don't faint by the way," encouraged Johan. "If we don't move too far away, we'll likely come to Philadelphia to check on our mail from time to time and we'll stop in to see how you and the boys are doing at the blacksmith shop. How does that sound?"

"That sounds wonderful, Johan. I believe the Lord has answered our prayers and given us a good master. I feel like praising the Lord for that. Couldn't we sing our praise song once more?"

"That we can," agreed Johan, and he immediately started singing "Praise God from whom all blessings flow, Praise Him, all creatures here below."

The whole group of friends joined in, singing heartily. The captain and Master Joel patiently waited with bowed heads.

"I'll sure miss your singing, Johan, and I hope you can come to visit before too long," said Pete, as he and the two boys gave parting handshakes to each of their friends. "But the boys and I will try to sing the songs you've taught us, even though we're not so good at it."

Pete turned to Master Joel and said with a smile, "I reckon we're ready to go with you, and we thank you for giving us a bit of time with our friends."

As they left the ship, they gave many a backward glance and just before turning a corner onto a side street, they turned and gave one last wave.

chapter twenty-three

Baby Joys

November 6, 1767, before the sun arose, the cry of a newborn baby was heard in the hold. "A-wha-a-a! A-wha-a-a!" Elizabeth was washing and dressing the baby.

Sitting beside the bed of a tired but smiling and flushed Margaret, Johan murmured, "I'm sure glad that's over and we now have a healthy son. What shall we call him, Margaret?"

"I've always liked the name Jacob. Would that be all right, Johan?"

"Margaret, I have two reasons for liking the name Jacob. First of all, it's a Bible name, and secondly, my boyhood chum, who was planning to be my brother-in-law, has the name Jacob. I know he will be pleased when our letter tells them the news. Yes, I like that name. I'm anxious to hold the little fellow. How are things coming, Elizabeth?" Johan stepped over for a closer look.

"As soon as I wrap him in this blanket, I'll be finished and then he's all yours, Johan." Elizabeth chuckled. She tucked the blanket snugly around little Jacob and laid him in Johan's arms.

Johan gathered the baby into his arms and murmured, "You're a precious gift from God, little Jacob."

He walked over where the light was coming down the gangway and studied his son. "Margaret, we have a beautiful son. He's wonderful!" He walked back to Margaret and sat on the side of their bed. He held little Jacob securely in his right arm and clasped Margaret's hand with his left. "Let's pray, Margaret, and thank God for His goodness to us."

"Yes, I'd like that, Johan," agreed Margaret.

"Hey, can I come down and see the baby too?" asked an excited voice in the bunk above.

"Oh, Tommy, do come down and see your little brother," invited Margaret.

Tommy swung out of his bunk and landed with a thump on the planking beside Johan and Margaret. He crowded close to Johan and peered in awe at the baby and whispered, "He's so tiny!"

"If God wills, he will soon be big enough to toddle behind you, trying to do everything he sees you do, Tommy," said Johan.

"Then I suppose I'd better be extra careful in the things I do," said Tommy, "not only because God sees everything I do, but also because I have a brother who will try to do what I do. It will be fun to teach him to do things. How long will it take him to grow?"

"We'll have to give him five or six months before he starts to imitate you, I should think," said Margaret. "Since I was an only child like you, Tommy, I don't know a lot about babies, so we'll need to learn as we go."

"I'm sure the Lord will give us the help we need," encouraged Johan. "We were just getting ready to thank the Lord for little Jacob. We would like to have you join us. Elizabeth, you may as well join us, too. The work can wait."

Elizabeth smiled broadly at Tommy, who was caressing the silky hair on the baby's head. *What a happy family!* she thought.

"Our precious Father in heaven," began Johan, "we thank you for our two young sons. They both have souls that will never die. It's a grave responsibility and privilege to have these two handed into our care. Margaret and I love them so much." Johan's voice choked. After a little pause he continued, "We need your help, dear Father, to guide them in the right way, so they can one day live in heaven with you. Please, Father, keep your protecting hand over them. Thank you for keeping us safe during the night. you've been so good to each of us and our hearts are bubbling over with joy this morning. Bless Elizabeth for her willingness to help us at this time. Give her a good master, who will show kindness and respect to her. Bless Tommy, too, for his willingness to help with the work wherever he can. Be with Pete and the two lads as they adjust to the ways of their master, whom we believe was sent by you. Again we pray, dear Lord, please send the right buyer—one who will need our services and will not object to our baby. We know there is nothing too hard for you. Also, bless Elizabeth's family in England and our families in Holland, dear Father. We pray through the holy name of Jesus. Amen."

After the prayer, Johan stood to his feet and asked, "Tommy, would you like to hold this little fellow?"

"Oh, yes, I'd like that!" Tommy reached out eager arms.

"Then sit right here beside Margaret and I'll finish the cleaning up so Elizabeth can get our breakfast." Johan tenderly placed the little bundle into Tommy's arms and said with a contented sigh, "My cup was running over on the day we married, Margaret, but now my saucer is running over too. God has blessed us with two sons."

"It makes me happy to see you so pleased, Johan. Yes, God has been very good to us."

"Hey, this little guy must be hungry," said Tommy with a giggle. "He's trying to eat his fist."

"I think I can do something about his hunger," said Margaret, reaching for the baby and cradling him to her breast.

Johan shook his head in amazement. "God thought of everything when He did His creation work. Then, too, He timed this birth just right so we could have some privacy in this hold and I was able to be with you and not working for some farmer chopping trees or husking corn. We also had the blessing of having Elizabeth with us. I've just got to sing a praise song or I think I'll burst."

Johan and Tommy burst forth in joyous thanksgiving as together they sang, "Praise God from whom all blessings flow, Praise Him, all creatures here below . . ." Margaret contentedly nursed her baby.

After breakfast was over, they spent some time on the deck so Margaret and the baby could get some much-needed rest. Repeatedly, a smiling Johan quietly crept down the walkway into the hold, and peeped behind the curtain to see how mother and baby were doing.

I just have to tell someone the good news, thought Johan. *I know! I'll get Elizabeth to finish those letters to our families back in Holland. They will want to know about little Jacob. Of course, I'll tell the good news to the captain. I wonder if he would let Tommy and me leave the ship long enough to look up Pete and his lads over on Walnut Street and tell them about our baby. Well, the letters must come first and then I think I'll ask him.*

With those thoughts settled, he found Elizabeth and together they discussed how to write the good news to their families. Tommy leaned close, watching every move of Elizabeth's pen.

The captain walked by and chuckled when he saw Tommy's interest as Elizabeth wrote. "I believe you'd like to learn to read and write, wouldn't you, Tommy?"

"I sure would!" exclaimed Tommy. "But I don't suppose I'll get the chance."

"Well now, there might be a way. It could happen," encouraged the captain as he hurried on about his duties.

"That would be wonderful!" Tommy shouted after the captain.

After the news was written in the letters, Johan said, "We're so thankful for your help in writing these letters, Elizabeth. Do you think we're ready to seal them up and give them to the captain?"

"I won't seal my letter just yet, Johan; not until I know who my master is. I want to add that bit of information in mine. I'm sure your family, as well as mine, will want to know where we are."

"That's good thinking. Of course our parents will want to know where we're all living, Elizabeth. Who knows, since your parents have plenty of money, they may insist that you return to England."

"Oh, I never thought of that," exclaimed Elizabeth, clapping her hand over her mouth, while her eyes enlarged at the thought. "But then, if I'm indentured, it would be impossible for them to take me back home and insist that I marry that older man. I suppose I needn't worry. Then too, this letter won't reach them for months. I would love to see my family again, that's for sure. It was the marriage that I rebelled against."

"Yes, I understand. Now that you're a Christian, Elizabeth, you must never marry a non-Christian man. Do a lot of praying about it. Be patient and wait on God's leading if you would have a happy life."

"I do want God's will for my life, Johan, and I want a happy family like yours," said Elizabeth.

"I have a request, Elizabeth. If the captain gives Tommy and me permission to leave the ship to look up Pete and his lads, would you be willing to stay alone with Margaret? I just think I've got to share our good news with our friends since they live here in the city," said Johan, while Tommy's eyes lit up with excitement.

"That would be fine with me, Johan. I'm sure Margaret and I would like to hear news about Pete and the boys, too. And it will give us some time to talk woman talk. We may not have many more times to be alone."

"All right, but first I want to step down and see if Margaret's awake and what she thinks of my plans." Johan turned and disappeared into the hold.

He pulled the privacy curtain aside and there was Margaret, checking over every part of their little son.

When Johan chuckled, she looked up, startled. "Is everything there?" teased Johan.

"Oh, Johan, he's perfect! He's a miracle when you think about all the many parts of the human body. We have a great Creator," murmured Margaret.

"Yes, little Jacob really is a marvel. He will have the special place of a firstborn in our family," said Johan, stroking baby Jacob's silky brown hair.

After a slight pause, Johan said, "Margaret, I have the urge to tell our ship family about our baby son. Since Pete and his lads live close by, would you mind if I left you with Elizabeth while Tommy and I asked permission of the captain to leave the ship for a short visit with Pete? Feel free to object if it makes you feel uneasy," insisted Johan.

"I think that is a wonderful idea, Johan," Margaret encouraged. "I'd love to hear how they are enjoying the work and how they're getting on with their master. Go today if the captain gives you leave. Elizabeth and I will have a good time together."

"All right, if you're sure you don't mind. I'll try to make a quick trip of it." After giving her a gentle pat on the shoulder, Johan left to ask permission from the captain.

chapter twenty-four

Surprise Visits

"So you have a baby son! Well, congratulations, Johan!" exclaimed the captain, clapping him on the shoulder. "And now you'd like to share the news with Pete? No reason why you can't. I'll give you permission to leave the ship for a visit, but I'll need to write out a pass for you and Tommy. I don't want you to be mistaken for runaway servants and get locked up in jail. I know you will return to my ship, because you're an honest man and you wouldn't consider leaving your wife and baby stranded here on my ship. Now this is the way to find Pete and the two lads," said Captain Boswell, pointing the way to Walnut Street.

"Thank you, Captain," said Johan. "We'll try to make our visit short."

"Take your time; just be back before dark. Tell Pete and the lads 'hello' for me," said the captain. Then he added, "If the right buyer comes along, I'll send one of my sailors to fetch you."

"Sounds good, and thanks for giving us the pass." After slipping the pass into his pocket, he waved a hand at Elizabeth, who was watching, then eagerly clasped Tommy's hand and hurried down the gangplank onto solid ground. Their walking gait was a bit awkward at first, but they soon adjusted to walking on something that wasn't continually moving.

"Won't they be surprised to see us!" exclaimed Tommy, chuckling with glee. "I can hardly wait to see Klaus and Ben's eyes when we step through the door."

"They'll be surprised all right," agreed Johan, smiling down at Tommy, who was stretching his legs to the utmost in an effort to keep up.

Their steps slowed as they turned into Walnut Street, trying to take in all the sights and watching for the blacksmith shop.

"Hey, there's a picture on that sign of a man shoeing a horse! That's probably the place," whooped Tommy.

"I think you're right," agreed Johan, increasing his steps to a faster pace.

When they arrived, they stood quietly in the large open doorway and took in the sight. Master Joel was showing Pete how to fit a shoe on an ox. The ox was held up with a wide belly-sling made of heavy canvas, and Pete, with his back to Johan, was intently working at applying the shoe while Master Joel patiently gave instructions. Pete seemed to be getting on well with the job and Master Joel was smiling with satisfaction.

Over in the corner, they could see Klaus adding coal to the glowing forge. Then he worked the bellows to make the fire burn more brightly.

The fourth shoe was finally attached to the ox and the sling was lowered so the beast could support his own weight. They unhooked the sling and Pete was just turning about to lead the animal over to the hitching post when he looked up and saw Johan and Tommy standing in the doorway. His eyes opened wide and he shouted, "Hey, Klaus, look who's here!"

Klaus gave a happy yell and came running. "Hey, Tommy, is that really you? Won't Ben be surprised? Can you stay awhile?"

Master Joel came over with a big smile and shook Johan and Tommy's hands. "Pete, we'll take our noon break right now, but first you'd better tie up the ox. Klaus, I want you to run into the house with the news and tell Minnie to bring some extra food and drink." Turning to Johan, he explained, "It's about lunchtime, and Minnie and Ben generally bring our lunch out to us in a basket, because we often get customers during lunchtime. It's good to see you folks again."

After tying the ox, Pete came back with a pleased grin and said, "I'm mighty pleased to see you both. Johan, were you standing there in the doorway very long?"

"Long enough to see that you're going to make a good blacksmith," praised Johan.

"That he is," agreed Master Joel, "and I'm right pleased with the way he's learning the trade."

His face beaming with pleasure, Pete spoke up. "I thank you, Master Joel; it's good of you to say so. I'd just like to give a return compliment. I couldn't have a nicer master, and I'm well pleased to work for you. And Johan, you wouldn't believe the good food his wife can cook. I've never had it so good. I know all these blessings are coming from the good Lord."

"I'm very happy for you, Pete," said Johan, "but you're not getting all the blessings. I got a great big blessing last night and I just had to come over to tell you about it."

"Well, out with it, man! What's the big blessing? We're anxious to know," urged Pete.

Minnie Bowman, Klaus, and Ben joined the group in time to hear Johan say, "My wife, Margaret, gave birth to a baby boy last night. Just wish you could come over and see him. We think he's wonderful."

"That surely is a big blessing and I'm happy for you, Johan. How does it feel, Tommy, to have a brother?" asked Pete.

"I'm mighty glad for a brother. I just hope he grows real fast," said Tommy, with a big smile.

"Minnie," said Master Joel, "this man and boy are some of the good folks I was telling you about. They were still on the ship when I was fortunate enough to get Pete and these two lads. From hearing Pete talk to them, I take it that this man is Johan and the boy is Tommy."

"I'm glad to meet you both. So there's a new baby in the family? That's good. Maybe we could walk over some evening soon and see him for ourselves." Minnie looked at her husband. After his nod of assent, she continued, "We had four daughters, but they're all married and have families of their own, and we don't see them often because they don't live close by. I'm itching to hold a tiny baby again."

"We'd be happy to have you come so we could show off our baby, wouldn't we, Tommy?" asked Johan. A smiling Tommy nodded his head vigorously.

"Oh, before I forget," continued Johan, "the captain said to say 'hello' to Pete and the lads."

"Did he really? That was good of him to remember us," said Pete with evident pleasure.

"Now, folks, we want you to eat lunch with us," invited Master Joel. "Let us pray."

After the prayer, he asked, "Is there enough food in the basket, Minnie?"

"If there isn't, I know where to get more," Minnie replied as she removed the cloth from the basket. She started handing out ham sandwiches and baked yams. When the last of those were finished off, she passed out half-moon pies, made with apple filling. There were two jugs of fresh apple cider to quench their thirst.

"Ah, this is better eating than we've had for months. Right, Tommy?"

asked Johan.

"That's right! My mother used to make half-moon pies like these and then I would sell them for her when I lived in Holland," said Tommy with a little tremor in his voice.

Johan saw the inquisitive looks on the Bowman couple's faces, but it hardly seemed wise to tell the family history right then, so he said, "Thank you for your kindness, Mrs. Bowman; you're a good cook. Pete has just been bragging about your cooking ability. I just wish my wife and our friend Elizabeth could have been here to enjoy it with us."

"I'll tell you what, I've got more in the house and I'll send a package of pies along with you for the women. That way they'll get to enjoy them, too," said kindhearted Minnie. "Then when we come to visit, maybe we can think up something else to bring. Your wife must be starved for good food after living on gruel for months and being with child."

Just then the owner of the ox walked up to claim his beast. While the man paid Master Joel, Pete untied the ox and brought it to his owner.

After the man left, Johan said, "Don't let us interfere with your work, Mr. Bowman. I would enjoy watching you work. And if it's all right with you, Tommy can help your lads with their work. He's a good worker."

Tommy gave Johan a pleased smile.

"That sounds good. Minnie, can you find jobs for these lads?" asked Master Joel, looking at his wife.

"I sure can," she replied. "There's never a lack of work at my house. Come on, boys, let's get at it." With a smile, she added, "We might even run across another moon pie for each of you after you work a bit."

The boys scuttled away with Minnie while Johan watched the men make horseshoes and fit them on a fine riding horse.

Finally Johan said, "I suppose I'd better get Tommy and head for the ship. I told Margaret I'd just have a short visit, so we'd best get back. She's going to be excited about your coming to visit soon, Mr. Bowman. We've certainly enjoyed our time here. May the good Lord bless you richly."

"Thank you, Johan, and I wish God's continued blessings on you and your family." Then, turning to Pete, he said, "Please go in and tell Tommy to come."

Tommy, with a package in his hands, soon returned with Pete. Quick good-byes were said, with promises of seeing one another before long.

While they walked toward the ship, Johan asked, "What all did you boys do for Mrs. Bowman, Tommy?"

"Oh, we had fun! Mrs. Bowman is nice. She kept us busy though.

We filled the wood box, split kindling, and washed and wiped dishes. We washed them in water instead of scrubbing them with sand, like we do on the ship, and we even scrubbed enough potatoes for their supper. Then she told us to sit at the table and she gave us a glass of milk and a moon pie. It was so good." Tommy looked worried as he gently shifted the package and said, "Pa, maybe you'd better carry this package of half-moon pies for Ma and Elizabeth. I'm afraid I might crush them. Won't they be pleased?" He lifted delighted eyes as the package changed hands.

"I'm sure they will. Well, that was a nice visit and I'm satisfied that Pete and his lads have a good home," said Johan with a contented sigh.

Margaret and Elizabeth were deep in conversation when suddenly the light was cut off, causing the women to look expectantly toward the hatch. As Johan and Tommy hurriedly descended, the women saw Johan hand a package to Tommy and whisper a few words.

Tommy's eyes were dancing as he rushed over and laid the package on Margaret's bed pillow. "A gift for you and Elizabeth!" he shouted. "Open it, quick!"

"For us?" asked Margaret, looking at Johan.

"It was given for you and Elizabeth," assured Johan.

As Margaret pulled away the wrapping, she gave a delighted sniff and said, "Oh, something smells good. What a treat! It's four half-moon pies, Elizabeth!" Passing two to Elizabeth, she bit into one of hers. She closed her eyes and with a dreamy expression said, "Ummm! Who sent them, Johan?"

Johan and Tommy told all about their visit while the women enjoyed their pies.

When the last crumb had disappeared, Margaret said, "I wish I could thank Mrs. Bowman for these delicious pies. She must be a very kind and thoughtful woman." After glancing at Johan, she could see he had something exciting to tell. "Come now, I can see you're holding back something special. What is it, Johan?"

"Tommy, why don't you tell our special news; I can see you're nearly bursting." Johan laughed heartily.

"They're all coming to visit us!" blurted out Tommy. "Mrs. Bowman wants to hold our baby! She said maybe she could bring something else along that was good to eat. She's a great cook! Pete, Klaus, and Ben have a nice place to live."

"Oh, that's wonderful," murmured Margaret.

"It sounds like we're about to get our first company in America. How exciting!" exclaimed Elizabeth.

Four evenings later, Tommy hurtled down the gangway and shouted, "They're coming! I saw them and they're carrying two baskets and some jugs of cider."

It was a cool evening, but they all gathered in a sheltered area on the deck. What a time of getting acquainted and exclaiming over the nice baby! Even Pete wanted to hold little Jacob.

They invited the captain and a few sailors, who were on ship duty, to enjoy the good food with them. The baskets contained ham sandwiches, hard-boiled eggs, pickles, cake, and apples.

They all had a good visit while they enjoyed the food, and then they sang several songs, and all who could, quoted some Scripture they had memorized. Then there was a time of prayer, with several different people leading out.

When it was time to say good-bye, Mrs. Bowman put her arms around Margaret, giving her a motherly embrace and said, "I hope we shall meet again, dear Margaret. We attend church over in Berks County when the weather is good. It would be wonderful if you could live close enough to attend the same church. That church could surely use some good singers like Johan and Tommy. But we can trust God to lead you each step of the way. It rests my mind to know you have a good husband—one who loves you."

"I do have a good husband, and oh, Mrs. Bowman, it's so good to feel a mother's arms about me again. If God wills, we shall meet again," agreed Margaret.

Mrs. Bowman embraced Elizabeth. "How I wish we were rich enough to buy your services also, dear girl, but we can't. We will trust our Lord to give you a good place to work. We'll be praying for you, Elizabeth."

"Thank you, Mrs. Bowman. Your prayers mean so much to us. We're trusting God to do what He feels is best for us."

Next she pulled Tommy into her arms and, not wanting the captain to hear, she whispered into his ear, "Pete and the lads told me why you're here instead of in Holland. It's tough, I'm sure, but the Lord is looking out for you, because He has put you into a family that will give you good care and teaching."

"I do miss my mother a lot," Tommy replied, his voice quivering. "But you're right and I'm thankful for my new ma and pa. Now the captain has become a Christian and is trying to help each of us find good homes. Elizabeth wrote a letter to my mother and the captain promised to see that she gets it," said Tommy, with a happy smile.

"That's good, very good," agreed Mrs. Bowman.

After everyone said a hearty "thank-you", the guests finally took their leave, giving final waves as they turned the corner toward Walnut Street.

"Wasn't that wonderful to have them come and bring food and stay for a time of fellowship and worship, Johan?" asked Margaret, as she sat on the edge of their bed, nursing little Jacob.

"Yes, it was! I'm sure you thought about Karl and Susie when Mrs. Bowman said they attend church in Berks County, because that's where Karl and Susie are living with their Herting cousins. It wouldn't surprise me a lot to learn that they attend the same church. I would be happy if we could attend the same church, but may the Lord's will be done."

"With God, all things are possible," murmured Margaret.

"If only the captain could find a buyer for us," Johan replied with a sigh. "This waiting is starting to wear me down."

As the days passed, the freight was unloaded from the ship and new freight was loaded for the return trip across the ocean. In another week or two, the ship would sail away, fully loaded.

Now and then an unlikely master would climb the gangplank and inquire about indentured servants, but the captain would shake his head. Although time was running out, he was still willing to wait awhile longer for the right buyer, one who was willing to take Johan's complete family, or one who would meet Elizabeth's requirement—a master who owned a Bible.

chapter twenty-five

One Man, Two Oxen, and God

Before the sun was up in Berks County, on a crisp November day, Pa Miller and his 21-year-old son, Joshua, were standing beside their mill, looking over a healthy pair of oxen. There was the comforting sound of running water close by.

"Son, you've done a good job of breaking these yearlings to pull the cart, but we don't really need them around the mill, since we have a nice team of horses to pull our carriage and wagon. What do you think we ought to do with them, Josh?" asked Pa.

"Our last customer said there's a ship in the Philadelphia harbor. Maybe I could make a deal with the captain. He might want to buy them and then swap them for something to take overseas. Some captains enjoy doing such things. It's worth a try, Pa. Should I take them over to the harbor?" There was eagerness in Josh's voice.

"Go ahead, Josh. It's worth a try. They are a beautiful and well-matched team; someone is sure to buy them. You need a break from the mill anyway, so get Ma to pack a lunch and be on your way. May the Lord help you to make a wise decision."

"Pa, I remember hearing you quote a Bible verse just this morning at the breakfast table that went something like this, 'If any man lack wisdom, let him ask of God, who will readily give that man the help he needs.' I plan to ask God for wisdom when I get to town," promised Josh.

"You're a good son, and I know I can count on you to do the right thing." Pa smiled broadly.

"Thanks, Pa! I'll get Ma to put up a lunch for me and I'll be on my way. I'll stay overnight in town and be back sometime tomorrow."

Turning, he took long strides toward their comfortable log cabin. In addition to its four rooms, the cabin had a loft, a lean-to kitchen attached at the back, and along the front was a porch with inviting chairs.

Ma was sitting in a rocking chair on the porch, cutting up cabbage for sauerkraut. She looked up and smiled. "What's making you step so lively, Josh?"

"Pa said I should take the ox team to Philadelphia and try to sell them. I need to leave as soon as possible."

"Well, then, I'll put a quick lunch together and you can be on your way." She dropped her knife along with the partial head of cabbage into the pan, brushed the damp, clinging cabbage from her hands, and hurried indoors. Josh pulled up a bucket of water from their well and filled some leather water containers so he could quench his thirst on his ten-mile journey.

In a short time his mother came bustling out with two leather bags containing food, which were tied at each end with a length of stout cord. "Make them secure," warned Ma, with a teasing laugh.

"Don't worry, Ma. One catastrophe was enough to teach me a lesson. I don't want them dropping loose and being trampled underfoot—again." They had a good laugh as they remembered the incident.

"Be careful, Josh. We'll be praying for you and looking for your return tomorrow." Ma returned to her cabbage cutting.

"I'll be careful, Ma, and thanks for your prayers." Quickly he walked over and secured the lunch and water to the backs of the oxen, and then with a wave of his hand and a gentle prick with the ox goad, Josh and the team of oxen started briskly down the road.

Josh smiled as he observed a few fluffy white clouds in the blue sky and the bare tree branches making sun and shadow patterns across his path.

Several hours later, the sun was high in the sky. When he came within sight of the town, Josh stopped and ate his lunch of biscuits, beef jerky, and apples, followed by a drink of cool water. He could see the sailing vessel docked at the wharf, so after a prayer for guidance, he was soon on his way with purposeful steps. He noticed a well-dressed man approaching the ship and ascending the gangplank. He also saw a young lad and a beautiful young woman standing by the ship railing. They were pointing his way.

Josh thought, *After I give these oxen a drink at the town watering trough, I'll tie them to the hitching post. Then I'll make my way into that ship. I hope the captain will give me a good price for these oxen.*

It was noontime, and with the weather being unseasonably warm, Elizabeth and Johan's family were up on deck enjoying the sea breezes—all except little Jacob, who was sleeping in the hold. Elizabeth and Tommy were over at the ship's railing, having a lively conversation. Johan saw them pointing at a man coming down the street with his oxen.

Margaret leaned over and whispered in Johan's ear, "Did you notice, Elizabeth is exceptionally pretty today? May the dear Lord give her a good master who will treat her with respect."

"Yes, she is a beautiful girl, and we'll continue to pray that God will spare her from a cruel master," murmured Johan, deeply concerned.

Footsteps sounded on the gangplank, and the little group turned to see who was coming. A man with glossy black hair and a waxed handlebar mustache strode along, carrying a gold-headed cane under his arm. He walked over and boldly looked Elizabeth up and down, then demanded, "Are you for sale?"

Oh, no, Lord, please not this man, prayed Johan.

Elizabeth replied in a trembling voice, "You must conduct your business with Captain Boswell, sir."

"Don't be saucy with me, girl. I'm not ignorant. I know I need to talk to the captain." He wheeled about and strode toward the captain, who had been watching Elizabeth's reaction to the man. The captain beckoned to Elizabeth, who came with faltering footsteps and downcast eyes.

Johan and Margaret moved closer, watching with troubled eyes. Tommy leaned hard against Johan and whispered, "Is that awful man going to buy her?"

"Shhh!" cautioned Johan and mouthed the word, "Pray," to Tommy.

"Captain, is this girl for sale?" demanded the man, leering at Elizabeth.

"Lucas, that all depends if you can meet the requirements for sale." The captain kept a steady eye on the man's face.

"Well, what are the requirements? Speak up; I'm in a hurry and I'm determined to have her."

At that precise moment, Josh Miller joined the group. He observed the serious faces and the trembling but beautiful girl being discussed. His heart cried out in pity. She was obviously distressed.

The captain acknowledged Josh's presence with a nod and then began explaining the requirements for sale to Lucas. "Her sale price is sixteen pounds and she will serve for seven years."

"That's fine with me! Sign up the papers! The sooner I get her into my pub, the sooner business will pick up, so get on with it." Lucas gave a harsh laugh.

"Not so fast, Lucas. There's one stipulation that I have agreed to before she can be sold. The buyer must own a Bible—one that she can read when her work is finished each evening." The captain's mouth was set firmly.

"Own a Bible!" snorted Lucas. "You're no goody-goody yourself. You've been in my pub and enjoyed every part of it. What's the holdup? I want this girl." Lucas stamped his foot.

"Lucas, I'm well aware of what I've done with my life in the past and I'm sorry. If you can't meet the requirements, then this girl is not for sale. Let that be final."

"Oh, all right! What Bible can she read?"

"It's up to you to tell us what the language is of whatever Bible you may have in your possession. And are you willing to sign a contract saying she has the right to read the Bible every evening when her work is finished? If so, she's yours."

Josh couldn't stand there and watch this girl being sold to this evil man. With a voice full of compassion, he offered, "We have a German Bible, which we'd be happy to let her read."

At the words "German Bible", Elizabeth lifted startled eyes and suddenly became aware of the young man.

"Don't listen to that poor man," growled Lucas. "He's only a miller; he couldn't afford to buy her. I said I'm determined to have her, so I'll give you twice the price—32 pounds. Is it a deal?" Lucas smiled at the battle on the captain's face.

As the captain raised troubled eyes, he saw Johan with bowed head and his lips moving in prayer. Suddenly he squared his shoulders, cleared his throat, and turned to Josh. "Young man, you've met one of the requirements, but what can you pay for this young woman?"

"Captain, that's what I came to talk to you about. I have a fine yoke of yearling oxen, which are broken to pulling a cart, and in another year, they can be used to pull logs from the forest. I would be happy to take the girl in exchange for the oxen. I'm a single man and live with my parents, but my mother isn't too strong, so she would be happy to have another woman's help in the house and garden. We are a church-going family that loves to read the Bible."

A smile broke over the captain's face. He turned to Elizabeth. "Which of these masters do you choose?"

"Please, Captain, the one with a Bible," begged Elizabeth, with pleading eyes.

"I might lose a bit of money, but I believe you'll be happy in the home of this young man's mother. Then, too, he can give you your heart's desire—a Bible. And I can sail away with a clear conscience. Let's get on with writing up the contract."

"But—but," sputtered Lucas in a shocked tone. His face turned red as he shouted, "You mean you won't take me up on my offer of double the money?"

"That's right, Lucas. Money no longer has control of my heart—God does," admitted the captain.

"I can't believe this. I've never been bested before. Never! Miller boy, you're going to be sorry when I get my grinding done at another mill from now on. Do you hear me?" He angrily shook his gold-headed cane very near Josh's nose.

Josh was silent. He nodded his head and gave Lucas a look of pity. With a final muttered oath, Lucas stomped away in a rage.

Josh explained that he lived ten miles out of town, right on the Berks County line. At that news, Johan and Margaret exchanged happy nods and smiles. They were well pleased, but when they looked at Elizabeth, tears were streaming down her cheeks.

Margaret rushed over and gathered her into her arms.

"Oh, Margaret, God is so good," said Elizabeth, her words coming out louder than she intended.

"Captain," said Josh, "I won't be leaving for home until tomorrow morning—early. Could Elizabeth stay on your ship until morning?"

"Certainly. Her friends will be glad to have her around a bit longer. We'll wait until morning to get the city mayor over for the final signing."

"That sounds good," agreed Josh.

It was obvious to Johan that the captain had taken a liking to this young man who had boarded the ship at just the right time. The worry lines had disappeared from his face as he informed Josh, "These folks have been a great blessing to everyone on my ship, and in the process I became a Christian. I'm finding it to be a good life. It has been real exciting to watch God work out the placement of each of these Christians. I'm still looking for a good place for Johan and his family, but after what just happened, I won't be surprised if God works things out for their good also."

Their attention was drawn to some activity on the shore. A man and woman were heading toward the ship.

"Captain," said Josh, "maybe they'll be the ones who will be just right for Johan's family. This is getting exciting! Do you mind if I stay a bit longer and see how things turn out?"

"Don't mind a bit. It's more enjoyable when there's more to share the excitement."

chapter twenty-six

Captain Keeps His Promises

Jason Cloud and his wife, Jean, left a wagon load of shelled corn at the mill to be ground. Then, adjusting saddles on their horses, they rode to the harbor.

"I'm just sure we're too late," grumbled Jean. "The servants will all be sold by now, and I wanted to get a good seamstress to teach our daughters how to sew. They'll soon be at the age when they will be going to special events and it would save much money if they could make their own clothes." Jean continued to vent her feelings. "But no amount of talking could convince you. Oh, no! You wouldn't budge until you had a full load of shelled corn." She looked at her husband with disgust.

Jason ignored his wife's complaining as he craned his neck for a better look at the ship. "It looks like there are still people on the ship; you may get your wish yet," he commented quietly as they dismounted.

"Well, let's hurry. I hope you're right." Jean lengthened her stride.

As they hurried up the gangplank, the captain motioned them to come near. "I'm Captain Boswell. How can I help you?"

"I'm pleased to meet you, Captain. I'm Jason Cloud and this is my wife, Jean. Do you have a woman seamstress for sale—one that could teach our daughters how to make clothes for special events?"

"Yes, we do have a seamstress," said the captain.

"Oh, where is she? We want to talk to her," insisted Jean, her eyes lighting up with keen interest.

"Margaret, will you step forward?" asked the captain.

As Margaret stepped forward, she gave a little Dutch curtsy and smiled.

"How do I know you really can sew?" sputtered Jean, as she looked at Margaret's simple and wrinkled dress.

At Margaret's questioning look, the captain interpreted, "She wants some proof of your ability to sew."

Margaret's face flushed, knowing how she must look, having had no access to an iron during their three-month sea voyage. Then, too, washing their clothes in salty ocean water had made them stiff, besides all the wrinkles.

"I'll go down in the hold and bring a sample of the kind of work my wife is able to do." Johan hurried away to get the satchel into which Margaret had put several articles of clothing for this purpose. He also snatched up their beautiful quilt, folded it neatly, and carried it along with the bag. He hurried to the deck.

Johan carefully displayed the articles on a bench. "Feel free to look them over."

Jean gasped with pleasure as she eagerly stooped to examine each piece, then turned astonished eyes on Margaret and asked—with the captain interpreting— "These are lovely! Are you sure you are the one who made all these?"

"Yes, my mother taught me to sew while we lived in Holland. I made all my clothes, even my wedding dress. I enjoy sewing," assured Margaret.

Jean looked at her husband and gave him a nod of assent.

"How much are you asking for her, Captain?" asked Jason.

Captain Boswell cleared his throat and said, "We have a rather unusual case here. Margaret is Johan's wife and they have two children—Tommy is ten years old and little Jacob was just born twenty-one days ago. We don't plan to split the family up. Would you be willing to take the whole family?"

"Oh, my, I didn't want a whole family—only a seamstress. A tiny baby could make things difficult," sputtered Jean.

"Now don't you worry about that tiny baby," assured the captain. "He doesn't do anything but eat and sleep. I hardly ever hear him cry. They are a Christian family and you would find it a pleasure to be in their company. I'm sure they would do their best to serve you well. Tommy, of course, must have the advantage of some schooling." The captain repeated this in Dutch so Tommy could understand.

"Does her husband know anything about farming?" asked Jason.

"He was a rich man's gardener in Holland," explained the captain. "On his own land he raised tulips—both the flowers and the bulbs to sell. Besides that, he cared for cows and sold milk and knows how to make wonderful cheese and butter."

"Can't they speak English?"

"They speak the Dutch language. Is that a problem?" asked the captain.

"Not a big problem, I guess." Jason slowly rubbed his chin. "Our family can speak some Dutch."

"That's good! Let's make it easier for everyone by using the Dutch language to finish our transaction," suggested the captain.

Jason nodded agreement to the captain and then turned to Johan. "Would you and Tommy be willing to work together on my farm? I'm a busy man, and I wouldn't have time to be telling a young lad what to do."

"That would be no problem. Tommy is obedient and a good worker," said Johan.

"I wouldn't expect Tommy to work constantly," explained Jason. "When the tutor comes to our house to teach our children, he could take advantage of some learning."

A look of excitement crossed Tommy's face.

Turning to the captain, Jason asked, "What kind of a price are you asking for these three?"

"I'm asking twenty-two pounds and seven sixpence for five years of service from this fine young man," said the captain. "And I'm asking eighteen pounds for Margaret and ten pounds for Tommy. Generally a seamstress like Margaret would sell for twenty pounds and an industrious lad like Tommy would sell for fifteen pounds. Since you may not keep any of them longer than five years, I'm willing to let you have them at a cheaper rate. Is it understood that when five years of service is completed they will all go free the same day?"

"I understand," said Jason, giving serious consideration.

"Oh, but Jason, we didn't come for a whole family," whined Jean, her forehead wrinkled. "Can't we just buy the seamstress?"

"You heard what the captain said," Jason reminded, looking keenly at Jean. "Do you want a seamstress or not?"

"Well, yes, but—."

"Then it's settled; we'll take the whole family, Captain. Our house is plenty big enough to accommodate four more people, and there's plenty of work to be done. There's one small problem though. I won't be able to transport these people to my house until tomorrow. I promised to pick up my ground corn at the mill and I need to bring it back to. . ." He paused as he cast an uncertain glance at Johan. "I need to bring it back into town tomorrow morning. Could they stay here until then?"

"Certainly! No problem at all," assured the captain. "I think these folks have some letters to finish anyway—letters I promised to deliver to their families when my ship docks at their home port. Do you mind spending another night in the hold, Johan?"

"No, we would prefer that. It would really be more convenient than leaving immediately."

"All right then, we'll see you in the morning, about daybreak," promised Jason. "Take your time with the contract, Captain. Get it ready to sign in the morning when I come by to get the family and I'll be ready to pay."

"Sounds fine and I'll have the city mayor here, so the signing will be legal," agreed the captain.

As Jason Cloud and his wife turned to leave the ship, Josh moved up beside them and asked, "Did I hear you say you left your corn at the mill? That must be my father's mill. Am I right?"

"Why, yes, you're right, and I recognize you now. You're Josh Miller. Are you in need of a lift? We're going right past your place," offered Jason.

"I'm not exactly ready to go at the moment; I have some business in town. But if the offer is still good in the morning, I would like transportation for Elizabeth and her luggage. You do pass by our mill on the way to your home, don't you?" inquired Josh.

"We sure do and we'll be glad to oblige you. We live two miles beyond your mill. Just be here at daybreak and we'll set off together," assured Jason.

"Thank you for your kindness, and if God wills, I'll be here." Josh smiled.

When Josh turned back to give the information to Elizabeth, he found Margaret and Elizabeth in exuberant conversation, while Johan, Tommy, and the captain looked on.

"Oh, Margaret!" Elizabeth was saying, her eyes aglow. "Did you hear the man? He said we'd be two miles apart! I'm so happy, I feel like laughing and crying at the same time. I knew God would take care of us, but I never imagined He would work things out in such a marvelous way."

"And I get to go to school!" shouted Tommy. "Elizabeth, I'll learn to read and write like you. Whoope-e-e-!" And Tommy leaped into the air, clicking his heels.

"I'm so happy for you, Tommy," said Margaret, chuckling.

Margaret turned to Elizabeth. "Just think, we'll be close enough that maybe I'll be allowed to visit you. Josh, do you think your mother would welcome me for a visit?"

"Certainly!" Josh replied. "Ma gets lonesome for visitors. She thinks it's not fair because Pa and I get so many men visitors at our mill. Visit any time. Johan, you come too." Then he turned to Elizabeth. "I have some business in town, but I plan to be back at daybreak tomorrow. I suppose you have some luggage, so I made arrangements with Jason Cloud to take your things in his wagon when he comes to take Johan and his family to his home."

"I'll be ready and waiting," assured Elizabeth. "Thank you for your kindness."

"Captain, we'd like for you and Josh to join us in a thanksgiving prayer," invited Johan, "and of course, we must sing a praise song. Our hearts are overflowing with gratitude."

"I would be pleased to join you, Johan," agreed Josh, while the captain, with a cheerful nod, joined the group after placing a heavy paperweight on his documents to keep the sea breezes from blowing them away.

"It looks like everyone is happy with the turn of events, and that makes me happy, too," said the captain, smiling.

"We surely thank you, Captain, for keeping your promise to us. May God bless you," said Johan fervently. "We realize it was in your power to let that evil man have Elizabeth, but you didn't. We are deeply grateful."

"Johan, I can't tell you how much it has increased my faith while I watched God working out a place for each of you. I'm more convinced than ever that God is all-powerful. It has given me pleasure to be an instrument in God's hand to help you find good homes. I just wish I had a Johan on each of my ocean voyages from now on. Thank you for the help you've been to me and my passengers."

"You're very welcome for what I did, but it was God who gave me guidance and strength, so may He get the praise. Let us all thank the Lord."

After earnest prayers, Johan led out in a fervent song of praise. God seemed very near.

chapter twenty-seven

New Home for Elizabeth

That evening, returning to the hold, Elizabeth sat near a whale-oil lamp and finished all their letters. As Elizabeth wrote to Tommy's mother, Tommy hovered near, watching each squiggly mark. "Be sure to tell my mother I will be learning to read and write before long. Then I will be able to write my own letters."

"That will make her happy, Tommy," encouraged Elizabeth.

Deep emotions were described on paper, especially about God's miraculous ways in finding good homes for them. They all hoped the letters would be safely delivered to their families and that there would soon be an answer in return.

After retiring for the night, Margaret said softly, "Johan, I can't forget how Jason Cloud stopped suddenly when he was telling the captain he would need to bring his ground corn back to town. He almost said where he was taking it and then he looked at you and changed the wording in his sentence. Why did he act like that?"

"I noticed how he stopped and looked at me, Margaret, but I have no idea what he was going to say. It did make me wonder though. Maybe he didn't want his servants to know his personal business. Otherwise he seems very nice and I think he will be a good master."

"Yes, we have much to be thankful for."

Before dawn, everyone in the ship's hold was scurrying around, gathering their things together. Little Jacob, who had nursed earlier, peacefully slept through all the commotion. They ate a cold breakfast and drank plenty of water in preparation for the journey ahead.

Four sailors came down into the hold and carried their two trunks up onto the deck, while Elizabeth and Johan's family followed behind. The little group approached Captain Boswell and Johan said, "Captain, we want to thank you again for all you've done to help us find good homes. You'll soon be sailing away, but our family will never forget you and we'll continue to pray that you will remain faithful to God."

"You're certainly welcome, Johan, and I'll be glad for your prayers. I've decided to buy a Bible and find out what God wants me to do. I aim to be faithful. After witnessing the miracles on this voyage, I know He is all-powerful and I want to serve Him." Then, looking at Tommy, he said, "I see you're loaded down with some of my pots and pans. Just set them down inside my cabin, Tommy." Looking intently toward the shore, he added, "That looks like Jason Cloud's rig driving up to the hitching rack now. Hurry, Tommy."

"I'll hurry," said Tommy, trotting away with his load.

Johan took the packet of letters from Elizabeth's hand and handed them to the captain. "We appreciate your willingness to see that these letters get to our people, Captain."

"I'll do my best and I hope you'll get letters from them in return." Captain Boswell shoved the letters into his coat pocket.

Jason Cloud came up the gangplank with Josh Miller and the city mayor following.

"Now this is what I call good timing," greeted the captain with a pleased smile, pulling out the documents for them to sign.

Authors' Note: *The old English reads like a copy of the original document which follows. Notice that Johan, who couldn't read or write, was allowed to sign with an X. Also, take note that many of the "f's" in the document would be replaced with "s" if it were written in today's English, which would make it easier to read, but the terminology is still difficult to understand. The ?? was a word that was indiscernible.*

(This document is a copy of the original selling of Johan. None was found for Margaret or Tommy.)

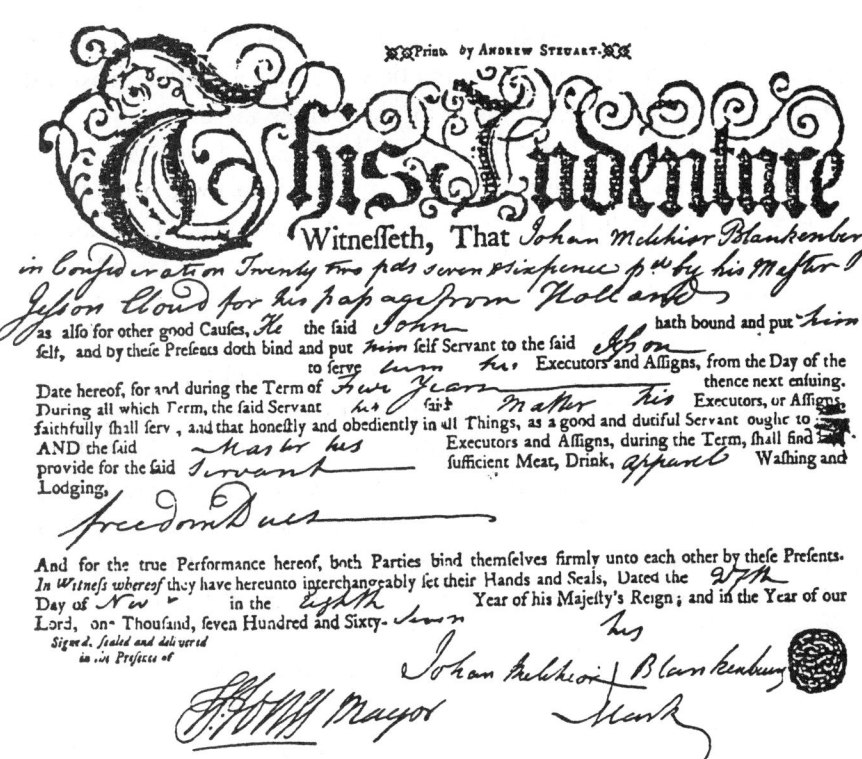

Below is the same document, in present-day English: Printed by Andrew Steuart.

This Indenture

Witnesseth, that Johan Melchior Blankenburg in Consideration of Twenty-two pounds and seven sixpence paid by his Master Jason Cloud for his passage from Holland as also for other good Causes, He the said Johan hath bound and put himself, and by these Presents doth bind and put himself Servant to the said Jason, to serve him, his Executors and Assigns, from the Day of the Date hereof, for and during the Term of Five years thence next ensuing. During all which Term, the said Servant his said Master, his Executors, or Assigns faithfully shall serve, and that honestly and obediently in all Things, as a good and dutiful Servant ought to serve AND the said Master, his Executors and Assigns, during the Term, shall find ?? and provide for the said Servant sufficient Meat, Drink, Apparel, Washing and Lodging, freedom dues.

And for the true Performance hereof, both Parties bind themselves firmly unto each other by these Presents. In Witness whereof they have hereunto interchangeably set their Hands and Seals, Dated the 27th day of Nov. in the

Voyage of No Return

eighth Year of his Majesty's Reign; and in the Year of our Lord, One Thousand, seven Hundred and Sixty-Seven.

Signed, sealed and delivered
In the Presence of ----------------Johan Melchior X Blankenburg
F. S. Jones – Mayor

Soon the documents were all signed and the captain gave orders to the sailors to carry the trunks over to Jason Cloud's wagon. Last handshakes and farewells were given and the little party followed their masters down the gangplank.

"If anyone wants to ride in the wagon, you may do so," offered Mr. Cloud, "especially the children and ladies."

After the tailgate was removed from the wagon, Johan held the baby while Margaret swung herself up onto it. Right behind Margaret, a heavy blanket from their trunk was used to make a soft bed for little Jacob.

"The roads may be rough in places, Margaret, so hang onto the side," Johan cautioned. "The baby should be comfortable and safe behind you."

"Margaret, do you mind if I walk for awhile?" Elizabeth asked. "It feels so good to be walking on something solid again, and the weather is crisp—just right for walking. I'll probably not walk the full ten miles."

"Sure, go ahead, Elizabeth. What about you, Tommy, do you want to ride?" asked Margaret.

"No, I'll walk for a while and maybe ride later," said Tommy.

Josh and Elizabeth walked in silence for a while. Finally Josh spoke. "I'm glad you can speak our native tongue, Elizabeth. I suppose it would be well if I explained a few things to you. My folks are going to be mighty surprised to see you, and I want you to understand why."

Elizabeth gave Josh a startled glance, but didn't speak.

"My pa didn't feel we had any use for the young pair of oxen I had gentled. When we heard from some of our customers that a ship had docked in at Philadelphia, I mentioned that maybe the ship captain would be interested in buying the oxen and then trading them for some needed cargo for his ship. We knew they'd been known to do such things. Pa encouraged me to inquire if I could sell the oxen to the captain. So I set out for Philadelphia yesterday morning. Just outside of Philadelphia, I stopped to eat my lunch and I don't mind telling you I prayed for God's guidance in finding a buyer for the oxen." He paused and cleared his throat. "Well, you know how things went between that vile man, the captain, and me."

"Yes, I know, and I don't know how to thank you. I am very grateful, but I'm sorry if I will become a problem when you get home," Elizabeth said shyly.

"Don't worry, I don't really think it will be a problem. But I'm sure they will be surprised and I wanted you to understand. They thought I would sell the oxen for cash. Ma isn't real strong; I think it's her heart. She works too hard. She has never asked for a hired girl, but I'm concerned for her. I feel she will be happy for your help. She's a good woman, and she'll welcome you with open arms. When I explain to my parents how things stood between Lucas and me, they will understand. So don't worry, everything will be fine."

"I'm very glad your mother is a godly woman," said Elizabeth, "for I have so much to learn about living for God. I only became a Christian while sailing with Johan and Margaret. They were such a blessing to everyone on that ship."

"From what you said on the ship, I take it the Bible means a lot to you. Is that right?" queried Josh.

"Yes, it does, I've learned to love that wonderful book; I'm glad you have one I can read," said Elizabeth, with a happy smile.

"Our family reads from it every day and we try to live according to its teachings," said Josh. Then, glancing ahead, he saw the frisky team and wagon widening the distance between them. "We've been busy talking and they're getting too far ahead. Maybe we should walk a bit faster and try to catch up, then you could ride for a while."

They ran to catch up with the wagon. Margaret reached out her hand and steadied Elizabeth while she jumped and landed safely by her side.

"That little run really made the roses bloom in your cheeks, Elizabeth," Margaret said, laughing. "You're the picture of health."

"That's right," Johan agreed. Then, turning to Margaret, he added, "Since Elizabeth is here with you, Margaret, I think I'll drop back a bit and talk awhile with Josh."

Still breathing hard from her run, Elizabeth shared with Margaret about her conversation with Josh and they both agreed that he seemed like a fine young man and most likely his mother would be a kind lady to work for.

"Margaret, I can't help but worry some, because I never learned the useful things about gardening and housekeeping. At home we always had servants to do that kind of work. At school, I was busy with my studies. I just hope she will be patient with me, because I do want to learn." Suddenly Elizabeth shuddered. "I don't like to think what my life would have been like if the captain had indentured me to that other man."

"Yes, you have reason to be thankful, but I wouldn't worry about learning how to take care of the house and garden. You're willing and quick to learn. I'm sure you'll do just fine." Glancing at Johan and Josh, she added, "It looks like the men are enjoying their visit, and look at Tommy—he's drinking in every word. I'm so glad we could keep him with us."

"Tommy is a very fortunate boy and I can see he will be good help for you and Johan."

"Yes, he's a good worker," agreed Margaret. "He had a good mother. She taught him to work and to have faith in God."

Jacob began squirming and sucking his fists.

"I believe he's hungry," Margaret said. She moved to the other side of baby Jacob and leaned her back against the sideboards before snuggling her baby close while he satisfied his hunger.

Tommy swung up and took Margaret's place beside Elizabeth. "It feels good to sit for a spell," he said with a sigh. "Those horses keep a fellow on the move."

"You've done very well. We must have traveled four miles at least. I'm glad you decided to take a rest and keep me company. I'm going to miss you, Tommy. I hope you can come and visit me sometime."

"I hope so, too. I don't think I ever told you, Elizabeth, but I'm glad you helped to keep me from being pitched out of my bunk during that terrible storm at sea."

"We'll never forget that night, will we? Since that night, you've seemed like my brother. I'm glad we won't live far apart. Just think, only two miles!" They talked of the scenery and the wildlife as they traveled through heavy woods. At times the forest was left behind and they saw log cabins and fields of shocked corn.

When Jason Cloud said, "Whoa there, Molly, Prince," the horses stopped. Beside the road was a stone mill, with a waterwheel turning in the millrace of swift-moving water. The mill customers suddenly stopped and stared at the arriving group. Elizabeth looked eagerly about, as though searching for something. A smile lit her face when she located a neat log cabin with a well and garden close by. She saw a woman with a pail of potatoes in one hand, a look of interest on her face as she studied the unusual group.

Josh stepped up to Elizabeth. "Just sit still until I go in and speak to my father." He quickly turned to Jason. "One moment, please, and my pa will pay you for our transportation."

"It was no trouble at all. Think nothing of it."

"We'll let Pa decide that." Josh moved swiftly toward the mill.

Shortly, Josh and his pa came out. Josh carried a 100-pound sack of ground corn over his shoulder. He set it in the front of the wagon.

"We don't aim to be beholdin' to our neighbors as long as we can give something to show our appreciation," said Pa Miller, giving Jason a friendly handshake.

"I was glad to help out, but the sack of meal will come in handy."

"It means a lot to us to have kind neighbors," said Pa.

"I want you to meet Elizabeth, Pa," said Josh.

After a friendly handshake, Pa Miller said, "Come, Elizabeth; you're welcome in our house. Josh, let's carry her trunk to the house and introduce her to your ma and then we'll get back and finish the work for these customers. We don't want to keep them waiting."

Elizabeth embraced Margaret, placed a light kiss on little Jacob's head, hugged Tommy, and shook hands with Johan, all the while thanking them for their kindness to her. Then she hurried after the men who were carrying her trunk to the house. She turned and gave her friends a final wave.

Elizabeth's heart was all aflutter. Now she was alone. *What will my future hold?* she wondered.

chapter twenty-eight

Welcome, Elizabeth

The woman who had been in the garden hurried in, donned a fresh apron, and was standing on the porch, ready to welcome this stranger. A question was plainly written on her face—*Who is this young woman?*

As the men and Elizabeth entered the yard, Josh said, "Ma, I want you to meet Elizabeth Hanley. She speaks our native tongue."

"Howdy, we're pleased to have you stop a spell with us," said Ma, clasping Elizabeth's hand in greeting.

"Ma," continued Josh, "Pa needs me to help him at the mill, so maybe Elizabeth can explain to you why she's here. I would like for her to have my bedroom while she's with us, and I'll sleep in the loft. Maybe she wouldn't mind moving my things up there sometime today and I'll get my things arranged in the loft tonight."

"We'll do just that," agreed Ma. "If you and your pa will set that heavy trunk in her room, we'll take care of the rest."

"We'll aim to be in at the regular time for dinner," said Pa. "If we can't get away, I'll send Josh in to tell you. Try not to overtire yourself."

As Josh passed his mother, she laid her hand on his shoulder and said, "I'm glad you're safely home, son."

"Home is a good place to be," said Josh with a smile.

It thrilled Elizabeth to see the parents and son display their love to each other. She silently purposed in her heart, *I'm going to do my best to help this frail mother.*

When the men were gone, Mrs. Miller sat down in a rocker and motioned for Elizabeth to take the other. "We've got a bit of time before I need to start dinner. Let's get acquainted. Tell me all about yourself." She gave Elizabeth an encouraging smile.

Ma sat spellbound while Elizabeth told of her well-to-do family in England, her schooling in a private school, the letter from her father telling her of her imminent marriage to an older man she didn't know, and how she had rebelled and gotten on a ship bound for America. She told how she became fearful of some criminals on the ship and how Johan and Margaret had protected her and helped her to become a Christian. From then on, how she had put her faith and trust in the Lord for each day and also for her future.

Finally she said, "There is so much I want to share, but I know the dinner will be late if I don't leave some telling for later; but before dinner, I do want you to know why I'm here in your house. I'm so thankful that you're a Christian; that makes it much easier for me to tell you. When the captain agreed to take me to America, I wasn't aware he would sell me for an indentured servant. He had agreed that I could get a job in America and pay him later, but I soon realized he had not been honest. Many things happened on that voyage; one was that the captain became a Christian through Johan's life and testimony."

"Is that right? How interesting!" exclaimed Ma.

"Yes, and after that, the captain was anxious to do his best in placing us into good homes. You see, he had kidnapped five young boys besides Johan, Margaret, and me. Two of the boys died of the measles. The captain said he didn't think it was possible to take us back to our homes, but if we had any special requests, we should tell him and he would try his best to help us find good homes. He wanted to do as much as he could to right the wrongs he had done to us. We all prayed about it and I know the Lord led us to ask for the right things. My request was that my master must own a Bible which was printed in the language I could read, and every evening after my work was finished, I could read from it. Well, to make a long story short, your son came up to the captain just after another man did. He was a wicked man from one of the pubs in town and was determined to buy my services, but he did not own a Bible. I was scared and refused to look at the man, so I was unaware that your son was present. Your son must have seen my fear and trembling and had a desire to help me, because he spoke up and said your family had a German Bible which I would be welcome to read. Then the man from the pub doubled the money for my services, for he was determined to have me."

"Oh, you poor girl!" said Ma, with tears in her eyes.

"The captain asked your son how much he could pay for me. He then explained about the yoke of oxen he had trained and that he would be glad to give them in exchange for my services to his mother. I know it was a temptation for the captain to accept the higher offer, but the Lord helped him do what was right. He let me choose which master I would rather have. Of course, I chose the one with the Bible. The other man was very angry and nearly hit your son with his gold-headed cane."

"Oh, my!" cried Ma.

"He declared he would do business at another mill and stomped off the ship. I'm so sorry if I have caused you to lose business," said Elizabeth sadly.

"Don't you worry about the business; we can do without the little business that man brings our way," said Ma, her eyes snapping.

"I'm glad about that," said Elizabeth, with a relieved sigh. "I can't tell you how relieved I was to see the last of him. Your son shared with me his concern about your heart. He feels you work too hard, so here I am. Put me to work—that is, if you feel you can put up with me, because I'll need much teaching from you."

"My dear girl, come," said Ma, standing and opening her arms to Elizabeth, who came without hesitation into Ma's embrace.

Leaning back, Ma looked Elizabeth in the eye and said, "Josh surely did the right thing and you're very welcome in our home. I'm glad you can speak our language, but we'll need to help you learn English, because that is the language most of the people speak."

"Oh, I can speak English, but it sounds some different than the way it is spoken here in America."

"That's good! Then you'll soon get on to our English. We'll help you all we can," encouraged Mrs. Miller. "And I want you to know that I'm glad you're here, but I can't ask you to do my work. I'm not used to having a servant; I've never had one."

"Well, you have one now," giggled Elizabeth. "You'll likely think I'm more trouble than I'm worth, but I'm not lazy and I want to learn all you can teach me. I want to somehow show you how glad I am to be in a loving, Christian home and not in that man's pub. Please tell me how I can help with the dinner, Mrs. Miller."

"Well, if you insist, but if we're going to work in the same kitchen and garden, I can't have you calling me Mrs. Miller. Let's see," Ma stopped and considered, "how would Ma Miller sound to you?"

"That's fine with me, and please call me Elizabeth, or just Beth. Take your pick."

"I believe I like Beth; that's quick and easy. So now, if you're sure you want to help, let's scrub some new potatoes for dinner. But first I'll go out to the well and show you how we get our water."

As Elizabeth watched Ma Miller pull on the rope, which hung over the pulley and saw the bucket of sparkling water appear, she saw what Josh meant when he said his mother wasn't well. The exertion had made Ma Miller's face pale and her lips turn blue.

As the woman stood there gasping for air, Elizabeth pleaded, "Please, Ma Miller, let me do all the pulling of water from now on. That job will be mine. I insist."

"Thank you, Beth. I'll not object. It seems it takes so little to wear me out, but I think I'm feeling better now, so let's walk back to the house. I believe God knew I needed you."

"I like to feel needed, but I'm sorry you don't always feel well," Elizabeth said as she carried the full pail to the house.

They quickly scrubbed the potatoes and put them in a pot with water. The pot was hung on an iron hook and swung over the fire in the fireplace. Elizabeth tended the sizzling ham in a skillet with its iron legs nestled in the hot coals. When the ham was done, she pulled the skillet away from the fire. Next she scraped some carrots, while Ma Miller sliced some fresh bread and got some pickles from a crock. After cutting the carrots into strips, Elizabeth quickly set the table.

"I declare, you can do a lot of work in a short time. I'm afraid you're going to spoil me, but it's a good feeling," said Ma Miller with a contented sigh.

As Josh and his father came through the yard, they removed their jackets and shook off the corn dust. Using their jackets, they swatted their britches to knock off as much dust as possible, and then they strode into the house. After washing their hands and faces and combing their hair, they sat down at the table. The women brought the hot food and quietly joined the men.

They bowed their heads while Pa gave thanks.

As soon as their heads were raised, Pa Miller said, "Elizabeth, I want you to know that you are welcome in our home. We're very glad that you are a Christian, and we want you to feel free to read from our Bible whenever you have a bit of time. There is no better book; we also love it."

"Oh, thank you. There is much I don't understand in the Bible, but there is some that I do. I want to learn all I can."

"That's good!" Pa drained the last drop of water from his cup.

"Oh, I forgot to place the filled water pitcher on the table." Ma started to get up.

"Please, sit still; I'll get it," offered Elizabeth, quickly rising.

"Thank you, Beth. You're very thoughtful."

Josh raised his eyebrows. "You called her Beth?"

"Well, she gave me the choice of calling her Elizabeth or Beth and I thought Beth would be quicker and easier. She started calling me Mrs. Miller, but I told her to call me Ma Miller. That seemed more comfortable since we would be working together."

"That sounds like a good plan," said Pa. Then smiling at Beth, he said, "I'm Pa Miller and here's Josh. If we're planning to live together for seven years, I think it's best to be more relaxed with one another. I'm really eager to hear all about your voyage from Holland, Beth, but maybe we'll need to wait until after the work's finished this evening. From what Josh has told me, it sounds like you've had some unusual experiences, but I'm sure he knows very little. Think you can stir up some good stories for us this evening?"

"I'm sure I have more than enough for one evening." Beth flushed with pleasure at the interest this family was showing in her. "Thank you for making me feel welcome in your home."

After the meal was finished, the men returned to the mill.

When the dishes were washed and put away, the women worked at getting Beth settled into her bedroom and moving Josh's belongings up to the loft. After making the last trip to the loft, Beth stood and thought as she looked about, *I hope Josh doesn't regret his offer to move up here, because it's not nearly as nice or convenient for him. This looks more like a place where a servant should sleep. But what can I do about it now?*

When Beth came down the loft ladder, Ma said, "Pa and Josh insist that I take a rest every afternoon, so while you get your room arranged, I think I'll lie down. I don't like to lie down for more than twenty minutes, because if I do, it just makes me lazy. But a short rest is just right to perk me up."

"I'm glad they insist that you take a rest."

A short time later, after Beth had finished sweeping and putting her room in order, she heard Ma again moving about. She quickly hung her dresses from pegs which protruded from the log walls and put clean sheets on her bed. She stood and considered her room. *It looks quite nice and I'm so glad there is a small mirror, so I can comb my hair in private.* Then she turned and went out to ask what else she could do.

"Are you tired? We don't want to expect too much," said Ma.

"No, I'm not tired. It's so good to be off that ship and have things to do. What's next?"

"Well, then, how much do you know about using a spinning wheel?" asked Ma.

"Nothing at all, but I'd like very much to learn," said Beth enthusiastically.

"Good! I think we have time before supper to give you your first lesson at the spinning wheel. While you were finishing your room, I was sorting some soup beans. We'll wash them, add the leftover ham with water, and set a kettle of soup beans to simmer over the fire while we're working at the spinning."

Ma sat down at the spinning wheel and demonstrated how to spin wool into yarn. Beth watched carefully and marveled at Ma's deft movements. Finally Ma got up. "Now it's your turn."

Beth tried her best to repeat what Ma had shown her, but it seemed impossible to spin a smooth yarn.

Ma saw her embarrassment. "Don't be discouraged, Beth. You're doing very well for your first try. Just remember, I've been doing this since I was twelve. You'll get on to it soon."

Finally, when Beth was able to make a fairly smooth yarn, Ma said, "We'd best quit and stir up some cornbread and stew some apples. I'll make the cornbread while you gather in some windfalls from the orchard. The good apples are already stored for the winter, but some of those lying on the ground still have some good parts; we'll just cut away the rotten spots. Here's a bucket. I'll show you where the orchard is." Ma led the way to the front porch. She pointed out the path that led to the orchard. "You may see some wild animals under the trees, but they won't bother you. They like the apples too."

Beth delighted in the crisp afternoon air and breathed deeply. "It's so good to be outside." Suddenly, she stopped, quite still, and stared. There were four beautiful deer standing under the trees. They looked at her with large, curious eyes, then flipped their tails and, with a snort, disappeared into the forest. Beth gasped, "How lovely!"

She would have enjoyed spending more time outside, but she quickly gathered the apples and carried them into the house. With two women working together, the apples with a bit of water and honey were soon placed into a kettle and swung over the fire.

While Ma sat on the stool by the fire, she watched over the baking cornbread and now and then gave a stir to the apples.

Beth set the table and then hurried out to pull up a fresh pail of water. The well was on the right side of the dooryard, so with her back toward the mill, she was unaware that the men had come into the yard and were doing their usual dusting off. When she was ready to lift the bucket, Josh quietly said, "Let me carry your bucket—just a little exchange for carrying my things to the loft." He chuckled.

"But," sputtered Beth, "I should be the one to sleep in the loft. After all, I'm the servant. I'll be glad to move your things back like they were. It will make it more convenient for you."

"I think it's best like it is. I was glad to do it. As an only child, I'm glad to have a sister—not a servant—in the house, Beth. Am I allowed to use that name too?" asked Josh.

"Yes, you're allowed to use it," Beth shyly agreed as they entered the kitchen.

Supper was an enjoyable time. The men shared bits of news that they had gathered from customers at the mill.

"Mr. Gordon, our nearest neighbor," Pa informed them, "wants us to be on the lookout for a tutor for their family. They have a large family and he wants them to be able to read and write. We promised to let him know if we happened to hear of someone who could teach them."

"Now that's interesting," mused Ma. "Beth just told me this forenoon that her parents sent her to a private girls' school in England, so I'm sure she would be qualified."

"But Ma Miller," protested Beth, "you're not strong and I enjoy helping you. I'm sure I would enjoy teaching, but my first responsibility is to spare you, isn't it? Then, too, the language might be a problem." Beth was looking from Ma to Pa.

"It so happens that the Gordon family is German speaking and I understand you are able to speak and read German," Pa replied. "We'll think and pray about it; God will show us what is best."

Beth knew the matter would not be settled at present, so she breathed a sigh of relief. She wasn't ready to adjust, so soon, to another family, but she had learned she could trust God with her life.

After the table was cleared and the dishes washed, they sat around the fireplace and Pa asked, "Beth, would you mind telling us first about your family in England, maybe some about your school life, and how you happened to be sailing alone to America?"

Beth nodded. She told the enjoyable things about her school and how the teachers encouraged her to learn a number of languages, since they saw it came easy for her. While telling about her family, the tears were near the surface. Questions were gently asked and readily answered. They also learned how her strong will had been the cause of her boarding Captain Boswell's ship and the dilemma that resulted from that.

Pa looked startled when he glanced at the clock. "It's hard to believe it's that late. I've really enjoyed your stories, but I suppose we need to wait for more stories until tomorrow evening. You're a good storyteller, Beth. I hope you don't mind entertaining us in the evenings. When you run out of stories, we may have a few to tell of our own. I think it's a good way to learn to know one another."

Beth nodded, well pleased. "I'm glad you like my stories; I will enjoy hearing some of yours too."

As time went on, the work schedule became routine. Each day began with Scripture reading and prayer. They ate their meals together and Beth thoroughly enjoyed her time at the spinning wheel. She learned to make fine yarns. Then every evening they had story time.

The family read each morning from their German Bible, but in their everyday life they spoke mostly English. English was a necessity when dealing with most of the customers at the mill. The people came to America from many countries, so they had to decide on a common language.

While Beth scrubbed the laundry on the washboard, helped with the ironing, and spun yarn, she sang the hymns she had learned on the ship. She learned to knit socks, caps, and mittens and tried her hand at weaving on the big loom that sat close to a window in the big living room. She found housekeeping enjoyable, but the thing she enjoyed most was watching Ma Miller as she applied the Scriptures to everyday living. She made decisions in the light of God's Word.

On a cold winter day, one such happening took place. Josh brought some Indians to the house—two young braves, a young squaw, and her baby.

"Ma," Josh asked, "will you give our friends some food? They're hungry."

Beth looked on with wonder as she observed Ma's reaction to her son's request.

Ma graciously invited them in and gave them all the food they could eat. She made a fuss over the cute, black-eyed baby, causing a smile to flicker over the young squaw's face.

Beth wrinkled her nose at the skunk skin hanging on the one brave's belt, but Ma ignored the bad smell as though it were of no consequence.

Later, when the Indians had silently passed single file from the house, Beth asked, "Ma Miller, how could you welcome those smelly Indians into your house and treat them like friends?"

"It's like this, Beth," explained Ma. "The Bible tells us not to be a respecter of persons. That means we should treat everyone with the same kindness. It also says we should give to every person that asks for our help and that we should give good measure. That means we shouldn't be stingy. It gives me joy to put to practice my Lord's teachings. He says we will receive the same measure that we give to others. You'll find these teachings in Luke 6; you might want to read them."

"I will read that passage while you take your nap this afternoon."

So while Ma took her afternoon rest, Beth read the Scripture passage. While meditating on what she had read, Beth nodded her head and thought, *Yes, Ma is completely right. How blessed I am to have her example before me each day.*

Beth was learning to walk daily with her Lord.

chapter twenty-nine

Settling In

When Jason Cloud's wagon halted in front of a large, two-story house, children peeped from the downstairs windows. Margaret, with fast-beating heart, gathered up baby Jacob in preparation to start her first job in a strange country—with strange people.

"Here, Johan," said Jason, "let's carry your trunk upstairs where you will be living and then you and Tommy may help me stable the horses and feed and water them. Most likely dinner will soon be ready, but you can begin to learn how things are done in the barn while your wife is getting her things organized in your room."

"Certainly, Master Jason!"

"Please drop the title master," said Jason. "I feel you will be respectful without using that word and we'll all feel more relaxed."

After an understanding nod and smile, the men grabbed a handle on each side of the trunk and headed toward the house.

The big house was furnished with fine furniture—better than any Johan and Margaret had ever seen. They were shown to a large upstairs room where a cheerful fire was blazing in the fireplace. Margaret quickly observed it all. There was a rocking chair with a cradle attached at one side and a sewing box on the other, a table and three chairs, and a large bed, with a trundle bed slid beneath for Tommy. A nice chest of drawers stood in the corner and over beside the window, a mirror hung above the washstand. Colorful rag rugs were scattered at the right places on the board floors.

"This is a lovely room, Mr. Cloud," Margaret said with admiration. "I'm looking forward to serving your wife and daughters."

Mr. Cloud smiled and said, "I'm glad you like it. Last night my wife and I moved some furniture around, hoping it would be right for your family needs." He turned to Johan and Tommy. "Let's head for the barn."

Margaret laid little Jacob in the cradle and bowed her head. *Thank you, Lord, for this nice room. I know I'll feel so alone while Johan and Tommy are out working and I must work with strangers, but Lord, you've directed us this far so I'm sure I can lean upon you for the future. You've been so good to us and I give you praise in Jesus' name. Amen.*

While Margaret busied herself with unpacking their trunk and putting things into the empty chest of drawers, she was thinking. *Mistress Cloud didn't seem very friendly, but she has certainly fixed this room to meet our needs.* Then the baby began to squirm, so Margaret dressed him in dry, clean clothes and satisfied his hunger while gently rocking him. When he was content, she laid him back in the cradle. Next she went to the washstand and washed away some dirt, put on a clean dress, and combed her hair. *I want to do my best to appear decent when I meet Mistress Cloud at the dinner table. But what shall I do with baby Jacob? Shall I take him down with me or leave him asleep in this room? I remember she said a baby would complicate things. I must do my best to keep him quiet. He has been such a good baby so far.*

When Johan and Tommy came to show her the way to the dining room, Johan advised Margaret to leave the baby in the room since he was recently fed. As they walked through the door, they were keenly aware that the Cloud parents, their two teenage daughters, and a five-year-old son, James, were looking them over with interest. They stared at their faces, their strange Dutch clothing, and their wooden shoes.

Jason motioned them to seats. "Johan, I believe the captain said you are a Christian. We will look to you to give thanks for our food each meal."

After a startled nod, Johan prayed, "Our kind Father in heaven, we do thank and praise you for this bountiful table and for a nice, warm place to stay. Bless this family for their kindness to us and help us to do our best to joyfully serve them. In Jesus' name we pray. Amen."

Margaret noticed the children could hardly eat for staring at Johan. *I wonder,* she thought, *did they never hear anyone pray before?*

When they were finished eating, Margaret said, "After eating gruel every day on the ship, this meal was like sitting at a king's table. It was delicious! Thank you."

"Yes, thank you! It certainly was delicious!" said Johan and Tommy together.

"We do have a good Dutch cook. Molly, standing over there in the doorway, is responsible for how it tastes," admitted Mistress Cloud, nodding toward the cook.

Margaret looked at the jolly, plump lady, who had a big smile covering her face and knew immediately they would be friends—and besides, they would be able to clearly understand each other's language.

"Well," Jason said, "if everyone is finished eating, Johan and Tommy may come with me. I'll instruct them as to their duties. Margaret, my wife will explain your duties."

The men were soon gone and Margaret was left to follow the mother and her girls upstairs. They entered a nice, well-lit room, with a large table and sewing supplies close by. A nice fire crackled in the fireplace.

"This is our sewing room, with plenty of material over on those shelves. Since this room is right next to your room," explained Mistress Cloud, "I thought that would make it handy for you since you have a small baby." She stopped and frowned. "I just hope he's as good as the captain said he was. Across the hall is the schoolroom. I heard my husband say your Tommy should have the opportunity to learn reading and writing, so when the tutor comes each forenoon—Monday through Friday—it will be Tommy's responsibility to carry enough wood for these three fireplaces and to be present for school by 9 o'clock. I just hope he considers it a privilege and doesn't make trouble for the tutor."

"I'm sure he won't be any trouble. He's very excited about learning to read and write, and he's a good worker," assured Margaret.

"Time will tell. I've had experience with boys." Then Mistress Cloud pointed to the folded materials on the shelves. "Here are some supplies you may use. I suppose you will want to use the cheaper material first until the girls learn more about sewing."

"Is there anything you would like for them to work on first?" inquired Margaret.

"We could use some more pillowslips and I would like a nice design, but not too difficult—embroidered or crocheted on the open end," explained Mistress Cloud.

"We'll do our best, won't we, girls?" Margaret asked, smiling at the two girls.

"But, Mother, we want to make beautiful dresses, not pillowslips," whined Betsy.

"It's important to learn the simpler things first," insisted their mother.

"I promise we will get to dresses," assured Margaret, with a bright smile. Turning to the mother, she asked, "Mistress, do you want us to start immediately?"

"Why don't you take the girls to your room and get acquainted. They want to see your baby, and then we'll plan to start tomorrow, right after dinner. I must go down and give directions to the cook." Mistress Cloud hurried toward the stairs.

As they entered Margaret's living room, the girls went straight to the cradle.

"Would you like to hold him?" asked Margaret.

"Oh, may we? We were seldom allowed to hold our brother. Mother was afraid we'd spoil him."

"I don't think holding him now and then will hurt," assured Margaret.

After both girls had a turn, Jacob was ready to eat, so while Margaret rocked and fed him, she had a good visit with the girls. She learned their names were Betsy and Charlotte, and that they had done very little embroidery and even less crocheting. They did know how to hemstitch handkerchiefs.

"I really enjoy sewing," enthused Margaret, her eyes sparkling, "and I hope you girls can learn to enjoy it too. If you have a desire to learn, then there is no reason why you can't learn to make beautiful dresses. We'll start with white pillowcases tomorrow afternoon and see how neat and attractive we can make them."

After a bit of silence, Margaret asked shyly, "Would you girls help me to learn how to speak English? If you would point to different things and then say the English word, I would be so happy to learn."

"Oh, that will be fun!" exclaimed Betsy. She pointed at Jacob and said, "Baby." Then she touched her nose and said, "Nose." She continued by saying the English word as she pointed to her eyes, mouth, teeth, ears, and hair.

Both girls were giggling as Margaret tried to repeat each English word several times. Yes, they decided, it would be fun to work with this seamstress.

"Probably that's enough English for one afternoon, but I really am serious about learning the language and I appreciate your willingness to help me while I help you learn to sew. Since we won't start before tomorrow, I wonder if I shouldn't do some laundry. It was difficult to do such things on the ship. Is there a place I could do laundry?"

"Yes, there is. Let's ask Mother if she would care if you did your laundry now," decided Charlotte.

When they approached their mother, she frowned. "We do have a lady who does our laundry every Monday morning, but I'm sure she will be glad to be spared the work of washing for your whole family. She expected only a seamstress—not a complete family. Well, so be it. Follow me," said the disgruntled lady as she flounced to the back of the house, all the way giving a volley of instructions. "There is hot water in the big kettle hanging on the hook in the fireplace. Be sure the kettle is filled again when you've taken what you need. Do your rinsing in cold water. The clotheslines are out back, and always hang the bag of clothespins on this peg when you're finished." She tapped the peg. "When the washing is extra big, we dry some clothes on the picket fence. You'll find the scrub board, soap, and tubs on the back porch where the washing is done until the weather gets too cold. Supper will be ready in four hours. That should give you plenty of time. You may use the wooden clothes rack upstairs in your room if you need to dry some things overnight."

When finally the woman stopped talking long enough to grab a breath, Margaret said, "The clothes rack for drying clothes will come in very handy, I'm sure. I'll get started right away, because I don't like to leave my baby for too long."

Within an hour, the clothes were washed and rinsed, the big kettle refilled, and the clothes carried to the upstairs room to dry on the clothes rack. Margaret piled more wood on the fire so the clothes would dry quickly. When she noticed the flatirons sitting beside the fireplace, she thought, *Mistress Cloud may not be the friendliest person, but she certainly is organized and has tried to supply our needs. It will be nice to wear an ironed dress again. Now, I think I'll cut out a shirt for Tommy from the skirt of one of my old dresses. He certainly needs more clothes. And to think I can even rock my baby, if need be, while I sew. God has wonderfully blessed us and I'm thankful.*

In the meantime, Johan and Tommy were out in the barn, and Jason was showing them how to care for the horses, two cows, a flock of chickens, and four sows. Then they found out that there were acres and acres of corn still standing in the field, and the corn would need to be husked.

Johan was curious. "Are you able to get rid of all your corn? I know your animals can't eat that much."

Mr. Cloud hesitated and then said, "I have no trouble getting rid of it." Then he clamped his mouth shut and Johan refrained from asking any more questions.

Turning to Tommy, Jason said, "You will go to school every forenoon, Monday through Friday. Besides learning to read and write, the tutor will teach you to cipher and to speak English. I'll also try to help Johan with English. Before school starts at 9 o'clock, you'll be responsible for carrying enough wood upstairs for three fireplaces—in the room where you'll live, in the schoolroom, and in the sewing room. There's a year's supply of wood in the woodshed next to the house." Then, turning to Johan, he said, "When the corn is all gathered in, there will be more wood to cut for next year's needs. I think I've told you all you need to know, so let's go in for supper. It will likely be ready very soon."

That evening, when they were excused to go to their room, Johan and his family enjoyed a time of worship—each one quoting favorite Bible verses, followed by prayer and then they sang "Jesus, Lover of my Soul". How their voices rang out in joyful praise!

When the song was finished, Johan spoke. "God is so good. He has shown us in so many ways how He loves and cares for us."

They discussed their various responsibilities and rejoiced at the prospect of learning to speak English.

"Margaret," Johan said, "you might be interested in one thing Tommy and I discussed with Josh Miller. He said if the weather is nice, his family and Elizabeth plan to drive their carriage to church on Sunday. They'll be glad to give us transportation, if it is agreeable with Jason. Would you like to do that?"

"Oh, Johan, that would be wonderful!" exclaimed Margaret, with shining eyes. "I wonder if it will be the same church that Karl and Susie attend. It will be great to see Elizabeth again. Oh, I'm so excited! I hope Jason will agree to let us go."

"I'll ask him tomorrow," agreed Johan. "Now I suppose we better get some sleep, because I believe Jason expects a good day's work. Tommy, how are you feeling about going to school tomorrow forenoon?"

"I'm so excited I don't know if I can sleep, and then on top of that, I might get to see the Herting boys on Sunday. Do you think Klaus and Ben might come too?"

"We'll just have to wait and see, but I hope they do come. It would be so good to see our 'ship family' again," said Johan, with deep feeling.

chapter thirty

Tommy Goes to School

The activities went well during that week. Margaret's enthusiasm for sewing rubbed off on Betsy and Charlotte, and they did their best at making beautiful pillowslips.

Even their mother, who was slow to give compliments, smiled and said, "I think they will do quite well. Margaret, I would like for the next project to be some pretty dresser scarves, like the one my girls have on their dresser. When you're ready to make them, ask the girls to bring the one from their room, so you can use it for a pattern."

"But—but when can we make dresses?" sputtered Betsy. "I thought that was why we got a seamstress, Mother."

"Don't be so impatient; give yourselves time. The dresses will come," assured their mother. "Some day you'll be glad you can make nice pillowslips and dresser scarves."

The next morning Tommy made many trips up the stairs with armloads of wood for heating the three big rooms. Then he scrubbed his face and hands, combed his hair, and anxiously waited for 9 o'clock, when Rawley Crumpet, the schoolmaster, would arrive on his horse.

Tommy intently watched out the front window. "Oh, I think he must be here!" he exclaimed, "'cause there's a man getting off his horse and tying it to the post. Now he's throwing a blanket over the horse. Shall I go over to the schoolroom, Ma?"

"Yes, as soon as your teacher goes into the schoolroom, you may go. Be sure to raise your hand if you need to ask Mr. Crumpet a question. I know you will be diligent and learn your lessons well," encouraged Margeret. "Just don't expect to learn it all in one day."

"I won't," Tommy said, grinning broadly, "but I wish I could."

Soon the tutor climbed the steps and passed their door. Tommy followed and was told where to sit. Mr. Crumpet put him to work on his lessons. Tommy soaked up reading, writing, and arithmetic like a sponge soaks up water. Before the week was up, he had memorized the ABCs. He found them rather hard to print, but pressing his lips in a firm line, he determined to master those tricky curves and lines. Before long he was sounding out a number of Dutch words as well as English words—words which meant the same thing in either language. He learned how to spell them aloud. He began writing his numbers one through ten and working on simple arithmetic. *I'll have something to tell Elizabeth if I see her on Sunday,* he thought.

While Tommy and the Cloud children were busy with their school lessons, Margaret cared for her baby's needs, and then set to work completing Tommy's shirt. By careful planning, she was able to cut two shirts from her old dress because the skirt was gathered full and long. Tommy had had no extra clothes with him when the captain kidnapped him, so he needed more clothes. She might need to ask Mrs. Cloud if her husband had some wornout britches; maybe she could use the good parts to make something usable for Tommy. As the shirt took shape, she prayed. *Please, Lord, help Tommy to be quick to learn his lessons. He has such a desire to learn and it would be so wonderful if he could read your Word to us. Do be with Johan as he learns how to shoulder his many responsibilities. Help him to be a blessing to Jason.*

Just as Margaret was finishing the shirt, Tommy came bursting into the room, thoroughly excited. "Ma, look at this slate! See my letters! After supper I'll show you lots of things I learned today. Learning is fun! The schoolmaster is very nice."

"I'm so happy for you, Tommy. I've been praying you would be able to learn your lessons well. How do you like this shirt I'm making for you?" asked Margaret, holding the shirt up for Tommy to see.

"Did you really make that for me? Oh, I was wondering how my clothes would last. Thank you for taking care of me. I'm glad when you let me do things for you too," said Tommy, "but I can't do anything as wonderful as making a shirt."

"Tommy, you work so willingly, and that means a lot to us. Now tomorrow you will have a new shirt to wear for school and while you're in school, I'll wash the one you're wearing, right here at the washstand. You'll need to wear your old shirt when you're out working with Johan. It's nearly time for dinner, but I think you have time to take the dirty water down to dump and bring up a bucket of fresh water, so we have extra for drinking and washing. Don't make the bucket too full. We don't want to spill water on the stair steps."

Margaret poured the last of the fresh water into the washbasin and handed the empty bucket to Tommy, plus the bucket with dirty water.

While Tommy was gone, Johan came in to wash for dinner and comb his hair. "Well, I've never husked corn before, and I'm finding out that husking corn is not too easy on hands that haven't been doing hard work for three months. I suppose I'll get used to it, though."

"Let me see," said Margaret, thoroughly checking his hands. "Johan, your poor hands are sore, that's for sure. I brought along some of my mother's healing salve. If you can stand it until evening, I'll doctor you up and you'll be much improved by morning."

When Tommy returned with the bucket of fresh water, they went down to dinner.

After Johan gave thanks, Jason asked, "How did the corn husking go, Johan?"

"I've never husked corn before, but I'm sure it'll go faster after I do it awhile. It's bound to go better this afternoon with Tommy's help. You know, after three months on a ship, I'm finding out that my hands are no longer tough like they were while I was working hard every day in Holland. Of course, on Sundays we didn't work real hard—only the necessary work."

"I must have forgotten to tell you about the leather gloves on the shelf in the barn. Feel free to use them; they will help a lot. I think there's another pair that will fit Tommy."

"Thank you. I'm sure Tommy and I will be glad for them," said Johan.

They ate in silence for a while and then Jason asked, "What was the necessary work you did on Sunday? And what did you do the rest of the day?"

"Our necessary work was milking eight cows," explained Johan. "We didn't sell milk on Sunday. That milk was used on another day of the week to make cheese and butter. My mother and sisters prepared Sunday's food on Saturday as much as possible. We tried not to work late on Saturday evenings so we would get a good night's sleep, in preparation for being alert in church on Sunday morning."

"So you really do come from a religious family. I can see the captain told the truth. We heard your family singing last night. Maybe some evening you can come downstairs and sing for us."

"We would be glad to do that," Johan agreed. "We love the Lord. He has been so good to us. Serving Him is a joy."

"Maybe when you sing for us some evening, you could tell us what made you decide to come to America and also about your voyage. I'm sure you have some stories to tell."

"Yes, we do have stories we will gladly tell." Johan thought a bit and then continued, "Jason, you remember the miller's son, who traveled with us from the ship? He offered to take us along to church on Sunday if the weather is nice. Would you have any objection to our going along?"

"Not if you can work it in between the morning and evening chores. No matter the day of the week, the animals must be cared for, you know."

"I don't think that will be any problem, because the Millers also have animals to feed. Thank you for giving us permission to go," said Johan gratefully. He smiled when he saw the excitement in Margaret and Tommy's faces.

Molly was bringing in more tea and heard the conversation. She patted Margaret on the shoulder and then offered, "I'll be up early Sunday morning anyway, so I'll be happy to bring an early breakfast to your room, since you're all fixed up there with a table and chairs. The rest of the household likes to sleep a bit later on Sundays, and then the mister takes his wife and children to the preaching in town."

"Molly, you're so kind. Tommy can come down and help you carry things up," offered Margaret.

"I'll let you know if I need his help," said Molly.

As soon as the meal was finished, they went about their various tasks. Johan and Tommy went to the field with the team and wagon to husk more corn, and Margaret, Betsy, and Charlotte went to the sewing room. Once during the afternoon, when Margaret stopped long enough to feed little Jacob, the girls joined her with their hand sewing and they taught Margaret more English words.

Johan's family was eagerly looking forward to Sunday. On Saturday,

Johan and Tommy did extra things in the barn; they threw down extra hay for the animals and mucked out pigpens, horse stalls, and cow stables in preparation for being gone on Sunday. Besides that, they even had time to husk more corn. That evening while walking in with two full pails of milk, Johan and Tommy stopped and studied the sky.

"See that red sky, Tommy?" asked Johan. "That means there will be good weather tomorrow. The Bible tells us, 'When it is evening, ye say, It will be fair weather: for the sky is red. But in the morning, it will be foul weather if the sky is red and lowering.'"

"Oh, goody! It must be true if it says it in the Bible? I hope I can soon read the Bible. I get so excited when I think of all the things there are to learn. I can read a little already," said Tommy, looking up at Johan.

"I know, and I'm glad. It will be good when you can read the Bible to us, son."

Sunday dawned bright and clear. Johan's family was up and dressed when they heard a light knock on their door. Tommy opened the door, and there stood Molly, with a big smile on her face. She carried a tray with their breakfast of buttered toast, fried eggs, and cooked oatmeal with cream and sugar.

"It smells so good," said Margaret. "Tommy can bring the dirty dishes down when we're finished."

"That's good," agreed Molly. "Likely, you won't be home for dinner, so I'll pack a lunch for you. Tommy can get the lunch when he brings the dirty dishes down to the kitchen. How does that sound?"

"That sounds wonderful," said Johan. "Thank you."

"Yes, thank you," said Margaret, throwing her arms about Molly and giving her a big hug. "You're so good to us. Is there anything we can do for you, Molly?"

"Well, now, I was just trying to get up enough courage to ask you to say a prayer for me at church. When I heard you singing last night, it gave me a longing to know more about God. I've always worked as a cook, so I don't get time off for going to church."

"We will certainly pray for you, Molly," Margaret assured her, "and we want you to feel free to come upstairs any evening it suits you to join us for our worship service." Turning to Johan, she asked, "We'd love to have her, wouldn't we, Johan?"

"Yes, indeed, Molly!"

"I can tell you really mean it and I'll probably come when I can," said

Molly. "Now you'd best be eating your breakfast while it's hot, and I need to get on down to my work."

Breakfast was soon over, and while Johan and Tommy were in the barn doing the chores, Margaret bathed the baby and dressed him in his Sunday clothes. Soon she was ready and waiting on the men. Since Tommy was busy helping Johan, Margaret took the dirty dishes to the kitchen and picked up the good lunch that Molly had packed in a basket. With another hurried "thank-you", she returned to her room just as Johan and Tommy were returning.

"Sa-ay, you look nice, Margaret," said Johan, with a pleased smile. "It's been so long since I've seen you in your Sunday dress. Ironing helps a lot too."

"Thank you, Johan. It is good to dress for church once again. Now, you and Tommy can wash over at the washstand, and then put on the clothes I laid out on our bed. I'll sit at the table, with my back to you, so you can have some privacy."

"That should work out fine. Right, Tommy?" asked Johan.

"Sure, we'll get this job over in a hurry. I hope they come soon; I can hardly wait."

"Don't hurry too fast," warned Margaret. "You might forget to wash your neck and ears real good."

"That's exactly what my mother used to say," Tommy said, his voice faltering.

Before long, they were all looking as good as possible, and Tommy was eagerly searching the road for the Millers' horses and carriage. Suddenly Tommy stammered, "Why, there comes a two-seated buggy pulled by one horse and right behind them is the Millers' horses and carriage. They're both stopping here. I wonder who owns the first buggy. Oh!" he exclaimed, clapping his hand over his mouth to keep from shouting. "I see Ben climbing out of the buggy!"

"Here, grab your jacket and our lunch and off with you," said Johan, chuckling. "We'll be right behind you as soon as we bundle up little Jacob."

When the Blankenburgs had joined the group and had given each one a friendly handshake, they decided to let Tommy ride with Klaus and Ben. All three boys crammed into the back seat of the buggy with a smiling Pete.

Pa Miller, Josh, and Johan sat in the front of the Miller carriage and the three women and little Jacob sat in the back. The lunch baskets were stored at their feet.

"Let me hold that sweet baby while you girls entertain me with all your chatter about the happenings of the past week," offered Ma Miller, reaching for the baby and tucking the blanket gently around him.

Five miles later they drove up to the meetinghouse, still wondering if Karl and Susie would be there.

chapter thirty-one

We Meet Again

Unloading the passengers at the meetinghouse door, the drivers drove their horses around back and tied them to the hitching racks. They removed the bridles and attached a nosebag of feed under each horse's mouth. Then they threw a blanket over each one so they would be comfortable until the service was over.

"We women will go in this door, because we sit on this side of the church and of course the men sit on the other side," Ma Miller informed them.

"I'm so glad you folks will be coming to this church," enthused Minnie Bowman. "Like I said when we were visiting together on the ship, Johan and Tommy will be a great help in our singing. Don't get me wrong, we have a group of good men, but they do lack singing ability."

The women filed in together and found seats. Margaret smiled when she saw Susie sitting with Mrs. Herting a couple rows forward. How her heart rejoiced!

When Mr. Bowman and Josh finished with the horses, they joined the waiting men and boys, and then they all filed in together and sat down. Johan was searching about for Karl, and to his surprise, he realized Karl was sitting right in front of him. He was tempted to tap him on the shoulder, but decided against it when someone started a song— "Praise God from whom all blessings flow;/Praise Him, all creatures here below;/Praise Him above, ye heav'nly host;/Praise Father, Son, and Holy Ghost. Amen."

The voices of Johan's family, plus their ship's family, rang out so joyfully that they caused the whole group to be blessed and drawn closer to God. During the singing, Johan noticed that Karl dropped his head and blew his nose in a large handkerchief. *He must have recognized my voice and he's just as excited as I am,* thought Johan. *Oh, thank you, Lord, for your goodness to us all.*

The minister preached a powerful sermon, which brought encouragement and strength, especially to those who were facing life-changing experiences as strangers and pilgrims in a new country.

At the close of the service, the minister looked at Pa Miller and said, "Brother Miller, would your guest be pleased to lead us in a closing hymn of his choice?"

Pa Miller looked at Johan, who nodded his head in agreement.

In soft, reverent tones, Johan led:

"When I survey the wondrous cross/On which the Prince of glory died,/My richest gain I count but loss/And pour contempt on all my pride."

They sang through all the verses—hearts and heads bowed.

"Brother Miller, will you lead in the closing prayer?" requested the minister.

After a nod, Brother Miller began, "Our kind Father in heaven, our hearts have been touched by the sermon—on the need of our being strangers and pilgrims here on this earth. Please forgive us where we've let the cares of life crowd you out of our hearts. The last song melted our hearts as we thought of that terrible death your Son was willing to endure for all people—yes, for me." He paused to gain control, and then continued, "We thank you and praise your holy name. Lord, help us to be faithful to the vows we have made to you. We want to love you more, for you alone are worthy of praise and honor and glory. In Jesus' name we pray. Amen."

After the "amen", what a time of rejoicing they had as the "ship family" shook hands and embraced one another! How they had longed and prayed for this day! The Lord had given them their hearts' desire. Everyone welcomed them and encouraged them to come again.

The minister approached the ones who had recently sailed from Holland, plus those giving them transportation and gave them an invitation. "I live closest to the church—just a mile. Why don't you folks come to our house for dinner, so you can be more comfortable while you visit? I can see you've got lots more to say."

That seemed to suit everyone, so they were soon sitting in the minister's large room, with a cozy fire crackling in the fireplace. The various lunches were laid out and added to the dinner, which had been cooking in the fireplace during church.

After the dishes were done, Tommy sidled over to Elizabeth and looked up with a big smile.

"Hello, Tommy," said Elizabeth, giving him a hug. "I'm so glad to see you again. What's been happening in your life that's put that big smile on your face?"

"Elizabeth, I'm learning to read and write," Tommy gushed. "I thought I'd burst if I couldn't tell you soon."

"Tommy, that's wonderful! You are a great blessing to Johan and Margaret, but you'll be a greater blessing yet if you can read the Bible to them. Are you learning your numbers, too?" asked Elizabeth.

"Yes, I am and I like every part—except writing my letters. But I'm determined to learn that, too," said Tommy, with a confident smile.

"Of course you will," said Elizabeth, giving him an encouraging pat on his shoulder. Then, noticing a commotion over by the door, she asked, "Are those boys waiting on you? I don't think it's me they're beckoning to, so it must be you."

"Yes, it's me they want; I promised to tell them all about our trip over from Holland." Tommy backed toward the door. "Well, I better go, but I just had to tell you about school."

"I'm glad you did," called Elizabeth as Tommy shot out the door with his friends.

Walking over to a window, she saw the five boys heading for the barn and thought, *I suppose they'll end up in the haymow and Tommy will give them some hair-raising adventure stories. Poor Tommy, he's such a brave boy, but I know he misses his mother, and I don't like to even dwell on how his mother must be missing him.* Elizabeth watched until the boys disappeared into the barn.

"What has your attention, Elizabeth?" asked Margaret, stepping up and slipping an arm about her.

"I was just thinking how much Tommy's mother must miss him. Tommy is such a brave lad. No wonder you and Johan love him."

"Yes, he's a blessing to us, but at times, during the night, I grieve for him and his mother. But we know the Lord never gives us more than we can bear. He always makes a way for us."

"It's so comforting to know He's always with us and He cares," agreed Elizabeth with a nod. "Please pray for me, Margaret. Our closest neighbor would like me to spend some time tutoring their children. I think I would like teaching, but I like it so well at the Millers. I don't look forward to adjusting to a new family. Ma Miller isn't very well, but if they say I should go, of course I'll need to go. They said I wouldn't need to stay all day. They have a horse they'd let me ride and I would just stay for the forenoon."

"You would make a good tutor, I'm sure," Margaret replied. "We'll be praying that God will make His will plain to you and the Millers."

"Thank you. I suppose we should join the others. I'm sure Susie will want more time to talk with you."

As they walked toward the group in the big room, Susie patted the empty chair beside her and beckoned to Margaret, who hurried to accept the invitation.

Elizabeth occupied the chair beside Minnie Bowman. That motherly soul asked how the Lord had led her to the Millers. After hearing the story, she laid a comforting hand on Elizabeth's arm, and said, "I'm rejoicing that the Lord spared you from a life with that other man. God cares for each of His children, and I'm so happy He answered our prayers and gave you a good place to stay. God is good."

All too soon the time came to leave, with promises to come the next Sunday if the weather would permit. Little Jacob had slept the afternoon away, though many hands had held him. Now he was wrapped in warm blankets, in preparation for travel.

Thankfulness was shown to the minister for his kind hospitality. "Just plan to do it every Sunday you can come," offered the minister.

With empty lunch baskets dangling from their arms, the group made their way to their rigs, while final good-byes rang in the air. The boys were called from the barn. Johan felt he should spend more time with Pete, so he and Margaret, along with the baby, went with the Bowmans, while the three boys rode in the back seat of the Millers' carriage with Elizabeth.

The arrangement was a happy one for all, but Pete was overjoyed. "Johan," said Pete, "the very thought of someone like me," he tapped his chest, "having a true friend like you just almost makes my heart melt to a puddle. I pray every day that God would let you help someone else like you helped me. I never would have known about Jesus if you hadn't told me. I feel so blessed. Then, too, the Bowmans are so good to me, and I enjoy my work. I had never experienced anything pleasant before I met Jesus. Things are wonderful here on earth, but someday, I want to see heaven and my Saviour face to face."

"Pete," encouraged Johan, "it blesses my heart to hear you talk of your love for the Lord. He alone is worthy of praise and honor. I, too, want to love Him more."

"I miss your singing, Johan. Could we spend some time singing?" asked Pete. "The boys help me sing, but we're not so good at it."

"Sure, Pete, we'll sing. I'm just glad God gave us voices to praise Him," said Johan. "Just remember, Pete, the Bible says, 'Make a joyful noise unto the Lord, all ye lands.' God doesn't require that we be great singers, but He does want us to make a joyful noise to bring glory to Him. Why don't you choose the songs and we'll sing."

The miles slipped quickly by while they sang one song after another, and all too soon, they were stopping in front of Jason Cloud's big house.

"Thank you! Good-bye!" the words rang out as they stepped from the carriage and buggy. It had been a wonderful day.

"We'll see you next week if the weather permits," they promised one another.

An early snowstorm moved in the next Sunday morning, causing them to remain at home.

"Margaret, why don't you invite Molly to join us for a time of worship in our room?" suggested Johan early on Sunday morning.

"I'll do that right after breakfast."

But while they sat at the breakfast table, Jason said, "Johan, I can see the weather is not fit for anyone to attend church today, so I'd like for you and your family to join us in the living room. While the storm roars outside, we can sit by the fireplace, and you can sing some of your hymns and have a little Scripture. Then you can tell us about your trip from Holland."

"We'll be glad to do that," agreed Johan.

They had an edifying time together while they sang and quoted Scripture verses.

Out of the corner of her eye, Margaret saw Molly hovering near the door. Now and then she would scuttle to the kitchen, but she was soon back, showing keen interest.

The Clouds were astonished to learn that Johan and Margaret had never intended to come to America and they were even more astonished to learn they had forgiven the captain. The fact that the captain had become a

Christian and did his best to find good homes for them was also surprising to the Clouds.

"Were you the only ones he kidnapped?" Jason asked.

"No, there was Tommy and four other boys. You see, it was this way: the captain promised free overnight lodging in his cabin, and then gave them drugged tea. Of course, they slept for some time. They had a rude awakening when they came out of their stupor. Two of those boys died from an epidemic of measles, and they were buried at sea." Johan stopped and blinked at the tears in his eyes.

"Well, of all things," sputtered Mistress Cloud, with a frown. "Now, I feel we've been tricked. We thought Tommy was your son. I only wanted a seamstress and now we have a child that isn't even yours."

"But he is ours," Johan insisted. "When Tommy realized what the captain had done, we promised we would be his parents and take care of him. We will never part with him. He'll always be ours, so he is part of our family. You see, we understood what he was going through; we were both in the same fix. Tommy has been a real blessing to us."

"Don't be so sure," Mistress Cloud said, with firm-set lips. "We could sell his indenture to someone who needs a young boy."

"No, Jean, that would be impossible," corrected her husband. "I promised the captain to keep the whole family together and I agreed to set them free on the same day. Just relax, Jean, Tommy is paying his way. He's a willing worker. And besides, if he was kidnapped, he likely didn't bring any extra clothes along. Jean, I want you to see that Margaret has material to make enough clothes for Tommy. If your children were kidnapped, wouldn't you be glad if there was someone who was kind enough to take care of them?"

"Humph!" was all she would say.

"And now," Jason continued as though there had never been an argument between him and his wife, "were there any storms on the way over?"

"Yes," said Johan, "we experienced a storm so wild that the captain tied himself to the helm so he wouldn't be pitched overboard. The luggage skittered back and forth across the floor and we all held on to anything that was solid to keep from being pitched out of our beds. Even though we were lying flat in our beds, there were times when we were nearly standing on our heads while going up a mountainous wave and the next moment we were standing on our feet when we cracked down into the trough of the next wave. Then right away we would be climbing the next mountain of water. For three months we lived in the ship's hold with very little light, but during the storm it was pitch dark; even the few whale-oil lamps needed to be extinguished so there would be no danger of fire. During good days, the open hatch door would leave in a bit of daylight, but during the storm, the hatch door had to be fastened down to keep the hold from filling with water. People were screaming and praying, and some were very seasick, but it was unsafe for them to leave their beds. We were glad we were Christians and prepared to meet our God. When the sailors finally opened the hatch, we knew the storm was over. How we praised God! The next day the captain told us about an unusual experience he had during the storm." Johan paused, lost in thought.

"And what was the experience?" prodded Jason.

"Well, the evening before, when the storm was approaching, I told the captain we would be praying that God would give him wisdom to bring us safely through. The next morning as Tommy and I were up on deck, marveling at the tranquility of the ocean after such a wild storm, the captain came and stood beside us. Finally he spoke and thanked us for our prayers. Then he said, 'There was one time during the storm when I thought all was lost, but I felt unseen hands clamp over my hands. Those unseen hands guided us safely through the storm.' That experience was what convinced him there is an all-powerful God, and he decided right then and there, he wanted to serve Him. He was a changed man after that, and that's why he tried to help each one he had tricked to find good homes."

"That's quite an experience," Jason said, shaking his head. "Thanks for sharing with us. You may be excused, as it will soon be time for dinner." Then, looking at Molly with a teasing smile, he added, "I just hope the dinner didn't scorch while Molly was trying to be in two places at once."

"You needn't worry, everything is progressing just fine," said Molly as she scurried back to the kitchen.

chapter thirty-two

Temptation Met and Refused

As the weeks and months passed, Betsy and Charlotte were exceeding Margaret's fondest expectations in learning to make dresses.

In the forenoon, while the children were in school, Margaret did sewing for Tommy. She made one pair of trousers from new cloth. By using the good parts of Jason's worn-out trousers, she was able to make two more pairs for Tommy to use when working outside with Johan.

Johan's family went to church every Sunday if the weather was nice, and Tommy was beginning to read from the Bible. He started out by reading portions that Johan or Margaret knew by heart, so they could help him if he couldn't pronounce a big word. He was learning how to add and subtract and was mastering the art of writing. Life was exciting! But would he ever get a letter from his mother? How he longed to write to her with his own hand.

Johan and Tommy had husked the many acres of corn and cut wood for another winter. In the spring, they had planted the fields back in corn again. Johan's hands had toughened up and the husking went well. Now the husking was nearly finished the second time. Of course, the corn needed to be shelled before Jason took it to be ground at the mill and then on into town.

One evening as Johan and Tommy were shelling enough corn to fill the farm wagon, Jason, with heavy fumes of whiskey on his breath, joined them.

"Well, looks like I can take another load to the mill tomorrow." Jason's words were slurred. "I'm anxious to get the woodcutting done for another year and then we might make some changes."

Johan looked up, waiting for further explanation, but Jason suddenly turned and left the barn.

"What changes is he talking about, Pa?" asked Tommy with concern. "And why does his breath smell so bad lately?"

"Tommy, I have no idea what the changes might be, but I do know what causes the bad smell on his breath," explained Johan. "What you smell on his breath is whiskey. I've vowed to the Lord and to Margaret that I'll never touch the stuff. Once a man starts down that road, he becomes a slave to it and his whole family suffers. He must have his whiskey even if his family must go without food and clothes. I feel sorry for Jason's family if he keeps on drinking. We need to pray for him."

As the weeks went by, more often than not, they smelled whiskey on Jason's breath. Also, when they were at the table, they noticed that his wife was more sharp-tongued than before. Jason looked sad and worried.

One evening, thirteen months after Johan and his family had come to work for Jason Cloud, the master brought a jug of whiskey into the barn and said, "Johan, you and Tommy have been working hard. It's time you took a little rest on that pile of hay. Here," he said, extending the jug, "take a drink with me—just to be sociable."

"Jason," said Johan, without hesitation, "I've always tried to obey you and to do my best to please you, but I cannot take a drink and sin against God. You see, I made a vow to God and my wife that strong drink would never touch my lips. I've seen the damage that strong drink can do to good men and their families."

A smile lit up Mr. Cloud's face. "I would have been disappointed if you had accepted my offer, Johan. You see, I have a problem and I need your help. I've never told you, but most of this corn we raise is used in my business in town. I own a still where whiskey is made from the corn. Here's my problem—the man that runs the still did fine at first, but now he's nearly always drunk and I can't trust him to do his work well. I feel I must taste the whiskey, to be sure it's all right, but this is causing friction in our house. My wife gives me no peace. She's worried, I suppose, but I know I'm a strong enough man. I don't intend to be a drunkard. I think the answer to my problem is for you to run the still. I can trust you to be sober and do your work well, so I won't need to taste the stuff, and my wife will be happy. I'll rent you a furnished house in town, close to the still, and pay you enough wages to keep your family in food and clothes. My wife is satisfied that our girls know enough to make some very nice dresses, so your wife's services are no longer needed. How does that offer sound?"

"I can see your problem, Jason," said Johan gently. "I also understand your wife's worries, and I would be glad for our own furnished house, but..." Johan hesitated as he sought for the right words. "I cannot be involved in making something that causes so much misery in the world. I'm sorry to disappoint you, for you've been a kind and considerate master to us."

Amazement registered on Mr. Cloud's face. "You mean you're refusing my fine offer? You know I could have you whipped and forced to do my bidding, but I'm not that kind of man, and I have a feeling that you would rather die than disobey your God."

"Yes, you're right about that," agreed Johan. "The Bible says it is better to never make a vow than to make a vow and not keep it. You see, God expects us to keep our vows."

Mr. Cloud's shoulders drooped. "Well, something must be done to pacify my wife. I'll sleep over it and maybe we can come up with a plan."

Softly Johan spoke, "Jason, God has the answer for your problems. If you will let Him, He is willing to solve them, every one."

"Oh, yes, I know, and He would want me to get rid of my still, but I refuse to do that. It's a good-paying business." Mr. Cloud stubbornly shook his head.

"I will pray and ask the Lord to show you how your problem can be solved," promised Johan.

"Thank you," said Mr. Cloud. Wearily he picked up his jug of whiskey and left the barn.

"The poor man," murmured Johan. "He needs God in his life. Money is his god. Well, Tommy, I think we're in for some changes. That's probably what he meant, some time back, when he mentioned there would be some changes after woodcutting."

Tommy looked at Johan with admiration. "The changes probably won't be too bad, 'cause he's always been good to us."

They were hardly prepared for the kind of changes that Mr. Cloud was making for Johan's family.

Two weeks later he came to the barn and explained, "Johan, I believe we have a workable plan. Yesterday I met Howard Hughes in town. After telling him what good workers you are, he agreed to take on your family and buy the rest of your indenture time, which would be a bit less than four years. You've been with us one year, one month, and ten days, and you've served us well, but as it is, we don't need all of you and we're not allowed to split up your family. I just hope Mr. Hughes treats you well; you deserve it. So, get your possessions packed this evening. Tomorrow, early, I plan to take another load of corn to the mill to be ground. When I get back from the mill, we'll load your trunk on the carriage and I'll take you and your family into town to meet with Howard Hughes. Jacob Morgan has agreed to witness the signing—to make it legal, you know. I don't like to see you go, but I must keep my wife happy."

"It's so sudden," stammered Johan. "But, yes, of course, we'll pack our things tonight."

Early the next morning, while Johan and Tommy were out doing the chores, Margaret heard Molly's heavy footsteps coming up the stairs.

After a light knock, she asked, "Are you there, Margaret?"

"Yes, Molly, come in," invited Margaret.

"I just wanted to come up and say good-bye. I want you to know I'll really miss you and your family. It was my first experience to watch a real Christian family. You've been a blessing to me. Last night I asked the Lord to forgive my sins and I promised to serve Him as near as I know how. I decided that when I hardly know what is right, I'd just ask myself, *What would Johan and Margaret do?* Then I think I'll know what to do most of the time. I never learned to read, you know. I sure hate to see you go." Tears sprang into her eyes and she was unable to say more.

Margaret gathered the plump woman into her arms and they cried together. "I'll miss you too, Molly. I'm happy you've decided to live for God; that news helps to cheer me up. Please pray for us, because I have a feeling this move may make things more difficult for us. I know we've had it so good here. But God has promised never to give us more than we can bear if we'll just lean on Him for strength. If He allows us to go through hard times, He must think we're strong enough to bear them. He's been faithful in the past and I know He will be in the future."

Mistress Cloud did not come to give them a good-bye, but Betsy and Charlotte hugged Margaret and said they wished she didn't need to leave.

With Jason's help, they strapped their trunk to the back of the carriage. Margaret climbed inside, carrying the bag with little Jacob's necessary things for the day. He was fourteen months old. Tommy lifted him up and placed him into Margaret's waiting arms and then he too climbed aboard.

"You may as well sit up here with me, Johan," offered Jason. After they had started down the road toward town, he added, "I just hope things go well for you and your family."

"We hope so too. You have been very good to us and generous and we want you to know we are grateful," said Johan from a full heart.

"After bragging your family up to Jacob Morgan yesterday, I wished I hadn't been so quick to promise you to Howard Hughes, but a promise is a promise. I, too, try to keep my promises," said Jason with a smile, "but I think Jacob Morgan would be the better master. I promise to stop in to see how things are going for your family after you're settled in."

When they arrived in town, they went to Thomas Willing's office to complete the transaction. Johan shuddered when he saw their master stomp through the door. He had a sharp, angry countenance which seemed to say, "No smiling allowed." He was carelessly dressed. He explained it away with, "I was too busy to be bothered with changing clothes, so let's hurry and get this over with so we can get back to work. I just hope these folks are as good at working as you said, Jason."

"Every one of them pleased me, Howard, and I tried to please them also. I find it works better that way," said Mr. Cloud, looking sharply at Mr. Hughes.

"Well, where is Jacob Morgan? I thought he was coming," stormed Mr. Hughes, impatiently rubbing his hands. "I have no patience with tardy people."

"What's this I hear about tardy people?" asked a jolly-looking man as he strode through the door. "My watch tells me I'm right on time." He paused and looked Johan's family over. "Are these the good folks you were telling me about yesterday, Jason? From the looks of them, I think you spoke every whit the truth. Just sorry I didn't know about them sooner."

"Let's get on with the business at hand," shouted Mr. Hughes. "We didn't come here to say nice phrases. I've got work that needs doing."

Soon the following document was signed. (The words are copied from the original one for Johan only.)

Below is the same document, in present-day English.

Berks County – In Consideration of the Sum of Twenty Pounds. I assign over the Remainder of the time of the within Indentured Servants to Howard Hughes to serve him, his heirs and assigns Witness my hand on the 16th day of January, 1769.
Came before me – Jacob Morgan
Jason Cloud

As the signing and payment was taking place, pity crept over Jacob Morgan's usually jolly face. He leaned over and whispered in Johan's ear, "If you ever need help, let me know."

"Thank you, my friend," Johan replied quietly. "I'll remember, but I aim to please him if at all possible."

Howard Hughes swung around and shouted at Johan, "If you have something to say, speak up so we can all hear."

"Yes, sir! I'll try to do better," Johan answered humbly.

"That's better! Now, let's get your trunk and be on our way." He motioned them through the door ahead of him.

There was no carriage to shield them from the harsh January wind, only a farm wagon drawn by a pair of bony horses. It was too cold to ride, and they had to walk so they wouldn't freeze. They wished for heavier coats.

Johan threw a blanket around little Jacob and held him close to share his own body heat. In spite of that, Johan could feel Jacob's little body shivering from the cold.

Ten miles later, as they were passing the mill, Josh happened to be standing in the doorway. He heard the approach of a team and wagon and thought a customer was coming, but when he recognized Johan, his mouth dropped open. He rapidly covered the ground between them and asked, "What's going on? Where are you going?"

"Mr. Cloud has sold the rest of our indenture to Howard Hughes—we have almost four years left. We refused to run Mr. Cloud's still in town, so he decided he didn't need us all—especially since his daughters have learned to make their own dresses now. I guess Margaret's such a good teacher that she worked herself out of a job. I think we'll need your prayers by the looks of our new master." Johan tried to smile but was unable to shake the sense of dread that had enveloped him.

"Whoa!" yelled Howard Hughes. He turned around and shouted, "What's the holdup? We don't have time for visitin'."

"Mr. Hughes," called Josh, running up where they could talk without shouting. "May I give these people transportation to your house in a closed carriage? The wind is terribly cold. These people are nearly frozen and the lady is limping."

"I'll thank you to mind your own business," Mr. Hughes snarled. "I never told them they couldn't ride on my wagon. If they want to walk, let 'em walk, I say. Giddap, Mac, Dick." He spit a wad of tobacco at Josh's feet as the team moved ahead.

"Go with God," said Josh, with tears standing in his eyes. "I tried, but failed. Just remember that God never fails."

"Yes, thank you, Josh. God will see us through. We trust Him."

As they started out, Josh risked walking along with them. "I've wanted to tell you that Beth is tutoring our neighbor children, and seems to enjoy it. But the main news is that she and I are getting married in early spring. I'm rejoicing over the day I traded those oxen to the captain. I hope you can be our witnesses at the wedding. We'll try to let you know when the date is sure."

The news was overwhelming. "Wonderful!" said Johan, when he finally found his voice. "We're happy for you and glad that Elizabeth is marrying a good Christian man. May the Lord bless you both with many happy years together. A Christian home is a wonderful gift from God. Now I think you better go back to the mill or Mr. Hughes will make it hard for us when we get to his home," said Johan.

"I hate to leave you, but I know you're right. We'll be praying for you every day; you can count on that." With that, Josh turned and walked slowly back to the mill, deep in thought. Before entering the mill, he gazed once more at the departing figures. Many depressing thoughts went through his mind, but one stood out with clarity—*those poor people.*

chapter thirty-three

Yet Another Life

Johan's tired family continued to follow Mr. Hughes' bony horses and wobble-wheeled wagon past Jason Cloud's big house. Molly came out in the side yard and stood with her fists propped on her ample hips and stared. Johan saw her shake her head. After another mile, the group turned to the left through thick woods and back a long lane. Finally, they came to a clearing with a dilapidated house and barn. Behind the house was a small log cabin, with a bit of smoke coming from the chimney. Johan saw Mr. Hughes looking at the smoke and then heard him growl, "There she goes, wastin' fuel again."

"Whoa, there, Mac, Dick!" shouted Mr. Hughes. He turned and looked at Margaret and said, "You and your young'un can go into the house. Johan and the boy will come to the barn."

Margaret stretched her arms out to take Jacob, but Johan said with deep concern, "No, Margaret, just hold his hand; I think he can walk that far. You're tired enough without carrying him." Johan laid the blanket which had been around Jacob over Margaret's arm. "Will you be all right?"

"I'll make it," said Margaret with a tired smile as she made her way to the door, holding Jacob's little hand.

Johan and Tommy followed the wagon to the barn.

The door opened slowly as Margaret approached and there stood the thinnest woman Margaret had ever seen. There were dark circles around her eyes. She looked toward the barn and then gasped, "You didn't walk all the way from town, did you?"

"Yes, it was too cold to ride," said Margaret. In spite of her own misery, her heart went out to this poor woman.

"Try to get warm over by the fireplace. I'm sorry there isn't a bigger fire, but Howard feels that would be a waste. My name is Allie. What's yours?"

"My name is Margaret and this is Jacob," said Margaret, holding her hands close to the fire and nodding at Jacob. "My, this heat feels good."

"I knew you'd be cold, so I started a little fire in your cabin. I just hope you don't find things too difficult here. I was looking forward to having another woman around; I never get to town," said Allie, checking out the window to see where Howard was. "They're carrying your trunk into the cabin now, so they'll soon be in." With a frightened face, Allie scurried to stir the bubbling mush that was hanging from a hook in the fireplace, as though she suddenly realized she had wasted time talking.

Oh, thought Margaret, *Allie fears her own husband. How terrible!* Aloud she said, "I'm glad you're here with me too, Allie. I'm sure we'll be good friends. Here, let me help you with the supper." While carrying a fearful Jacob on her hip, she placed the plates and spoons on the table. "I hear the men coming in. Shall I fill the cups, Allie?" asked Margaret.

"Yes, there's some hot tea in the container sitting next to the fire, but we're out of sugar, so we'll need to eat our mush and tea without it. I'm sorry about the lack of sugar, but we do have a bit of salt for cooking." Allie's voice trembled.

The men came in, bringing with them a large bag of flour and one of cornmeal. After setting them on the floor, Howard Hughes marched to the table, dipped liberally for himself and started to eat. Allie didn't speak, but motioned for Johan's family to sit on the bench and she took the other chair. She handed the bowl of mush to Johan first, casting fearful glances at her husband, who was shoveling the food in as fast as he could. It was obvious there would be no talking at this table. Johan's family bowed their heads and prayed silently. When they raised their heads, both Mr. Hughes and Allie were staring at them, dumbfounded. Mr. Hughes growled and then continued to shovel in his food, but there were tears in Allie's eyes. Quickly Johan and Margaret dipped out their food for their family, making sure there was some left for Allie. They knew they had better hurry if they wanted time to eat.

As soon as Mr. Hughes was finished, he pushed his chair back with a loud scraping sound and stared at Johan's family hurriedly eating their food. Johan found it difficult to enjoy the meager meal while the man's piercing eyes were on him. *Does he begrudge us this little bit of food? Will we be able to maintain our strength with this kind of diet? We must trust God in a new way,* Johan thought.

When the last bit of food had disappeared, Mr. Hughes growled, "Well, I thought you'd never get done. In the future, you'll need to eat faster; I've been done for some time. We can't be wasting time like this."

Turning to Allie he said, "Put another stick of wood on the fire. You can't even keep a decent fire going. That woman's not much good for anything; she can't even raise a young'un. Keeps losing 'em. Instead, we have to waste our money buying strangers' help. Well, so be it!" he said with disgust, spitting a stream of tobacco juice on the floor while leaning back on the back legs of his chair. "This is the way I have things planned; Johan, Tommy, and my woman will work with me in the fields. We still got acres of corn to husk from the shocks. Margaret, you and your young'un will stay in and do the housekeeping—cooking, cleaning, mending, laundry, and setting rabbit and bird snares for meat. In summer there will be plenty of berries in the woods you can pick for some variety. Right now, we'll be eating corn porridge for supper and fried mush for breakfast. There's flour for biscuits and brown gravy for dinner. The chickens have quit laying eggs and the cow is dry. I reckon they'll pick up come spring. Do you know how to make sourdough bread?"

"Yes, I can make bread," said Margaret quietly.

"Well, then, let's get to bed, so we can get an early start tomorrow. I'll blow my horn when it's time for you to get up. Your cabin's small, so Tommy can sleep in the haymow; he can burrow into the hay to keep warm."

"We'll make room somehow for Tommy in our cabin," said Johan with firm resolve.

"After one night, you'll change your mind," said Mr. Hughes with a careless shrug.

"Allie, would you show me where your supplies are, so it will go quicker with meal preparations?" asked Margaret.

"I'll help you get breakfast in the morning," offered Allie. Then she showed her the flour bin and meal bin, the lard bucket and salt crock, and the lump of sourdough that was saved for fermentation in the next baking. After putting on their jackets, they carried a candle out in a cold back room and Allie showed her the pile of dirty clothes, the washtub, and the scrub board. "Don't get too liberal with the soap. Howard is mighty close on soap," cautioned Allie. She showed her the rabbit and bird snares and how they worked.

Oh, thought Margaret, *this way of living is all new, but with God's help I'll do my best.*

"You can check the two I have set out in the woods behind your cabin. I hope you're successful in getting some meat," said Allie wistfully.

"I'll do my best to get you some meat, Allie; you need better food," said Margaret, clasping Allie's hand with compassion. "I wonder if you're strong enough to stand the cold and work in the fields. I'll be praying for you."

"Thank you," whispered Allie with trembling lips. "It's been so long since I've heard a kind word."

"What's taking so long?" roared Mr. Hughes from the other room. "You've had plenty of time to tell her two or three times over. Get in here and settle down."

The women hurried back in and Margaret joined Tommy and Johan, who were waiting for her with a bundled-up Jacob. Tommy was carrying a tin candle-lantern as they went out the door.

"Now mind, don't burn that candle longer than necessary. You'll get one candle a week," warned Mr. Hughes as they went out the door. "Be saving on the amount of wood you burn in your fireplace too."

After they were safely away from the house, Johan comforted, "I'm sorry for you, Margaret. You have such few supplies in that kitchen and you'll have no meat unless you learn how to catch it. I wish we had a gun; we could shoot a deer."

"You and Tommy won't have it easy either if you must work every day with him," Margaret replied. "That poor Allie! I have it easy compared to her. I thank God for a Christian husband."

"He's one mean old scoundrel!" Tommy burst in. "Did you see how skinny his wife is? He doesn't even give her enough to eat! I think it would be good for him to go hungry for a while!"

"Tommy!" Johan reprimanded. "There's no doubt it'll be hard to get along with him, but that's no way to talk. He is our master, so we have to show respect to him even if he is mean at times. Let's remember that even though we are slaves in Mr. Hughes' sight, we are totally free in our Christian lives. We're free to live or die for God, no matter what we must bear. Nothing can separate us from the love of God.

"By the way," Johan continued, "did you notice how much interest Mr. Hughes showed in our trunk? I don't think we can trust him, so we better keep it locked again. All our small savings from Holland is in that trunk, and I'd hate to lose it. Could you hang the key around your neck, Margaret? I might lose it while working in the fields."

"Yes, but I think I'd best fasten it inside my dress somehow. The yarn around my neck might be noticeable to Mr. Hughes, and I have no desire to attract his attention." Margaret shuddered.

The cabin was small, but not ice cold—thanks to Allie's kindness. There was no bed for the boys, so for this night, they would need to make do as best they could by rolling up in a blanket close to the fireplace and sleeping on the floor.

"I'm sorry, Tommy, but this is the best we can do tonight. Let's pray about it and I'll see if I can think up a better arrangement for tomorrow night," encouraged Margaret. "I hope Jacob will be content to sleep with you. You and Jacob keep each other warm."

"I'm just glad I don't need to be alone in that cold barn," Tommy replied.

Johan laid another chunk of wood on the fire and blew out their precious candle. "Let's quickly get ready for bed, and then we can worship without a light."

They recited Scripture, sang songs of praise and thanksgiving, and then ended with "When I Survey the Wondrous Cross". Their voices rang out clear and sweet.

Then Johan prayed, "Dear Lord, you've promised to never give us more than we can bear. Our trust is in you. Keep us strong in spite of our poor food. We are thankful for the food you supplied on the ship and then the bountiful supply at Mr. Cloud's, and now it's right meager, Lord, but we're thankful for what we have. Lord, please help Margaret to be successful in snaring some kind of meat tomorrow. Allie especially needs it. And help Margaret to think of a way to make better sleeping conditions for our boys. We pray that we will each one show love and respect to our master and his poor wife. Give us opportunities to let your love shine through us. Pete said he has been praying every day that you would give us the privilege to help someone else like we helped him. So maybe you're about to answer that prayer. Help us to be strong and not faint under our hardships, but rather bear them patiently. We praise you for your promise to be with us always, even unto the end of the world. Now watch over us tonight and give us rest for our tired bodies. In Jesus' name we pray. Amen."

Margaret lay awake even after Johan's breathing told her he was asleep. Silently she prayed, *Thank you, Lord, for this little cabin, where we can have a time alone with our family. Please help me learn how to catch enough meat to feed our hungry stomachs. This is a different kind of life, Lord, and I'll need your help in a special way. My faith and trust is in you, the all-powerful One. Praise your holy name!* Without realizing it, her tired body relaxed in sleep.

chapter thirty-four

A Friend Indeed

Early the next morning, the loud blast of a horn caused Johan and Margaret to sit straight up in bed. It frightened Jacob, who started crying. *Is Mr. Hughes standing right outside our door?* Johan wondered. *It surely sounds like it.*

"Are ya' awake in there?" shouted Mr. Hughes, hammering his fist on their door.

"Yes, we're awake and we'll be about our chores as soon as possible," said Johan patiently.

"Well, get a move on and get them horses fed and watered. The boy can carry in wood for the big house and a little for your use. I'll expect breakfast to be ready when the chores are finished."

It was a relief to hear his footsteps returning to the house. Johan wondered, *Why does he need to be so gruff and tell us our chore duties again? He told us yesterday what we should do.*

After Johan and Tommy had dressed and were out of the cabin, Margaret locked the trunk and tied the key in a corner of her handkerchief and slipped it temporarily into her deep pocket. Then she hurriedly prepared herself and Jacob for the day. She hugged him close, and murmured, "You're such a good little boy." Then after helping him into his coat, she threw a heavy blanket over him and hurried to the house.

Allie was already placing two skillets with legs amongst the coals in the fireplace. Margaret hurriedly laid Jacob on the blanket, close enough to get some heat. Kneeling beside him, she flopped a piece of the blanket over him, then gave him a kiss and a few pats. He yawned and soon returned to dreamland.

Quickly, while the skillets were heating, Margaret set the table. Allie looked tired, like she hadn't slept well. "I wish," said Margaret, "you wouldn't need to go to the field and we could work together in the house. I'll try my best to have something special for supper, Allie. Right now, I don't know what it could be, but I will pray and if it's God's will, we'll have something special."

"Do you really think God hears your prayers?" asked Allie wearily.

"Oh, yes. I have many stories I could tell you about God's marvelous answers to our prayers. Maybe you could go with us to church and we could talk along the way," said Margaret cheerfully.

"Go to church?" Allie was incredulous. "We never go to church. I have nothing fit to wear. I doubt if you'll be allowed to go either. It would certainly be a miracle if such a thing ever happened."

"Well, that's something else for us to pray about," said Margaret, while turning the frying mush.

"I wish you'd pray for me, Margaret," implored Allie. "I feel so weak, especially in the mornings." Her hands shook as she turned the mush in the other skillet.

"I'm glad you want us to pray for you, Allie. We already prayed for you last night. We prayed for your husband too. It's good to have faith in God, because He's promised to care for His children. He's all-powerful; He keeps every one of His promises. Our family is determined to trust in Him, no matter what comes." Then, listening carefully, she said, "I believe the men are coming in, so let's get this fried mush on the table." They placed two plates of mush on the table.

Mr. Hughes shrugged out of his coat, dropping it on the floor, and strode to the table. He slid more than half of one plateful of mush onto his plate and started shoving it into his mouth.

Johan and Tommy also dropped their coats on the floor, since there were no nails or hooks for hanging them. They hurried to the table and helped themselves to the fried mush. Johan slid some onto Margaret's plate while the women were getting seated. Then he pushed a good portion over to Allie. Again, Johan's family bowed their heads and silently prayed. Mr. Hughes loudly cleared his throat. When the prayer was ended, they quickly and silently ate.

While the men were still swallowing the last of their meager breakfast, they grabbed up their coats and headed for the barn. After the team was harnessed and hitched to the wagon, Allie heard her name angrily bellowed from the barn. Margaret helped the trembling woman into her coat, gave her a hug, and then Allie scurried out the door to do her husband's bidding.

Margaret breathed a sigh of relief when she was alone. *How can one man make everyone in the house so miserable. Well, I do have my work cut out for me, so I better get started. I don't think this fried mush will be the best for Jacob, so I'll cook some corn porridge for him.* When it was cooked, she set his bowl of porridge close to the fire to stay warm and proceeded to wash the dishes. She saved the grease that was standing in the mush skillets. She could use that again later.

Jacob yawned and sat up, rubbing his eyes. Margaret swept him up into her arms, making him giggle. "Now, my little one, you need some food and then we'll go out and check the snares. Maybe we'll have rabbit for dinner. That would taste good."

After feeding and bundling up Jacob, she grabbed up a couple more snares from the back room and poured a cup of cornmeal into a leather bag for bait, then stuffed it into her jacket pocket. She eyed a small pile of very dirty clothes on the floor near the washtub and shook her head. "Why does he wear his clothes until they get that dirty? Well, if I catch some meat, the clothes will need to wait until tomorrow."

She banked the fire with ashes, gathered up Jacob in one arm, the snares in the other, and started out the back door.

Suddenly she stopped in surprise as Mr. Hughes rushed from their cabin. He was breathing heavily, as though he had been running. He saw Margaret and growled, "Just thought I'd check on how much candle and wood you're burning." Then he hurriedly disappeared around the corner of the cabin.

To herself, Margaret thought, *I wonder what the real reason was that he was in our cabin. He looked very guilty.* Out loud she said, "Let's go check on our cabin, Jacob."

When they stepped into the cabin, Margaret noticed her trunk had dirty fingerprints on the top and it was moved out of its place. She nodded with firmly pressed lips and thought, *That's what I thought he was after. I'm glad the key is safe in my pocket.*

She didn't want to frighten Jacob so she tapped her foot on a spot on the floor and said cheerily, "Right here is where I hope to make a bed for you and Tommy."

"Me! Tom, Tom!" Jacob shouted and clapped his hands.

"Now we'd better check the snares and set some more, and then maybe we can think of a way to make you a bed," said Margaret, holding the door open for Jacob to slip out ahead of her.

She looked for the snares behind the cabin like Allie had said, but there were none. *Well,* she thought, *maybe she meant a good ways behind the cabin.* She followed the path, looking right and left, intent on finding the snares. Suddenly she saw one snare and, sure enough, there was a big rabbit caught in it. Margaret set Jacob on a log, then gathering up more courage than she thought she had, she snatched up a stick to put the animal out of its misery. Just as she was wringing the head off the rabbit, she thought she heard someone moaning in pain. Quickly she carried the bleeding rabbit over to the path and hung it head down from a small sapling.

I wonder, did I really hear someone moan, or was I just imagining it? No, there it is again. I did hear it. She followed the sound, with Jacob toddling after, now and then falling and bravely picking himself up. They came to a swamp and there was an Indian woman, who had broken through the ice and was sinking to her armpits.

"Oh, you poor thing," cried Margaret. Then, turning to Jacob, she set him safely on a log close by and told him to stay put. Then she found a smaller log, which she tugged and rolled over beside the woman. "Grab hold of the log," she instructed, thankful that she had learned some English.

It was evident that the woman had no strength to help herself, so Margaret stretched out on the log, grasped the woman's arms and pulled with all her might. Hope suddenly leaped into the woman's eyes and she struggled to help. Finally she was partway out, but Margaret needed to rest. While the woman leaned over the log, Margaret gasped for breath. Soon she was able to try again and succeeded in pulling the woman free of the mire and then dragging her to solid ground.

Catching their breath, Margaret noticed a bad bruise on the woman's face, but she thought she looked able to walk, so she motioned for her to follow. On their way to the house, Margaret picked up the rabbit and snares. *I'll need to wait and set more snares this afternoon. This poor woman needs care now.*

When they got to the house, Margaret helped the woman get the mud washed away. She gently touched the bruise on the woman's face and said, "That's a bad bruise."

Suddenly the woman began to talk haltingly. "Bad white man. Hate Indians. Throw rocks at Morning Star. Cause Morning Star to stumble into swamp. Break through ice. Sink down. Bad man laugh. Leave Morning Star to die."

"I'm so sorry," said Margaret. "I will help." To herself, she thought, *That's why Mr. Hughes was breathing so heavily. He was throwing rocks and chasing Morning Star.*

After the woman was washed clean, they wrapped Jacob's heavy blanket snugly around her, and Margaret helped her over to the cabin. It would never do for Mr. Hughes to find the Indian he hated being cared for in his house. Margaret placed another log on the fire and hung the Indian woman's leather clothes by the fire to dry. She motioned for the woman to rest on their bed, but she shook her head. Instead, she wrapped the blanket tightly around herself, then lay on the floor by the fireplace and stretched her bare feet out toward the fire.

Then Margaret said, "I must make food for six people. I must go to house." The woman nodded in understanding, so they turned and left her to rest alone.

Margaret skinned the rabbit very carefully, because she hoped the soft fur could be used to some purpose. She handed the fur to Jacob to feel and then they hurried into the house. She cut the rabbit into as many pieces as she dared, then floured and salted each piece and placed it into a hot skillet with a little grease to brown. When all was nicely browned, she poured in a little water and clapped a lid on the skillet, pulling it back so it would slowly simmer and get tender. Next she mixed up sourdough bread, so it would be ready to bake for their supper. Margaret set aside a mixture of flour and water in preparation for making the gravy when the rabbit was removed from the skillet and placed on a platter. She stirred up some biscuits so they could later be placed in the covered iron container to bake over the fire.

Thumping noises caused Margaret to look out the window toward the cabin. The Indian woman clutched the blanket about her with one hand, thrashing her leather clothes against the cabin, causing the dry mud to fly. She then reentered the cabin and was soon outside wearing her own clothes. She walked toward the house with the blanket over her arm. Margaret met her at the open door with a smile as the woman handed her the blanket.

"I go now. I better," said the woman. Then she spied Jacob with the rabbit skin. Holding out her hand, she said, "I take. I fix like this." She showed the softness of her own leather clothing.

"Oh, thank you," said Margaret, gently pulling the rabbit skin from Jacob, who was loath to give it up. Giving the fur to the woman, she invited, "Come in, I will give you food."

"No, one rabbit feed six, not seven. I go and come again." The woman swiftly disappeared amongst the trees and bushes.

Well, thought Margaret, as she sat down to nurse Jacob, *that's my first encounter with an Indian woman. She seems nice. I'm sure she could teach me many things. I'm glad she can speak some English. That will be nice when we meet again.*

When Jacob was content, she set him on the floor and slid the biscuits into the iron container they used for an oven, then she added a couple more chunks of wood to the fire. The rabbit was tender, so she put it on a platter, then covered it with a lid to keep it from drying out and set it on the hearth to keep warm. The field workers came stomping in just as she finished making the gravy. She smiled when she checked the biscuits; they were nicely browned.

Again, one-third of the food landed on Mr. Hughes' plate and was fast disappearing into his stomach before the others could be seated. This time he paid no attention to their prayer, but continued to stuff the food in. After prayer, the rest ate with relish. Allie looked at Margaret and smiled. The food was delicious, but hardly enough for hardworking people. The meal was soon over and the field workers left to husk more corn.

While Margaret washed the dishes, Jacob fell asleep on his blanket. Leaving her sleeping son, Margaret went outside to set some more snares. She hurried, so as to be back when he awoke. She found a quail in the other snare that Allie had set. She wrung its neck and then set the other snares.

After dressing the quail, she checked in on Jacob, who was still sleeping soundly. Grabbing up the hatchet from the back room, she hurried out to cut evergreen branches and carried them to their cabin, in an effort to make a more comfortable bed for the boys. She pulled a mattress tick from her trunk and stuffed the ticking with leaves from the forest. After sewing it shut with large stitches and laying it on top of the branches, she smiled with satisfaction. *Thank you, Lord, for that idea.*

When she came in, Jacob was sitting up and yawning. He smiled at his mother and came toddling to meet her. She leaned down and kissed his warm forehead.

The sourdough bread turned out well, and they consumed two full loaves besides the evening porridge.

The men quickly ate the food and went out to do the evening chores.

"You sit still and rest, Allie, while I wash up these dishes," Margaret insisted.

"Oh, thank you, Margaret. You're so kind," said Allie, her voice trembling as a tear slid down her cheek.

When the dishes were washed, Margaret went to the well and pulled up several extra buckets of water in preparation for doing the laundry in the morning. When she came back in, Allie was still sitting with her elbows propped on the table and her head leaning on the backs of her hands.

"How did your day go, Allie?" asked Margaret.

"It wouldn't be too bad if my hands weren't so sore. I never can work fast enough to please my husband, though," she sighed, shaking her head. "Sometimes I wish I were dead, but I know I shouldn't think like that. But it is better with you here, and that rabbit you fixed sure was good. I wish I could just once have all the food I could eat."

"I'll run out and get some salve and bandages for your hands," offered Margaret.

"But Howard might not like that," Allie worried.

"We can't have you getting infection in those hands. I'll explain to your husband if he gets too hard on you." Margaret raced for the cabin and soon had Allie's hands doctored up.

When the men came in from the barn, Mr. Hughes stopped and stared at Allie's bandaged hands, then stamped his foot. "Now what! I guess you think you won't need to go back to the field tomorrow. Well, you're going! It's time you got toughened up." He slouched into a chair and gave her no more attention.

Allie sadly smiled at Margaret and then Johan's family left for their cabin.

"That poor woman!" mourned Margaret. "I feel terrible about leaving her there with that man. I wonder why he's so mean. Mr. Cloud wasn't a Christian, but he wasn't mean."

"I know," sympathized Johan. "We can't do too much, but God can. We will continue to pray."

"This morning Allie asked me to pray for her, and I told her we had already started praying for her and her husband last night, so, yes, we must keep praying for them," agreed Margaret.

As they walked into their cabin, there was a strong smell of evergreens. Tommy held the lantern high and shouted. "Look at our bed, Jacob; let's hurry and get ready for bed, so we can try it out."

They quickly slipped into their nightshirts and Margaret tucked the heavy blanket around them. They giggled and snuggled into their nice-smelling bed.

"Good for you, Margaret," praised Johan. "That's a big improvement over last night. We'll sleep better if we know our boys are comfortable."

After laying more wood on the fire, the candle was blown out and they enjoyed a time of worship. Then Margaret said, "Boys, would you like to have a bedtime story? I have an exciting one for you."

"Yes, please tell it," pleaded Tommy.

"I talked to an Indian woman today," said Margaret. There were warm smiles in her voice.

"An Indian?" said Johan and Tommy together in astonishment.

"Yes, and she was very nice. She said she would come again."

"Where did you see her? Could she talk English?" asked Tommy.

Margaret saw Tommy in the flickering firelight, sitting straight up in bed, looking her way. She started at the beginning and told the whole story.

"The poor woman," murmured Tommy.

"Yes, the poor woman," repeated Margaret. "Morning Star then asked for the rabbit skin Jacob was holding. She said, 'I fix. Like this.' She pointed to her soft leather clothes. 'I bring. I come again.' So that's my story. I could hardly wait to tell you. Helping that woman seemed to brighten my whole day."

"That was some experience," said Johan. "I'm glad you could help her. I'm sure she was thankful you came when you did. That was kind of her to offer to cure the rabbit skin."

"That was a good story, Ma. I hope you have one every night. That rabbit was delicious. I just wish there was more," said Tommy. "I get so hungry between meals."

"Maybe tomorrow will be better. I'll do the washing the first thing tomorrow, but after that, Jacob and I will check the snares. I set four snares instead of two, so maybe there will be more," encouraged Margaret.

"That sounds good," said Johan. "You surprise me with all the things you're able to do. You're such a blessing to our family, Margaret."

"Thank you, Johan."

After the boys were sleeping, Johan quietly told Margaret the other side of the Indian story. "Allie and Tommy were working at one corn shock and Mr. Hughes and I were working at another one when Mr. Hughes reached into his pocket for a fresh plug of tobacco. His pocket was empty, so he stamped his foot and cursed, and then jogged to the barn where he had left his tobacco. It seems his tobacco is even more important than making another penny."

"I'm sure glad you don't use that filthy weed, Johan," said Margaret.

"I'm glad too, Margaret. Well," continued Johan, "Mr. Hughes was gone longer than I expected. When he returned, although he was gasping for his breath, he was still cursing—about Indians this time. I understood enough that I know he hit someone with a rock and knocked her into the swamp. He hoped she would die there. He thinks all Indians should be killed. I've learned that it's better not to say anything when he's so angry, but I sure prayed for him and also that someone would help that poor Indian he had mistreated. And God answered my prayer by letting you be the one to help her. God is so good."

"Oh, Johan, I'm so glad you could tell me the other side of my story."

Then she leaned close to Johan's ear and whispered, "I caught Mr. Hughes coming out of our cabin today."

"You did?" Johan gasped.

"Yes! He looked confused and guilty, but he grumbled something about checking to see how much candle and wood we were using. I didn't believe that was the real reason, so I checked the cabin and, sure enough, there were dirty fingerprints on the trunk and it was moved out of its place."

"Well, I believe the Lord prompted us to lock the trunk just in time. Then too, when he returned to the field and was done raving about the Indian, he said we should be more saving on the candles and wood. I couldn't understand why he would say such a thing when we've used so little, but now I think I understand. He was trying to cover his tracks. I'm glad you told me, Margaret. He won't likely try it again, but we'll pray about it anyway."

"It's so good to have an understanding husband who shares my concerns, and now I think I can sleep," murmured Margaret.

chapter thirty-five

Good-bye, Allie

The next morning started out with a loud blast of the horn. To keep Mr. Hughes from banging on their door, Johan quickly shouted, "We're awake!"

Allie's sore hands were better, but she felt too weak and sick to eat much. Margaret's heart went out in sympathy as Allie struggled to obey her husband when he shouted from the barn. As she went out the door, Margaret thrust a couple pieces of fried mush, sandwiched between two pieces of bread, into her hand. "Here, Allie, put this in your pocket. Maybe you'll feel like eating later on in the morning. I'll be praying for you."

"Thank you, Margaret, for caring. I wish I knew your God. I heard your family singing the last two nights. It must be wonderful to have a family like yours." Allie's voice trembled. She turned and hurried toward the barn.

Margaret watched her go and thought, *I believe Allie is with child, but things will not go well if he doesn't take better care of her.* After breathing a prayer for the poor woman, Margaret scrubbed their own clothes first and then went to work on the pile of filthy clothes in the back room. The morning was cold, but the sun was shining brightly, so Margaret hung the clothes outside over the rail fence. She poured another cup of cornmeal in the leather pouch, stuffed it into her jacket pocket, wrapped up Jacob in his warm coat, and headed out the game path to check the snares. Margaret was pleased with her catch. Wildlife was plentiful, because there was an animal in each of the four snares—two rabbits and two quails. They hurried back to the house where she butchered them. She hung the quails up in the back room with yesterday's quail for later use and fixed the two rabbits with more biscuits and gravy.

As the days went by, Allie became weaker, but she kept on as best she could.

Mr. Hughes was a miserable man—never cracking a smile as he forced his workers to their fullest potential, driving for every dollar he could make, and spending only enough to keep body and soul together.

Johan's family tried to work hard and to be as cheerful as they were allowed. Tommy, however, found it hard not to complain. One day, Johan tried singing out in the field and Mr. Hughes shushed him with, "Shut up! Working and singing don't go together."

"I'm sorry about that, Mr. Hughes. I find I can work better when I sing. It puts new life into me," said Johan, with a smile.

"Well, I never!" snorted the master, and after some thought, he grudgingly conceded, "If it makes you work harder, I guess you can try it."

And so Johan and Tommy sang while they swiftly husked corn. Johan was rewarded when he saw Allie smile, and her eyes lit up with a trembling hope. They were happy to give her this small pleasure. It was evident her soul was hungry for God.

The singing did improve the morale in the field, but they were never allowed to stop for a rest except when they sat down to eat their meals. They were relieved that Mr. Hughes gave them one day of rest from field work on Sunday. As Allie had predicted, her husband would not allow them to leave the farm, even for a church service, so Johan's family did their necessary chores and had a worship service in their cabin. Mr. Hughes slept the day away except for eating his meals, but Allie accepted Margaret's invitation to join them for worship. She came in fear and trembling, lest her husband should find out and be angry.

The day finally came when Allie accepted Jesus as her Saviour and Lord. She experienced wonderful sweet peace in her soul. It was a great day when her love for her Lord exceeded her fear of her husband.

Finally the corn husking was finished. Next they shelled the corn by hand, using a corncob to rub the kernels off of each ear of corn.

Mr. Hughes took wagon load after wagon load of shelled corn to sell in town.

Is he selling it to Mr. Cloud? Johan wondered.

One evening in February, Josh Miller and Elizabeth came to visit. They were nearly bursting with good news.

Mr. Hughes saw them coming and growled under his breath. He threw down the ear of corn he was shelling and stomped out to meet them. "What are you doing on my property?" he shouted. "Still minding other people's business, are you? Well, speak up. Don't just stand there with your mouth hangin' open. Can't you see we're busy?"

Finally Josh found his tongue and said, "We just wanted to tell Johan and his wife we're getting married the first Sunday in March, and we want them to be our witnesses."

"They're not comin'! You'll have to get married without 'em. They'll not be leavin' this farm as long as I'm their master. Now be gone! You're wasting my time! And don't be stopping at the house, 'cause Margaret's busy." He stared fiercely at the astonished couple until they turned to leave.

When Josh and Elizabeth heard Mr. Hughes stomping back to the barn, they whirled around and waved at Johan and Tommy, who didn't dare return the wave, but they smiled and gave a slight nod. As they passed the house, the worried couple smiled when they got a glimpse of Margaret and little Jacob waving from a window in the house. With heads bowed and hands clasped as in prayer, they conveyed to Margaret that they would be praying for them. They saw her smile and nod.

"So that's the kind of place they have. And to think, he won't even allow them to attend our wedding," lamented Josh. "I'm disappointed."

"I am too," sighed Beth, "but I'm more concerned about their living conditions."

They were out of sight of the barn when they suddenly heard something that caused them to stop and listen. It was singing! Johan and Tommy were singing, "When I survey the wondrous cross, on which the Prince of glory died."

"Oh, those dear people," gasped Elizabeth. "What a testimony! I think they're trying to tell us they'll make it with God's help. Surely some good is bound to come from all of their suffering."

"May it be so," agreed Josh reverently.

One day Margaret saw the Indian woman peering through the kitchen window. She hurriedly opened the door and invited her in.

"Morning Star not come in. Bad white man. Not like Indian." She pointed toward the barn. She held out the beautiful rabbit skin to Margaret.

"Oh, it's lovely," cried Margaret, holding it against her cheek.

"You have more?" asked Morning Star. "I make more."
"I have a bundle of rabbit fur."
"I take. I come again."

When the corn was finished, the field hands went to the forest to cut firewood. Lifting heavy chunks of wood was too much for Allie in her condition. As a result, she lost her fourth child. She cried out her grief on Margaret's shoulder.

While she was trying to get her strength back, her husband ranted and raved day after day and finally on the fourth day he snapped, "You'll never toughen up lying in bed. Tomorrow you'll get back to work in the woods." He slammed the door for emphasis as he went back to his work.

How Margaret's heart ached for her, but Allie smiled sweetly and said, "I was just thinking of the story you told Tommy and Jacob last Sunday—the one about Queen Esther. I understand how she felt when she said, 'If I perish, I perish!' It's wonderful to know I'm ready to die and I need not fear what man can do to me."

So Allie went back to work in the woods.

It seemed the months and years moved on at a snail's pace as the weekly grind of work continued. Johan's family had lived on the Hughes' farm for more than three years when Margaret, in the year 1771, gave birth to their second son, Christian. Fourteen-year-old Tommy and four-year-old Jacob were very pleased to have another brother.

With the longing of a mother's heart, tears slipped down Allie's cheeks as she hovered over the tiny bundle and remembered her little ones who were not.

Soon after baby Christian was born, Allie lost her fifth child. Margaret, still weak from her own delivery, laid the dead child in Allie's arms and then worked frantically to keep Allie alive.

"It's no use, Margaret," gasped Allie. "I'm going home to be with my Lord and my babies. So - glad - my - babies - are - dead." With a sweet smile Allie was gone.

Margaret wept. How she had loved Allie! How she would miss her!

Mr. Hughes refused to let Margaret prepare Allie's body for burial. He said it was a waste of precious time. He ordered Margaret to stay in the house and work, while Johan and Tommy were given the job of digging the grave behind the barn. Then the horse, Dick, was hitched to the mud sled, on which the bodies of Allie and the baby were loaded and dragged to the gravesite. With his foot, Mr. Hughes rolled the bodies into the grave.

Johan's shoulders shook with silent sobs. *How can the man be so cruel and heartless?* Tommy's lips quivered as he studied his bare toes. Feelings of hate and revenge struggled to rise in his heart. His fists clenched and unclenched. *Oh Lord,* he finally prayed, *help me not to be bitter.*

On the first Sunday after Allie's burial, a beautiful early summer morning, Johan's family held a worship/funeral service beside her grave. They felt free to shed healing tears with no one to interfere, for their master was snoring the hours away in the house.

After the service, Johan looked earnestly into the face of Margaret and Tommy and said, "Let's never regret the suffering we've endured on this farm. We were sent here by God to tell poor Allie about Jesus, so she would be able to meet her Lord with joy. We haven't suffered like our Lord; He willingly suffered and died that we might experience salvation. God is so good in letting us see at least one of the reasons why He sent us here." Johan brushed the tears from his eyes. "With God's help, let us be faithful unto death and after that we, also, will receive a crown of life!"

After Allie's death, Mr. Hughes was more cantankerous than ever, causing added stress in Margaret's life. She was forced to work hard before her full strength had returned. Little Christian was fussy, not at all like Jacob. Mr. Hughes stormed and raved about the trouble "that young'un" was making. Margaret did not have enough nourishment to give her baby. *What can I do?* she fretted. *Will our dear baby starve to death?* Her worrying and fretting only increased the problem.

One morning after the men had gone to their work, Margaret washed the dishes and then attacked the laundry, rubbing the clothes on the scrub board. Her steps were slow as she hung the clothes to dry over the rail fence. She had been up most of the night trying to quiet little Christian so the others in the little cabin could sleep. Now the baby was fussing again. Margaret knew he was hungry and she was sick with worry. *Oh, what shall I do?*

Regardless of her problems, the work must be done, so she held her crying baby in one arm and grabbed up some snares with the other and said, "Come, Jacob, let's check the snares."

"I want to help," said Jacob, tugging at the snares in her hand.

"Thank you, Jacob," said Margaret, giving him one snare to carry. "You're a good helper."

As Margaret plodded along the game trail, baby Christian was now crying in earnest. Suddenly she felt unable to go on. She collapsed on the ground and leaned against a tree, crying out in despair, "Lord, help me. I can't go on." Great sobs shook her body.

Jacob, distressed and frightened, dropped the snare and threw his arms about his mother's neck, sobbing with her.

Morning Star was bringing a bundle of tanned rabbit skins to Margaret when she heard someone crying. She quickened her steps and found Margaret and her children. Without a sound, she came and sat beside her friend.

Finally the storm subsided and the exhausted baby's crying ceased. When Margaret had wiped away her tears, she was surprised to see Morning Star sitting by her side, looking at her with concerned eyes.

"Big trouble?" asked the woman.

"My baby," gulped Margaret. "No food. He will starve."

Morning Star smiled. "I help." After leaving the bundle of furs with Margaret, her Indian friend arose and began searching, studying plants on the ground. Suddenly she crouched down and began plucking leaves from a plant.

When she had both hands full, she came back and said, "Make much tea." Then pointing to Margaret, she said, "Drink big. Make milk. Papoose not starve. I bring more."

Tears streamed down Margaret's cheeks again, but this time they were tears of relief and joy. "Thank you, oh, thank you!" she exclaimed, smiling through her tears, while rising to her feet. "I go now and make tea." Then, looking at the bundle of furs, she said, "You are a good friend, Morning Star."

"You save life," said Morning Star, tapping her own chest. "Now me save papoose. Little Brave carry furs. Not heavy. I come, bring more tea. Get more furs later." She placed the furs in Jacob's arms, causing him to smile as the soft fur brushed his cheek. Giving Margaret a gentle push, she said, "Go. Make tea. Drink big."

Margaret's feet moved with renewed determination. She hurried along the path, with Jacob trotting to keep up. Soon she was drinking cup after cup of the strange tasting tea, and all the while thanking the Lord for sending Morning Star and praying this would be the answer to her problem.

She hurried to have dinner ready on time. Little Christian continued to fuss while they ate dinner, and Mr. Hughes drummed his fingers on the table in frustration while glaring at Margaret. She saw Johan's smile of relief when she refused to be disturbed by it.

The tea had relaxed Margaret and while she was tidying the kitchen, she suddenly knew all would be well. She snatched up her baby and smiled as she snuggled him to her breast. "Oh, thank you, Lord, thank you!" Her happiness was nearly overwhelming. "Maybe tonight we'll all get more sleep."

Once again she and her sons took the snares down the game trail. Now there was a spring in her step, and they soon returned with their game. She decided to put the boys to bed first and then butcher the rabbits and birds later.

The two little boys were soon sleeping soundly. Margaret smiled and drew a long, relieved breath as she tucked a thin blanket over them. "Life is hard," Margaret murmured, "but now I feel I can face tomorrow. Thank you, Lord."

chapter thirty-six

Promise Made, Promise Kept

Jason Cloud was getting another grinding done at Miller's mill. As Josh was loading the bags of ground corn onto his wagon, he asked, "Mr. Cloud, have you seen Johan and their family since they left your place?"

"No, why do you ask?" inquired Mr. Cloud.

"Well, my wife and I, before we were married, stopped in at Howard Hughes' place to talk with Johan about being witnesses at our wedding," explained Josh. "Mr. Hughes wouldn't even allow us to talk to Johan or Margaret. He said they were too busy and ordered us to get off his place. He said Johan's family would not be allowed to step off his farm as long as he was their master."

"Hm-m-m..." Mr. Cloud frowned. "I've got a bit of extra time today. I think I'll go back there and see if I can have a word with Johan."

"It would be a big relief if you would," encouraged Josh.

While delivering his ground corn to his still in town, Mr. Cloud's conscience was giving him a hard time. *I promised Johan I would come and see how they were doing and I meant to get there a long time ago. I've regretted many times that I sold their indenture to that tightwad.*

When Mr. Cloud arrived at Mr. Hughes' farm, he saw the men hoeing weeds in the cornfield. Seeing the horse and rider turn in his direction, Mr. Hughes threw his hoe down in disgust and came striding with swift steps to meet the rider.

"Now what do you want?" demanded Mr. Hughes when he recognized Mr. Cloud.

"I just wondered if I might have a few words with Johan?" replied Mr. Cloud.

"No, you can't; you can see they're busy. We have no time for visiting on this farm. I bought them to work for me and that's what I expect. Now I have work to do," growled Mr. Hughes.

"Tell them I stopped in," said Mr. Cloud, who turned his horse and left.

Mr. Cloud was in deep thought as he traveled out Mr. Hughes' long lane. *I think I'd better get in touch with Jacob Morgan. Maybe he can be of some help to Johan and his family.* So instead of stopping at his own home, he went on to Jacob Morgan's farm.

Jacob was repairing his rail fence when he saw Jason riding up. He stopped his work, wiped the sweat from his brow, and smiled at Jason. "What brings you here, my friend?" he asked.

"Do you remember when you were my witness at the signing of a family's indenture from me to Howard Hughes, over three years ago?" asked Mr. Cloud.

"Yes, I remember, and a nice family they were too," said Mr. Morgan.

"Well, I'm concerned for them. I don't think things are well with them and they still have more than five months to serve. He'll likely send them away without their freedom dues; he's so tight-fisted."

"Well, why didn't they come to me? I promised to help them," said Mr. Morgan.

"They're not allowed to leave the farm for any reason," said Mr. Cloud. He shared the experiences that he and Josh had when they tried to talk with Johan.

"Well, something must be done," said Mr. Morgan with determination. "It so happens that I'm looking for an honest man like Johan to work my farm. There's much unrest over the high taxes which England is demanding, and I'd like to become more involved if I could find someone to care for my farm and see that my wife's social and material needs are met when I'm absent from home. I must talk to Johan. Could you let me know when you see Mr. Hughes head for town?" asked Mr. Morgan.

"Yes, that would be a good time for you to hurry back there and talk to Johan. But Mr. Hughes doesn't go to town very often at this time of year. In the fall, when he has corn to sell, I see him quite often, but I'll keep my eyes open and let you know," promised Mr. Cloud.

It was two months since Allie had died. One evening after supper, Mr. Hughes cleared his throat and asked, "Margaret, did you make Johan's shirt and pants?"

"Yes, I did," said Margaret, wondering what he was leading up to.

"Well, I bought some good strong material the other day in town and I want you to make three new shirts and pants for me. I'll expect one set to be done by Saturday evening." He stalked off to his bedroom.

While Margaret put away the last cup, she looked at Johan with raised eyebrows. Johan shrugged his shoulders and shook his head.

After they were settled for the night, Margaret whispered, "Johan, I think that man has courting on his mind. What else would cause him to spend money for new clothes? Really though, I've applied so many patches to his clothes, it will be a relief to make some new ones."

"You may be right, Margaret. I can't help but pity any woman he might persuade to marry him though." In spite of his pity, Johan's tired body cried out for rest and he was soon sleeping soundly.

By noon the next Saturday, Margaret was nearly a nervous wreck from overwork, but she had completed the shirt and pants for the master.

After a shave and bath, he donned his new clothes, saddled a horse, and gave orders to Johan. "I'm going to town. I may stay and come back tomorrow evening—then again I may be back this evening. I want you and Tommy to finish the field work and do the chores as usual and don't go wandering off the farm. I want you to carry some of those big rocks up to the house and lay them on either side of the path that leads to the front steps. I want those stones whitewashed with limewater and the yard swept before I get back. Be quick about it!" He turned and rode down the lane.

"Well, Tommy, he sure enough has some plans, but he's not sharing them with us," said Johan. "Let's get the field work done and then tackle this yard. We'll likely need to work after supper, but isn't it wonderful to be here on our own?"

"It sure is, Pa! Let's sing!" shouted Tommy.

Margaret watched from a window and gave a relieved sigh as Mr. Hughes rode away. Then her attention turned back to Johan and Tommy. Poor Tommy was so thin but growing taller. His pants were much too small, but Mr. Hughes had said nothing about making a bigger pair for him. Then she smiled and her nervous tension drained away when she heard Johan and Tommy joyfully singing. *Oh,* she thought, *I can hardly wait till we can be alone and have our own home.* She clasped her hands in prayer. *Thank you, Lord, for giving us this bit of time alone.* Then her thoughts continued as she picked up the scissors. *I think I have time to cut out the other two shirts and pants for Mr. Hughes before supper. I want to get those done as soon as possible. I believe from the way he's acting, we're in for some changes.*

Mr. Hughes went to town and came home without Mr. Cloud or Mr. Morgan seeing him. When he returned Sunday evening, he had a smug look on his face. He seemed to be deep in thought and forgot to be cantankerous, much to Johan and Margaret's relief.

The following week, Mr. Hughes kept Johan and Tommy busy repairing the rickety front steps and a number of other things around the house. They even fixed the wobble-wheeled farm wagon so the wheels ran true. Mr. Hughes pounded some large square nails into the kitchen wall to hang coats on and more were pounded into the two bedroom walls. They made two bed frames from saplings and carried them into a spare room. To both bed frames, they strung ropes, making a springy webbing, which they overlaid with a thick mattress tick stuffed with corn shucks.

When they were away from Mr. Hughes' hearing, Tommy asked quietly, "Why does he need three beds, Pa?"

"Time will tell, Tommy," said Johan. "He's planning something, that's sure."

While Margaret was intent on hurriedly sewing Mr. Hughes' clothes, he came in and sternly shook his finger in Margaret's face and demanded, "In two weeks, I want this house cleaned from one end to the other; the bed covers and sheets must be washed and be sure the three beds are made up by that time. My clothes must be finished then too. So get a hustle on. Don't be so slow." He whirled and stalked out of the house.

"Oh," moaned Margaret, "how will I get it all done? I need your help, Lord." She brushed a tear from her eye and went back to her sewing. In her hurry, she accidentally poked the needle into her finger. "Ouch!" she hollered, and stuck her finger into her mouth.

Jacob came running. "What happened, Mommy?"

"Mommy has an ouchy. See?" Margaret showed him her bleeding finger.

"I'm sorry. Don't cry, Mommy," comforted Jacob, while searching his mother's face and leaning against her knee.

Laying aside her sewing, she pulled her son up onto her lap. "You're such a precious gift from God, Jacob. My finger will soon be fine. I wish I had time to hold you more and tell you Bible stories."

"I like your Bible stories on Sundays. I love you, Ma." Jacob gave her a big hug.

"Thank you, Jacob. Now I must get back to this sewing. See, my finger is no longer bleeding." She slid her small son to the floor and hurriedly returned to sewing one seam after another. Mr. Hughes still wanted more patches applied to his old work clothes. "I can't afford to be wasteful just because I have some new clothes," he had said.

The next Saturday afternoon Mr. Hughes bathed, shaved, and dressed in his best. He rode away again on his horse toward town. This time, Mr. Cloud saw him go. He didn't even take time to saddle up, but rode bareback and before long he was tying his horse at Mr. Morgan's hitching post. He gave the message and then returned to his own work. Soon after putting his own horse in his stall, he saw Mr. Morgan's cheerful wave as he galloped past—heading toward Howard Hughes' farm.

Mr. Morgan slowed his horse to a walk as he went up Mr. Hughes' lane. He was a fair man, even to his animals. He considered walking a horse for a spell to be a good way to cool down a lathered animal.

Margaret answered his knock. "Yes, may I help you?" she asked shyly.

"Is Johan here? I would like to speak to him. I'm Mr. Morgan. Do you remember me? I was the witness when your indenture was signed over to Howard Hughes from Jason Cloud."

"Yes, I remember you. I don't know what to say. Our master doesn't want us to talk to anyone. We haven't been off this farm for three and a half years. I know Johan would like to speak to you, but I…" Margaret's voice trailed off.

Mr. Morgan glanced toward the field. "Oh, I see Johan now. I'll just ride out there and have a chat. That way you won't be blamed for sending me out there." Giving her an understanding smile, he hurried away.

"Oh!" gasped Margaret, "I do hope. . ." Then she bowed her head in prayer. *Please, Lord, make a way for us to leave this place.*

After Jacob Morgan rode away, Johan and Tommy made the work fly. They had new hope for the future. When they came to the house, Margaret was full of questions, but she knew the men would be hungry, because they worked so hard on little food.

When the last bite was eaten, Margaret eagerly leaned across the table and asked, "What did Mr. Morgan want, Johan? I can see you're nearly bursting with a secret."

"Yes, Margaret, I am. Mr. Morgan wants us to come and work for him," said Johan with shining eyes.

"But—but," sputtered Margaret, "we still have five more months to work here."

"I know, but he's willing to pay off our indenture. He said he would offer Mr. Hughes five pounds—enough to pay for one year, not just five months. Mr. Morgan feels sure Mr. Hughes will snap up such an offer in a hurry, especially when he realizes he won't need to give us our freedom dues. How does that sound?" Johan slapped the table with the palm of his hand and smiled broadly at Margaret.

"But can we live without our freedom dues, Johan? You know, tools, land, clothing, and food are necessary and useful things when it comes to supporting a family," stated Margaret, afraid to believe the good news.

"Mr. Morgan says we can use the tools on his farm," assured Johan. "He has an extra house on his farm which he will furnish for us to live in. He will supply us with food and clothing the first year and after that we will work the farm on shares and take care of our own needs. He says there's a lot of unrest in the colonies over the heavy taxing from England, so he'll be gone from home a lot and he wants us to be close friends with his wife and see that her material and social needs are supplied when he is away. He even said we would have our own horse and buggy to drive."

"Just think," said Tommy, smiling broadly, "what it would be like to get away from the old grouch." Before anyone could reprimand him for voicing his true thoughts, he continued, "We could go to church again and I would get to see Klaus and Ben. I wonder how much they have grown in the last three and a half years."

"Those boys have probably stretched up just like you have, Tommy, but likely they're not as thin. Oh, this seems too good to be true," said Margaret. Her lips trembled as tears streamed down her cheeks. Suddenly she sat up straight as a thought struck her. "But how will Mr. Hughes get all his work done? He might not let us go, Johan."

"This may surprise you as much as it did me," explained Johan, "but Mr. Morgan said the rumor in town is that Mr. Hughes has been courting a widow woman, ten years his senior. She has three strapping sons in their early teens and they are good workers."

"Well, that explains a lot," said Margaret, with a sigh. "Things might work out for our good if that's the case."

"Margaret, I feel it's an answer to our prayers. I've prayed many times that I would get to talk to Jacob Morgan and God brought it to pass today. I told him we would be glad to come if Mr. Hughes will release us."

"May God bring it to pass," said Margaret earnestly.

"Since Mr. Hughes is not here, let's have our evening worship time here in the big house. We have much to talk to the Lord about and to praise Him for," said Johan.

"Amen!" said Margaret and Tommy together, followed by an "amen" echo from little Jacob, who looked up from his play with some sticks on the floor. Johan smiled and reached down and patted Jacob on the head.

chapter thirty-seven

Winds of Change

Sunday evening arrived, but Mr. Hughes did not return home as at other times. On Monday, Johan's family continued on with the work as always, with one exception—they enjoyed a relaxed atmosphere. While Margaret was getting the skillets out to fry the mush for breakfast, she heard a loud "Whoa!" at the front of the house. She peeked out a window, and there on the wagon was Mr. Hughes, with a woman on the seat beside him, and three sturdy boys sitting amongst the things piled high in the wagon.

Quickly Margaret put lard into two big skillets and placed them in the hot coals to fry the mush. There would be four more mouths to feed. *So, thought Margaret, this must be the family Mr. Morgan was talking about. I wonder if the woman will be kind, like Allie. Does she know what kind of man she has married? I hope she's strong in more ways than one.*

The wagon was unloaded while Margaret was busily setting the table and frying the corn mush. Finally, when everything was set inside the house, the woman strode over to Margaret, and with a smile, shook her hand. "I'm Nettie, and you must be Margaret. I used to be Nettie Jenkins, but now I'm Nettie Hughes and these are my fine boys." Beckoning with her hand, she said, "Step up here, boys, and meet Margaret. The youngest is James, the next one is William, and the oldest is Jonas. My boys know how to work; we all do, and that's a fact!"

"It's a pleasure to meet you all," said Margaret, with a Dutch curtsy. Then pointing to her own boys lying on a blanket, she continued, "Those two little boys who are still sleeping belong to Johan and me. The older one is Jacob and the baby is Christian. Our older son, Tommy, is out in the barn helping Johan." With a glance out the window, she continued, "I see the men coming in now, so I better get breakfast on the table."

"I brought along some extra chairs, so I'll just slide them up to the table, and then tell me how I can help," offered Mrs. Hughes. She seemed to be a bundle of energy.

"You may pour the tea if you want to," offered Margaret.

When the men came in, Mr. Hughes didn't drop his coat on the floor as usual; he hung it on a nail. Neither did he march over and start dipping out more than his share of food. He said, "Let's all be seated."

After everyone found a place to sit, he started reaching for the food, but Nettie exclaimed, "Why, Howard, shouldn't we give thanks first? The Lord has given us so many blessings."

"Oh, yes, I reckon we should," conceded Mr. Hughes, refusing to meet Johan's eye. They all bowed their heads in silent prayer.

After the first bite, Nettie stopped and looked at her sons, who also had stopped eating. She asked Margaret, "Is there any syrup or butter on the shelves?"

"No, this is the way we always eat it," said Margaret, embarrassed. She glanced at Mr. Hughes and saw the red creeping up his neck.

"Well, never mind, I can remedy that problem." Nettie hurried over to her pile of belongings and produced some syrup and butter. "There, that will help the mush a whole lot. And here's a bit of sugar; it will improve the tea." She smiled sweetly at her husband as she poured syrup on his stack of fried mush and added sugar to his tea. "See if that doesn't taste better, Howard. I brought all kinds of things along to help with the cooking. I always keep a big garden and we will eat well as long as the Lord gives me strength." Then, turning to her husband, she asked, "You do have a garden spot, don't you, Howard?"

The red was creeping up his neck again. "Well, no, we don't, but I'll have Johan plow up a spot if that's what you want," offered Mr. Hughes as he rubbed his hands in agitation. "But what about garden seeds?"

"Oh, I brought plenty of those with me. I always save my own seed and sometimes trade with my friends. Johan, please put plenty of manure on the ground before you plow it," instructed Nettie.

"I'll be glad to do that for you, Mrs. Hughes," replied Johan with a smile. "In Holland, I enjoyed taking care of a rich man's gardens. He had orchards, flowers, and vegetables."

It was evident that Mr. Hughes felt ill at ease and hardly knew how to react to this new kind of energetic wife—one who knew what she wanted and went after it. He cleared his throat and after a bit of hesitation, he said, "Nettie, maybe your boys can come out in the field with me and we'll hoe weeds in the corn. Johan and Tommy can spread the manure and while Johan is plowing, Tommy can pick up the rocks and put them on a pile. You just tell them, Nettie, how big you'd like your garden to be." With that, he swung around as though fleeing from a lion and headed for the tool shed.

Nettie's boys stood still, looking at their mother, until she said in a loud enough voice for Mr. Hughes to hear, "Go with him, boys, and do your work well. I'll be checking to see that everything goes well."

After the boys seemed secure in their mother's promise, they hurried after Mr. Hughes, who handed each boy a hoe.

Then, turning to Margaret, who was nursing her baby, Nettie said, "You can finish feeding your boys while I'm outside determining where and how big the garden will be. You can do the dishes and then we'll work together putting my pile of things away. How does that sound?" She stooped to give a hug to Jacob, who was just waking up.

"That sounds fine," said Margaret, "but when shall I check the rabbit and bird snares?"

"Check the snares? What do you mean?" asked Nettie, in shocked surprise.

"For over three years, it has been my job to bring in the meat for our table, so every morning I check the snares and reset them. But most always there are rabbits or quail in the snares," said Margaret cheerfully. She liked Nettie and hoped she wouldn't get discouraged.

"Do you mean Mr. Hughes doesn't raise any pigs? You bring in all the meat? Well, I never!" Suddenly Nettie laughed. "It looks like there will be lots of changes around here. My boys and I aren't rich, but we know how to work and how to have plenty to eat. Growing boys need plenty of food, and I don't see any reason, with all this land, why we shouldn't eat well. Suppose you tell me what you've been used to cooking, Margaret."

"When we came," replied Margaret, "I was told what to cook, and every day it is the same. We have tea and fried mush for breakfast, rabbits or quail with brown gravy and biscuits for dinner, and sourdough bread with cooked mush for supper."

"Well, cheer up, things are going to change. I brought a couple cured hams, dried apples, dried beans, and lots more. With a bunch of willing hands, there's no reason to skimp along like that. Well, I see your men are ready to work on the garden. I'll try not to be gone very long." So saying, Nettie hustled out to join the men.

Johan and Tommy, with one of the horses pulling a load of manure on the mud sled, arrived just as Nettie came bustling out of the house. She showed them how large the garden should be. After hauling several more loads and spreading it over the ground, they hitched the horse to the plow and soon the garden was taking shape.

After the door closed behind Nettie, Margaret could no longer contain her laughter. She didn't laugh aloud, but silent laughter shook her shoulders. Never in all her days had she witnessed such surprise on a man's face as she had seen on Mr. Hughes'. *Yes, indeed, there are going to be a lot of changes on the Hughes' farm.*

When Margaret looked out the window, she saw huge smiles spread over Tommy and Johan's faces. Her shoulders began shaking, and her silent amusement gave way to a burst of laughter. *Oh, my, I can just imagine what they are thinking.* Margaret wiped tears of mirth from her eyes.

"Mommy, what's wrong with you? You're making funny noises," cried Jacob, rushing to his mother's side. "You're not crying, are you?"

"No, Jacob, I'm not crying; I haven't been so tickled in a long time. Let's celebrate!" She grabbed Jacob by his hands and swung him around in a circle, causing him to shout with happiness while his legs flew off the floor amidst Margaret's swirling skirts.

She didn't hear Nettie come in, but suddenly she was aware they weren't alone. Fear washed over her face as she steadied a dizzy Jacob on his feet. Slowly she looked up and saw Nettie smiling broadly.

"That's more like it," said Nettie, nodding her head vigorously. "Every family should know how to have fun together. My first husband and I had learned that secret, and after the Lord took him, I thought I'd lost the knack, but my boys and I, together, have learned how to enjoy life. We worked hard, yes, but we took some time to play games and even go fishing now and then. Money is nice to have, but having a loving family is much more important. Watching Johan and Tommy working together told me that they had learned the secret. You've done a good job training Tommy."

"Thank you, Nettie, but we don't deserve all the credit. Tommy wasn't ours until he was ten years old," confessed Margaret.

"Is that so? Tell me about it."

The morning passed swiftly as Margaret shared how they had come to America and how Tommy came to be theirs and what a blessing he had been to them.

"You sure have an interesting story, Margaret; I want you and Johan to share at least one of your experiences every evening after supper. That will give my boys something enjoyable to look forward to each evening. It takes some planning if we want an enjoyable life. I've had lots of experience with the planning." Nettie chuckled as she put some apples in a kettle to stew for their dinner.

"Why don't you run out and check the snares," suggested Nettie, "and maybe we can have some fried meat along with some potatoes. I'm sure Jacob will want to run along and get some exercise, but just leave Christian with me, and I kind of hope he cries so I get to hold him. I'm very glad we have a baby in the house."

Hand in hand, Margaret and Jacob tripped lightly down the game trail, each carrying a snare just in case one should be damaged and a new one was needed.

"We're having lots of fun today, aren't we, Mommy?" chortled Jacob as he skipped to keep up with his mother.

"Yes, we are," said Margaret, pulling the animals from the snares and swiftly setting them again. "I'm very glad we learned how to catch animals with snares. Maybe someday we'll be thankful that we know these things."

Soon they returned to the house with three butchered rabbits. Nettie had the skillets hot and the grease sizzling. Margaret quickly floured and salted the pieces of meat and placed them in the iron skillets and popped on the iron lids.

"I'm glad you found three rabbits in the snares," praised Nettie. "While you were out getting the meat, I went out to see how the garden work was coming. It's looking good. I believe I can plant the garden after dinner; that is, if Howard can spare my youngest son and Tommy. If we plan our supper right now, could you be responsible to have it ready at the usual time?"

"Sure, I'll be happy to do that," agreed Margaret. "Just tell me what you want fixed."

"You noticed we hung several hams in the back room. Just cut off a couple slabs of ham, chunk it up, and put it in an iron kettle with dried beans, onions, salt, and water. Let them simmer over the fire all afternoon. You can cook some corn mush to get cold and stiff for frying in the morning, but I think corn pone is a must when we have ham with soup beans. While the beans are cooking, you may sew or mend. I saw what fine work you did on Howard's new shirts and pants." She smiled at Margaret as she continued. "Then if you have time, you can sweep the floor. If you run out of something to do, you can come out and see how we're doing in the garden, but I know you won't want to leave your sleeping boys for long."

When they all sat down for dinner, Margaret couldn't help but see Mr. Hughes' mouth twitch as though he were struggling to control a smile when he saw the potatoes and stewed apples. There was plenty of rabbit for all to have their fill.

"That was certainly a good meal, Mrs. Hughes and Margaret," praised Johan.

"I agree," said Tommy, patting his stomach.

The women smiled with pleasure.

Nettie turned to her husband and said, "Johan and Tommy did a wonderful job preparing the garden this morning, Howard. If you can spare two boys, I'd like to have Tommy and James' help this afternoon. If I can get the garden all planted, then tomorrow afternoon I'll come out and help in the field. How's that for a bargain?"

His wife's winsome smile caused Howard to drop his eyes like a confused schoolboy. He nodded his head and said, "I reckon that could work out all right. You sure you want to work in the field?"

"Certainly, I don't mind hard work, and I feel it is my duty to work with my boys as much as possible. We've learned to enjoy working together; I'd miss it if I couldn't. Then, too, I'm anxious to enjoy working with you too, Howard."

When Margaret saw the red creeping up Mr. Hughes' neck again, she suddenly coughed to keep a giggle from bursting out. She didn't dare look at Johan or Tommy. She did look at Nettie's three boys and saw the happy, relieved smiles on their faces. Those boys loved their mother; that was clear from the way they smiled at her. *Well,* thought Margaret, *I think Mr. Hughes has married a jewel.*

chapter thirty-eight

Life Renewed

It was suppertime when Nettie came in with a satisfied smile. "Well, that's one job out of the way. Planting a garden is more like fun than work. Now if the Lord blesses us with rain and sunshine, we'll likely have lots of food. We planted potatoes, sweet corn, three kinds of beans, late cabbage, tomatoes, pumpkins, cucumbers, and melons. I even planted some popcorn that a kind Indian woman gave me. Those people can teach us a lot if we're willing to listen."

"Yes, I've learned if we treat them right, they will treat us right," agreed Margaret, looking at her contented baby, cooing and playing with his bare toes.

After an enjoyable supper of ham with soup beans and corn pone, Nettie turned her radiant smile on her husband again and said, "Howard, I'm sure you've heard the wonderful stories that Johan's family can tell about their voyage from Holland to America, but my boys and I haven't and I know we would enjoy hearing all about it. Would it be all right with you to have a story each evening if Margaret and I hurry and wash the dishes? If they run out of stories, maybe you and I could tell a few."

"If they want to tell a story, that's all right, but I'm no storyteller, so don't count on me," said Mr. Hughes, fear plainly written on his face.

After snatching up a yarn ball from her box on a high shelf, Nettie turned to the boys and said, "Here, boys, I made this rag-and-string ball. There's a small rock in the center to give it some weight. Take Tommy along and go outside; it's not too dark to play some pitch and catch while we women do up the dishes." She handed the ball to Jonas.

The boys rushed out the door, forgetting they had worked hard all day. Johan picked up Jacob, and they went out to sit on the front steps to watch the fun. Margaret smiled as she noticed Mr. Hughes get up and walk over to watch out the window.

The dishes were soon done and the boys came in with happy smiles. They eagerly leaned forward while listening to Johan tell about the storm at sea.

When the story was finished and many questions answered, Jonas asked, "What made you decide to come to America?"

"Hold everything," said their mother, with an easy laugh. "Let's save that story for tomorrow evening. Hardworking people need their rest."

"That's a good idea, Mrs. Hughes. We'll answer your question tomorrow evening, Jonas," said Johan. "Light the lantern, Tommy, and let's be on our way to our cabin."

During their time of worship, Margaret had noticed Johan's lips twitching in an effort to keep from laughing, but it wasn't until they were all settled in their beds that she felt their bed shaking.

"Are you laughing, Johan?" whispered Margaret, giving him a little punch in the ribs with her elbow.

Johan completely lost control and a snort erupted, causing Margaret and Tommy to quietly join him in good, belly-shaking laughter. Through it all, the two little boys slept soundly. Finally Johan gasped, "I've wanted to laugh all day, for I never in all my life saw anything like the way Nettie Hughes handles her husband. He knows he has a good wife, and three hardworking boys besides, and he wants to keep it that way. I wouldn't wonder if Mr. Hughes might turn out to be a decent man yet. We can learn a lot from Nettie on how to get along with difficult people. Just don't forget, it wouldn't do at all to laugh in front of Mr. Hughes. Margaret, for a little bit there at the table, you had me scared. I didn't know if you would be able to control yourself or not."

"Well, from my side vision, I saw you and Tommy intently studying your empty plates," said Margaret with a giggle.

After another siege of laughter, Johan said, "Well, I think we got that out of our systems now and we'll be better able to handle any shocking developments tomorrow. Let's see if we can get some sleep now."

The days became a pleasant routine. Nettie and Margaret worked happily together in the mornings, and if the garden needed hoeing she kept one or two boys to help her, then in the afternoon she would go work in the field. The woman seemed to have all kinds of energy and to spare.

Their evenings became a time of enjoyment as Johan and Margaret told stories about their life in Holland, about their dog team which was used on their milk route, and about their voyage—even Tommy helped at times, telling about his mother and how he was kidnapped. While they loved to talk about their homeland, there were times when tears needed to be wiped away.

One evening Tommy turned to his ma and asked, "Will you tell the story about Daniel in the lions' den that you told the children on the ship?"

"Sure, Tommy," Margaret replied with a smile. "I'll be glad to tell it. As a little girl, my mother told me that story repeatedly. I never grew tired of it."

That evening Margaret had no trouble holding everyone's attention. Even Mr. Hughes got so caught up in the story he forgot to look disinterested. Thanks to Nettie, the home atmosphere was becoming a happy one.

A month went by, and one day Johan saw Mr. Morgan come riding in. He rode out to the field, within calling distance, and hollered, "Mr. Hughes, could I talk to you about some private business?"

Mr. Hughes dropped his hoe and hurried over to Mr. Morgan. Johan noticed that Nettie not only hoed her own row, but she kept hoeing her husband's row so they would be side by side when he returned. Of course the rest of the crew got ahead, because they had only one row to hoe.

Johan called back to her, "Nettie, do you want me to help you with your husband's corn row?"

"You can if you want to. It looks like they might be talking for awhile, but when you see him coming this way, just go back to your own row," instructed Nettie.

Johan dropped his hoe and came back and took Mr. Hughes' hoe. They worked side by side in friendly silence for a while and then she said, "I hear your family singing each evening before you go to bed. I enjoy it, Johan. You have a nice family."

"I feel the Lord has richly blessed me," said Johan. "You have nice boys too."

"Yes, I do and I'm thankful. Oh, I see Howard is coming now, so you can go back to your row. Thanks for your help, Johan."

As Johan started hoeing in his own row which was close by, he heard Nettie say, "Well, you look mighty pleased, Howard. That was Jacob Morgan, wasn't it?"

"Yes, and he wants to buy the rest of the five-month indenture for

Johan's family. He needs help on his farm as he is giving more of his time to the problems in the government. He's willing to pay more than double for the five months just to get them, and that will save us the expense of giving them their freedom dues. It's a pretty good deal, don't you think?"

Wonder of wonders! Johan marveled to himself. *Is that man actually asking advice from his wife? He probably sees she's got a business head on her.*

"Well," Nettie was saying, "if Johan's family leaves, I surely will miss them. They are a pleasure to have around, but we could get along, I suppose." After a short pause, she added, "How's this for an idea, Howard? If you are willing to let the boys take turns helping me every morning, then we could all be out here together in the afternoon. I'm sure we could get the work done and get along just fine."

"I believe we'll do it then, if you're satisfied. It's nice having you out here in the field, Nettie."

"Why, Howard, that's the best compliment you've paid me yet. If you're not careful, you'll be spoiling me."

When Johan heard a soft chuckle from both of them, he shook his head. *Will wonders never cease? Nettie is helping her husband to know how to respond to love. I wonder what Mr. Hughes' boyhood was like. Maybe it was a bit like Pete's boyhood; he never had anyone to care for him.*

Thoughts of moving to the Morgan farm gave Johan much to think about. They would soon be seeing their friends at church. Glory hallelujah! He began to softly sing, "Praise God from whom all blessings flow/Praise Him, all creatures here below,/Praise Him above, ye heavenly host,/Praise Father, Son, and Holy Ghost."

Nettie's voice floated up to Johan again. "That singing is so beautiful, Howard. Do you think we could attend church on Sundays while the weather is nice?"

"Might be. I guess we could go sometimes."

"That would surely please me, and I know my boys would enjoy being with some of their friends again," said Nettie.

"Let's plan on church this coming Sunday then," consented Howard.

"How soon does Mr. Morgan want Johan's family?" Nettie asked.

"As soon as possible," Mr. Hughes replied. "Tomorrow morning I'll need to go over to his farm and have a paper drawn up in the presence of a witness, to make the transaction legal. I'll tell him to bring his horses and wagon to move Johan's family to his place this coming Saturday afternoon."

Johan decided the conversation was over, because he noticed they seemed intent on finishing their long rows before suppertime. His heart was bubbling over with joy. *What will the next year hold for my family?* he wondered. *I can hardly wait to tell Margaret and Tommy.*

The very next morning, Howard Hughes and Jacob Mogan met in town to sign the following paper in front of a witness to make the transaction legal. He then collected the five pounds that Jacob Morgan had promised to pay so Johan's family could be set free from being indentured servants.

Below is the document in present-day English.

In Consideration of the Sum of five pounds In bond paid by the within Indentured Servant or secured to be paid. As is also requiting his freedom dues. I do hereby Discharge the Said Servant from the remaining part of the within Indenture written by my hand the 22nd day of June, 1772.
Howard Hughes
Witness present – Josif Millard

Margaret's heart was light as she went down the game trail with Jacob. The night before, Johan had shared the good news with her. Suddenly Morning Star stepped silently from some trees with another bundle of rabbit furs and approached Margaret.

"White friend have good news? Eyes shine. Footsteps light."

"Yes. This Saturday we are moving to Jacob Morgan's farm. Do you know where that is?" asked Margaret.

She nodded her head. "Morning Star know. Him good white man."

"Will you come to see me sometime?" asked Margaret, eagerly searching her friend's face.

"Morning Star come see white friend," agreed the Indian woman. Placing her hand on Jacob's head, she said, "Little brave big. Papoose big! Bring more furs." She held out the bundle of fur.

"Morning Star, you help white friend much. Thank you," said Margaret, giving the bundle of furs to Jacob to carry.

"Thank Great Spirit." Morning Star disappeared among the trees as quietly as she had come.

The sun peeked above the horizon as they finished the breakfast dishes. Nettie said, "Let's sit down, Margaret; we need to talk. Howard asked me to explain some things and then you can tell Johan." After settling themselves in straight chairs at the table, Nettie continued, "This isn't easy for me to say because I've learned to love you and your family, but Mr. Morgan was here the other day and made an offer to my husband. He doesn't feel he can turn it down. Mr. Morgan wants your family to finish the last five months of your indenture on his farm. I believe he is a kind man and will treat you well."

"I've learned to love you too, Nettie, and life has been so nice since you came here to live," said Margaret, "but I know you don't really need us since your boys are here and they're such good workers, so we do understand. I met Mr. Morgan a time or two and like you said, he seems like a kind man."

"Well, that's a relief! I hated to tell you, but I do believe you understand, don't you? Mr. Morgan will come with his wagon and take your family to his place on Saturday afternoon. Now," said Nettie, with a sigh of relief, "we'll have three more days together and I want you to take my three boys, one each morning, on the game trail. You can teach them all you know about snares and how to mend them. Howard is planning to get two small pigs, but they won't be ready to butcher until fall, and besides, it's good to have rabbit and quail meat for a change sometimes. They're real tasty."

"Yes, they are, especially with some of the spices you put on them. You're a good cook, Nettie. I've learned a lot from you."

"Thank you, Margaret. I just hope you'll come and visit us sometimes." Suddenly her eyes lit up with excitement and she leaned toward Margaret and exclaimed, "I have some good news to share with you! I'm so excited! Howard has promised to take us to church on Sunday. My boys think it's wonderful, too. God has been very good to me and my boys and I'm thankful."

"That is wonderful!" enthused Margaret. "And I hope you'll stop in for a visit some Sunday afternoon. We would be happy to have you come."

"Well, maybe we will. It could happen, you know," said Nettie with a chuckle. "But, right now, I reckon we better scurry around and get a good meal prepared for our hungry men."

chapter thirty-nine

It's Moving Time Again

The Blankenburg family passed their last three days on the Hughes' farm with mixed feelings. Margaret took Nettie's boys, one at a time, on the game trail. She taught them how to use the snares in catching wild animals and how to mend the snares. As she walked along, she was thinking, *I will surely miss Nettie! And Tommy will miss her boys. He has really enjoyed working with them. Johan and I have enjoyed the change of atmosphere in the home, but there's no doubt we are really looking forward to the freedom we will enjoy on Mr. Morgan's farm. It makes me happy to see Mr. Hughes responding to his wife's love. From all appearances, things will go well for Nettie and her boys. No doubt the Hughes family will miss the story time each evening, but with Nettie's keen imagination, she will think up some game or story of her own.*

On Friday Margaret did the laundry. It was a good drying day. That evening she packed all their clothes into the trunk. She eyed the pile of soft rabbit skins with satisfaction. *I'll make something warm for my little sons this fall. What a blessing Morning Star has been to me!*

As they settled into their beds, Johan said, "Well, if God wills, this will be the last night we'll be sleeping in this little cabin. Maybe we'll have a bit more room in the Morgan house. I've been thankful many times that even though it was a tight fit, we had somewhere to be alone as a family."

"And I was thankful you squeezed me in instead of sending me to the barn to sleep," Tommy put in. "You've been so good to me."

"Yes, and you have been a blessing to us, Tommy," said Margaret. "You and this tiny cabin have both been a blessing. Now in the morning we'll need to fold our bed covers and dump the leaves out of the boys' mattress and put the covers and ticking into the trunk. Tommy, you can drag the evergreen boughs out into the woods, and sometime during the day I'll try to get over here and sweep the cabin. I'm so excited! Just think, we'll get to see Elizabeth again and ever so many of our friends."

"I'm just wondering," murmured Tommy, a worried frown puckering his brow, "if I can still read and write. Maybe I forgot a lot during these three and a half years. If I did, maybe Elizabeth will help me remember what I forgot. I wonder why my mother never answered my letter. I thought we would all hear from our families. Didn't you think we would, Pa?" Tommy bit his lower lip.

"Yes, I thought we would, and it's been a real disappointment to Margaret and me too," said Johan. "In God's good time, we may hear yet; if not, we'll write again. Maybe the captain's ship went down in a storm and our letters never arrived."

After the dinner dishes were done the next day, Nettie said, "You know, a couple days ago I was going through everything in our bedroom and I came across three letters. It looked to me like they belonged to your family, so I talked to my husband and he said I was right."

"Oh!" gasped Margaret, suddenly turning pale and sitting down heavily on a bench. "Do you mean they really are addressed to us? We've wondered why our families didn't answer our letters. The ship captain who brought us over to America promised to take our letters back to our families in Holland." With beseeching eyes, Margaret begged, "Where are the letters; may I see them?"

"Yes," agreed Nettie, her hands sticky with biscuit dough. "Howard said I may as well give them to you. He knew that neither you nor your husband could read or write, so he thought he'd keep them until your time was up on his farm. He thought the letters would only distract you from your work, but I convinced him of the opposite. I'm sure those letters could have been a comfort to you. Sometime you'll be sure to meet someone who can read them to you. I may as well get them right now." Nettie hurriedly washed and dried her hands and disappeared into the bedroom.

When she came out holding the letters, Margaret sprang to meet her and clasped the letters to her breast, her face aglow. "Oh, thank God for this great blessing. And thank you, Nettie, for making sure we got them. I can't begin to tell you how happy I am to know we have letters from our families."

"I'd be glad to read them for you, Margaret, but I can't read that language." Nettie gave her hand a comforting squeeze.

"Oh, we'll get them read, all right. We have a good friend who can read and write. She came with us on the ship and wrote our letters for us. I know she would be delighted to read them for us," assured Margaret. "Then, too, maybe Tommy might be able to read them. He was learning how to read and write quite well before we came here. I'll just slip them into my pocket and keep them for a wonderful surprise when we get to our new home. Oh, I'm so happy, Nettie! God is so good."

In the middle of the afternoon, Nettie approached Margaret with two pairs of pants draped over her arm. She handed them to Margaret and said, "I noticed that Tommy has grown out of his pants. Here are two pairs that don't fit my boys anymore. They may be a bit too large in the waist, but I'm sure you can figure out a way to hold them up. You may have them if you think they would be suitable."

"Oh, Nettie, I am so grateful. Yes, they will be suitable. How very kind and thoughtful you are. Tommy will be so pleased. I know the pants he has been wearing must be very uncomfortable, but I didn't know what to do about it."

"Well, I'm glad if Tommy can make use of them," said Nettie. "Now, I want you to feel free to go to your cabin if you have some last-minute things to tend to. Mr. Morgan should be here before long."

"Thank you, Nettie. I was hoping for a bit of time to sweep our cabin. I'd like for it to be tidy when we leave." Grabbing a broom, she hurried out and gave the cabin a thorough cleaning. She heard the letters crackling in her pocket, making her heart thump. *Oh, joy! I can hardly wait! How happy Johan and Tommy will be!*

Taking the broom back to the house, she saw Mr. Morgan driving up the lane with his team and wagon. She looked toward the field, and noticed Johan and Tommy on their way in, with Nettie's boys running to catch up. Margaret walked out to meet them.

When the boys caught up, James got his breath back first and gasped, "He gave us permission to see you off, Tommy; we'll sure miss you and Johan. We especially liked your singing while we worked. We'll miss the evening stories."

"Yes, I'll miss you, too," said Tommy. "We don't live that far apart, so maybe you can come over to see us sometime. I hope you can."

Nettie came out, looked toward the field, and asked her boys, "Isn't Howard coming to see them off?"

"No," William replied, "he said he talked to them before they left the field. He didn't want to leave his work. He said we could come, though, but as soon as Johan and his family leave, we're supposed to go right back. You'll go back out with us, won't you?" He was searching his mother's face.

"Yes, I'll come out for a while. Just think, boys, we're going to church tomorrow. It's good to have something to look forward to."

Jacob Morgan stopped his wagon beside the little group. "Howdy, folks. I see you're all here but the little ones. Where are they? You're not planning on leaving them here, are you, Johan?" He had a twinkle in his eye.

"We wouldn't consider such a thing, Mr. Morgan. They are more precious than gold. It so happens that they are taking their afternoon nap. We're all ready to go as soon as Margaret gets the boys and we load our trunk."

In short order, the family and their trunk were loaded onto the Morgan wagon. A pile of soft hay was provided for Margaret and the little boys to ride on. Mr. Morgan looked at Johan and patted the seat beside him. Tommy sat in the front corner of the wagon so he could hear the conversation of the men.

As the wagon started down the lane, Nettie and her boys called after them, "Good-bye, good-bye! Thanks for all the good stories you told us. Thanks for the singing every night. Come back for a visit." Margaret saw Nettie grab her handkerchief and wipe her eyes. They gave one last wave just before the woods cut off their view.

The men rode in silence for a while, then Mr. Morgan said, "It appears like Mr. Hughes married a good wife—and got some strapping sons besides."

"Yes, he did," agreed Johan. "It has been a different place since Nettie and her boys came there to live. Nettie is the perfect wife for him and she has brought about some changes for the better in Mr. Hughes too. He's even promised to take his family to church tomorrow. We're happy about that."

"I'm glad to hear that. Now maybe I can quit feeling sorry for his wife and boys. I noticed he didn't come in from the field to give you a send-off. Why not?" asked Mr. Morgan.

"I was just glad he allowed Nettie's boys to come up to see us off," Johan replied. "Nettie asked why Howard didn't come along, and the boys told her he didn't want to be leaving his work. He said he had talked to us before we left the field," said Johan.

"Do you mind telling me what he said?" asked Mr. Morgan.

"He said, 'Your time's up. So get.' And Tommy and I lit out for your wagon." Johan chuckled.

"That's all he said?" Mr. Morgan's eyes were big in amazement.

"That's all! It could have been worse, so I am thankful," said Johan, with a sigh of relief. "I don't know how to thank you for making it possible for us to leave."

"The only thanks I want is for you to be an honest, faithful worker on my farm. I plan to treat your family right, and I believe we'll get along well. The Lord hasn't blessed us with children, so my wife and I are hoping we can all be sort of like 'family'."

"Well, we plan to be honest and faithful. We'll work as though we are working for the Lord Himself, and with His help, we're bound to get along well together. Then, too, we'll be glad to be included in your family."

As they were nearing the Millers' property, they could see Josh and Elizabeth talking together beside the mill. At the sound of the team, they whirled around. Suddenly they began waving.

"Whoa!" Mr. Morgan said. He turned to Johan and said, "I take it you know these folks."

"We sure do and thanks for stopping." Johan reached down and gave Josh a hearty handshake, while Elizabeth ran around to hug Margaret.

"We're planning to be your near neighbors again, Josh," Johan informed him with a big smile. "We'll just be a mile on the other side of you—toward town. Do come and visit us."

"Yes, please do, Elizabeth," begged Margaret. "You can help me get settled into our new house."

"That would do you a world of good, Beth," encouraged Josh. "Why not? I'll take you and baby Isaac over on Monday morning. You can spend the whole day and then I'll come and get you in the evening. Pa and Ma might want to come in the evening too. We'll bring enough food along to celebrate this happy time."

"That's a wonderful idea, Josh," said Beth, her eyes glowing. "It will give us something wonderful to look forward to. We don't want to keep you folks any longer, because Mr. Morgan will want to get home. But, oh, I'm so excited! I'll hurry into the house and prepare enough food for both our families tomorrow when we eat together at the preacher's house after the church service, and then I'll fix some more food for Monday when Josh brings me over."

Giving her a parting hug, Margaret said, "Thank you, Elizabeth. You are a wonderful friend. It will be a great help if you can pack our Sunday lunch." Then she pushed Elizabeth back, still holding to her shoulders and asked, "Did I hear right, Elizabeth, do you really have a baby?"

"We sure do! We have the sweetest little boy, just about the size of your smallest one." Laughing gaily, Elizabeth headed for the house and shouted, "Oh, won't we have a good time tomorrow at church and then again on Monday?"

With a "gid-dap", they moved on down the road. Mr. Morgan chuckled and said, "Well, Johan, looks like you stirred up some excitement at the mill. Evidently your friends are glad to have you back in circulation again."

"Yes, it looks that way, but you're the one who triggered off the excitement. God is so good to give us a caring friend like you."

"Well, it seems your friends here at the mill spoke of their concern to Jason Cloud," explained Mr. Morgan. "When Josh and Elizabeth walked back to Mr. Hughes before they were married and he wouldn't allow them to talk to you, they eventually told Mr. Cloud about it. He decided to pay a visit to the Hughes' farm, and he too was not allowed to speak with you. When he found out you weren't allowed to leave the farm, he came and talked to me. I guess you know the rest of the story."

"So, that's how the Lord answered my prayers. I wondered how it all happened. It sure pays to trust in God." Johan sat back with a contented sigh.

Before long they were turning into Mr. Morgan's place. They passed his two-story house, and went on back a short lane to a four-room log cabin, with a loft. The grass was freshly cut around the house and fresh curtains hung at the open windows.

"Oh, how nice," Margaret quietly said to Tommy. "We won't know how to act with all that room. Won't it be wonderful?"

Tommy gave a quick nod while a smile spread over his face.

As the two men carried the trunk into the house, Mr. Morgan said, "We tried to think of all the things you might need. There's a spinning wheel in your sitting room, and a barrel of wool out in your storage lean-to, but we didn't give you a loom because it might crowd you up a bit. My wife is hoping that Margaret will come over and use our loom when she wants to weave some cloth. She wants Margaret and the children to feel right at home in our house, especially so since we have no children of our own." Pointing to the bed, he continued, "There's a trundle bed under your bed, Johan, for your little boys. We put another bed in the other room for Tommy. If all five of you lived in that tiny cabin behind Mr. Hughes, I wouldn't wonder if it might feel good to spread out a little."

"It will be wonderful," said Margaret, with a sigh. "I don't want Tommy to feel lonely, though; he might want Jacob to sleep with him at times."

"I'm glad you like it," said Mr. Morgan, opening another door to a lean-to. "We put a lot of shelves in this room off from the kitchen; it's something like a pantry and cold room for hanging your hams in winter. It will help to keep things from spoiling. We tried to think of the food you would need for now. I think you'll find plenty to hold you over for a while. But for this first evening, if you don't mind, my wife and I would like for you to eat your first meal with us."

"Oh, how nice! I'm very anxious to meet your wife." Then, peeking into an empty water bucket, Margaret asked, "Is there a well close by?"

"Better than a well! There is a spring and a little house over it—to keep animals out, you know. The spring runs all the time. That way you can keep your food from spoiling in the summer. Follow me," said Mr. Morgan, stepping outside and pointing. "The spring is in that small building, a short piece down that little hill. I also want to show you the garden."

"The garden!" exclaimed Johan. "Is there really a garden?"

"Yes," Mr. Morgan replied, nodding his head. "As soon as I felt sure you would be coming, I put in a garden for you. That should give you a nice variety. Jason Cloud told me you were once a gardener in Holland, so I wouldn't wonder but what we'll be learning some things from you. When I'm gone from home, my wife might need some help with her garden too."

"We are overcome by your kindness and the goodness of our God toward us," said Johan. "I know we'll enjoy working for you and your wife. Whenever you're gone, we'll be asking her from time to time if she has needs, but we also want her to feel free to ask for our help at any time—just as she would if we were her son and daughter."

"That sounds good," said Mr. Morgan with a pleased smile. "There are four pigs being fattened in the barn, and in the fall we'll do our butchering together. Then the women will set aside a day to make the candles. My wife has the candle mold, plus some beeswax and tallow saved back for that purpose. Now, while Margaret gets used to the surroundings in the house, we men will go to the barn and I'll explain some things there."

Margaret and Jacob watched the men head for the barn.

"Ma," Jacob asked, "are we going to live in this nice house?"

"Yes, we are," she replied with a smile. "God is so good to us! Mr. Morgan seems like a kind man, too. I must go to the spring and get a bucket of fresh water, Jacob. You stay here with Christian and I'll soon be back. You boys may sit on the doorstep and watch me get the water."

Margaret hurried down the hill, entered the springhouse, and looked around. There was a pool with a natural rock basin for the spring water to run into and an overflow pipe for the water to flow outside—down to a pond for the ducks, geese, and farm animals. The temperature was cooler in the springhouse, and there was a ledge of rock at the water's edge to place crocks and containers of food. "This is wonderful," murmured Margaret, while dipping in for a full pail of sparkling water.

As Margaret carried the pail of fresh water toward the house, she waved at her faithful little son, who had his arm around his little brother as they waited on the doorstep. She used the dipper and gave them each a drink and then took the bucket in and set it on the table. The boys came in to watch as their mother put sheets and covers on their beds. She pulled out the trundle bed and explained, "This is a bed for you boys. We'll pull it out at night and push it under our bed during the day. Jacob, you're used to sleeping with Tommy, so you may sleep with him sometimes. We don't want Tommy to be lonesome over there in that room all by himself." She led the way to Tommy's room.

"This is a nice room," said Jacob. "I suppose I'll sleep with him sometimes, but I'd like it better if we were all in one room."

Margaret chuckled. "You'll soon get used to a bigger house, Jacob."

After the beds were all prepared for the night, she took her sons outside and looked at the garden, which was growing well. What bounty! There was even a row of colorful hollyhocks blooming along one end of the house and a rosebush on either side of the front door. She could see where tulips had bloomed earlier. On impulse she reached down and patted the plants. It was like a bit of her home from Holland. The letters in her pocket crackled as she straightened up. A happy smile spread across her face.

"Are you happy, Ma?" asked Jacob, always watchful of his mother's moods.

"Yes, Jacob, I'm very happy!" said Margaret, dropping to her knees and hugging a son in each arm.

"Now, let's go into the house and get washed up and put on some clean clothes, because we'll be going to the big house to eat our supper with the Morgans. We will meet Mr. Morgan's wife this evening and we want her to see some nice, clean boys."

After a quick washup, Margaret took the rest of the clean water to the two bedrooms and poured it into the pitchers, which were sitting in large washbowls on their washstands. Now, she must get more water. While she was getting another bucket of fresh water from the spring, she saw the men returning from the barn.

As the men came in, Johan said, "Say, you three are all spiffed up. Tommy, I reckon that calls for some washing on our part."

"You can wash right here at the washstand in the kitchen," offered

Margaret, "and then use the towel I hung on the nail above it. Your fresh clothes are lying on your own beds."

"And how does my good wife like her new home?" asked Johan, vigorously scrubbing his face, neck, and arms.

"Johan, it's wonderful! It seems like the Lord is pouring out so many blessings that we can hardly contain them," marveled Margaret, secretly placing her hand over the letters in her pocket.

"Yes, it seems the Lord is paying us well for all we endured the past three and a half years. I'm glad we didn't let it make us bitter; instead, we worked together and did our best with the Lord's help. Then, too, Allie was able to meet her God in peace."

"Yes! Dear, dear Allie! And while thanking the Lord for all His goodness, we never want to forget the kindness of Morning Star. She was such a blessing to me, just when I thought I couldn't go on," said Margaret, while hugging plump little Christian.

Margaret left the men to their washing and walked into the living room. She rocked Christian while she waited for Johan and Tommy to get dressed and join her. She felt she couldn't wait another moment to share her secret.

When the men came striding into the living room, wearing clean clothes, Margaret pulled the letters from her pocket and handed them to Johan.

"Why—why, this looks like letters!" gasped Johan.

Tommy rushed over to peer closely at the letters. "They are letters! Three of them!" Barely above a whisper, he said, "Maybe one is for me from my mother? Maybe I'll be able to read them!"

"Here, son, let's open them carefully and then we'll see if you can read them." With trembling hands, Johan slit one open with a knife and said, "Quick, Tommy, see if you can read it!"

"Oh, this is from my mother," Tommy said excitedly as he continued to study the letter. "I know it's mine because I can read my name at the beginning and it says Mother at the end. I can't read every word, but I think it says she married the preacher and he is writing the letter."

"Don't worry, Tommy," comforted Johan, "if you can't read every word, we know that Elizabeth can read them for us on Monday. Stick it in your pocket and take it along to supper; maybe the Morgans can read them for us tonight and then Elizabeth can read them to us again on Monday. Tommy, can you tell if the other two letters are for Margaret and me?"

Tommy carefully studied the letters and then with a nod he handed one to each of them and said, "You each have one, that's sure."

"It's time for supper, so let's head for the big house, but while we go, you can tell us how you got the letters and pulled off this wonderful surprise, Margaret," said Johan.

So after closing the door behind them, Margaret told them the happy story as they walked along.

"So Mr. Hughes had those letters in his possession for some time! All I can say is that Nettie came into that home at the right time and she brought many big blessings to us, as well as to Mr. Hughes."

chapter forty

Letters from Home!

Mary Morgan looked out the kitchen window and saw Johan's family coming up the lane and thought, *My, what a happy family. They seem mighty excited about something.* Turning to Rachel, the thirteen-year-old blond, blue-eyed indentured girl who was helping her in the kitchen, she said, "Rachel, I think we can dip up the food and place it on the table. The family will soon be here. You're a good worker and you've helped me well with this meal."

The praise made Rachel's cheeks flush with pleasure and she said, "You're very kind to say so, Mistress."

Jacob Morgan swung the door open and gave Johan's family a hearty welcome into their home. He nodded at his wife and the young girl and said, "This is my wife, Mary, and our indentured friend, Rachel Van Dooren from Rotterdam, Holland. She is a great help to my wife." Then, tapping Johan on the shoulder, he said to his wife, "Mary, this young man is Johan; he's holding little Christian and beside him is his wife, Margaret, with Jacob next. Their older son is Tommy."

"It's a pleasure to meet you, Mary," Margaret said. Then she smiled at Rachel and they exchanged a customary Dutch curtsy, while Johan and Tommy acknowledged the introduction with a nod and smile.

"Well," said Mary, with a happy chuckle, "it looks like the ladies from Holland have something in common. That's nice and I'm very pleased to meet each one of you. I'm excited about having your family living close by." Catching her husband's eye, she gave a slight nod toward the table.

"It seems the food is ready, so just be seated," invited Mr. Morgan, "and we'll see if this food tastes as good as it smells."

After enjoying the delicious meal, which included fresh wild raspberries with whipped cream for dessert, the men went to another room while the women cleared the table and washed the dishes.

When the women joined the men, Johan said, "We had a wonderful surprise today. Mrs. Hughes gave Margaret three letters that her husband was holding in his bedroom for quite a while. Mrs. Hughes found them, and after talking to her husband he agreed that she could give the letters to us today. Our problem is that my wife and I cannot read or write. While we lived with Jason Cloud, he made it possible for Tommy to get some education, and he learned a lot in the short time we were there, but there are a number of words in these letters he is unable to pronounce. We know that Josh Miller's wife can read them to us on Monday when she comes to spend the day, but we think we can't wait—that is, if one of you can read the Dutch language."

Johan's family waited anxiously, with bated breath, looking from one to another.

Mr. and Mrs. Morgan sadly shook their heads. "I'm sorry," Mr. Morgan said. "We can speak the Dutch language, but we have never learned to read it well. Oh, I was tutored enough to understand official documents, but that is all. I'm sorry."

Finally Rachel spoke up. "My mother was well educated and she taught me to read and write when I was very young. I always enjoy reading in my own language. Three years ago, when I was ten, I was kidnapped and put on a ship and brought to America, but I can still read the Dutch language. You see, I get a letter from my family once or twice a year."

"Rachel, if you can do that for us, we would be mighty pleased. Tommy, you go first," encouraged Johan.

So Tommy's precious letter was handed over and Rachel cleared her throat and began:

My dear Tommy,

I was so happy to get your letter. I cried all day. This time my tears were tears of joy.

I watched for you continually on the day I was expecting you home from the docks, but you didn't come that day—nor the next. I knew something terrible had happened to you. The preacher and I walked all the way to Rotterdam to try to find you. We were hungry, so we stopped in at the inn on the docks and asked the owner if he had seen you. He told us what might have happened. I can't tell you how I grieved. It was worse than a funeral, because I wondered who would care for my dear son. I prayed mightily to my God and He finally gave me peace. Then when your letter came and you told me about Johan and Margaret being so kind to you and taking you for a son, I rejoiced greatly, especially when you told me they were good Christian people. Dear Tommy, always be true to God.

I think you will be happy to know that I am no longer a widow. The preacher, Peter Koch, and I were married soon after you were missing. He's a good man, Tommy, so you needn't worry about me. He is writing this letter for me. You were a good lad while you were here, and you took good care of me by selling my baked goods. Please write again. I long to hear from you.

I think of you every day with love,
Your mother, Katrina Koch

"That was wonderful to hear news from my mother. I've waited four and a half years for this day. Thank you, Rachel, for reading it to us." Tommy reached for his letter and carefully slipped his precious treasure into his pocket.

"It was a great privilege to read it for you, Tommy," said Rachel. "Just think, your mother and the preacher might have walked right by my parents' house in Rotterdam. We didn't live far from the docks. Oh, that letter was like a visit from my own home. I'm so glad you folks will be living close by." Rachel looked at Johan and said, "Are there more letters to read?"

"Yes, Margaret and I both have a letter. Let her read yours first, Margaret," offered Johan.

Rachel eagerly reached for the letter and read:

Our dear and only child, Margaret, (written by your Aunt Molly)

It was with great joy that we read your letter. We are sorry that you are so far from us, but so thankful that you have a kind Christian husband. We are very thankful you were not separated when you were sold as indentured servants. I'm glad you could tell us about the birth of baby Jacob. So we are grandparents! How we long to hold him in our arms!

As you remember, we were supposed to meet you with our donkey and cart in Rotterdam after you had seen your friends off to America. We were so excited about having you spend the weekend with us. I understand you brought your trunk and among many other things you were bringing some baby clothes you had made and a beautiful quilt you wanted to show us. I know you are a good seamstress, Margaret, so I know they were lovely. As it turned out, we're so thankful you brought your trunk with your clothes and probably the medicines I gave you. No doubt, you have found a way to use some of them.

Very early, on that fateful morning, we arrived at the dock because we wanted to see the big ship set sail, but there was no sign of a ship anywhere. We looked everywhere for you and Johan. We finally inquired at the inn and the owner was very distressed. He told us he felt sure the captain had tricked you and your husband into sleeping on his ship. He said he started to come to your table to warn you about the ways of that captain, but a very sick woman was brought in just then and her husband was demanding a bed for her. He said while he and his wife were up tending to the sick lady, the ship left the dock sometime around midnight. He said the captain often kidnapped young children too.

The innkeeper was very kind and brought us a cup of coffee and even packed us a free lunch. Your father and I sat awhile on the bench and prayed for strength. We knew Johan's family would want to know, so we started on a journey we hadn't planned to take. Your father insisted that I should ride in the cart until I felt stronger. We rode outside Rotterdam, where there was a quiet spot in a little grove of trees and there we fell on our knees and cried out to God to help us through our grief and to help you and Johan cope with the shock of going to America. We begged the Lord to spare you from being sold to separate masters. We thank God He didn't allow you to be separated. God did strengthen us after we prayed. I was able to walk most of the way from that point on and make it easier for our little donkey, but our hearts were heavy.

We dreaded to tell Johan's family the terrible news, but it was something that had to be done. Jacob Boekman, Greta's special friend, was there and they all rushed out to meet us. When they saw the tears streaming down our faces, Johan's mother invited us in. She knew something terrible had happened, and asked us to tell her all. We did and after many tears were shed, that dear mother requested a time of silent prayer for you and Johan asking God to help you through this shocking experience.

Little Jacob snuggled up to his mother, who was wiping her tears. After blowing her nose, Rachel continued:

After much crying and praying, the Amen was said, and then Johan's mother said, "This makes me think of Job in the Bible. The Lord gave us Johan and Margaret and He has a right to take them away. Blessed be the name of the Lord. I'm sure Johan didn't plan to go to America, but God must have a special plan to fulfill in their lives. She asked each one to try to think of some possible blessing that could come from this terrible experience. She led the way and said, "I know they'll be a great blessing to Karl and Susie. Susie seemed so broken up about leaving."

Hilda was next and said, "Maybe there will be kidnapped children on the ship and I know Johan and Margaret will be a comfort to them."

Margaret, I rejoiced when you told me about your love for ten-year-old Tommy. I thank God you were there for him. How that boy must have suffered!

Jacob said, "I'm sure it's a blessing that they took their trunk with their clothing and valuables—even some bed covers and baby clothes."

Greta said, "It's a blessing that Johan taught Hilda how to handle the dogs and to run our milk route. It seems God was preparing us for this day. But how I will miss my dear brother and his precious wife!"

Then Johan's mother said, "Yes, I believe God was also preparing Johan when Grootvader told him stories of the persecution he had suffered."

Then she remembered that Mynheer Voosterman must be told so he could get another gardener to take Johan's place.

Jacob decided he might like the job and planned to go right over and apply for it. He enjoys gardening, but besides that, he wanted to do something for Johan.

Then, Margaret, your dear father said, "I would like to add a blessing we experienced because of this terrible disappointment. We thank God for a family like you to share our sorrow. It was wonderful to hear you mention the various blessings from the past, present, and future. I can see why Johan is such a godly man—he has a godly mother."

His mother murmured, "May God be praised! He alone is worthy."

It was hard to leave this grieving family, but we felt we needed to get home to care for our animals, as we didn't expect to be gone so long.

You can imagine how wonderful it was to receive your letter and to know you were alive and well; also that God had blessed you with a dear little son to join Tommy. You're in our thoughts and prayers daily. Please write to us again. We're anxiously waiting for another letter.

We love you dearly,
Your parents, Peter and Annie

"Thank you, Rachel," said Margaret, reaching for the letter. "It was so wonderful to hear from my parents. While hearing Mother's letter, it was almost like hearing from your family, wasn't it, Johan? Mother was always so good at telling stories."

"Yes," agreed Johan, "it was almost like being there with them when they heard the news." He pulled out his letter and said, "Here, Rachel, this is the last one. I hope we're not asking too much of you."

"Not at all! In fact, I feel honored that you trust me with all this information about your lives. These letters make me feel like I've known your family for years." She opened the letter and read:

Dear Johan, your precious wife, and family, (written by the schoolmaster, Hans Kuipers)

We praised God and rejoiced greatly when we received your letter. Just to know you were safe and well meant so much to us. We were happy to hear about the birth of baby Jacob!

Margaret's mother said she would tell about how it went when they came to bring the shocking news about you and Margaret, so I will leave that to her. After they made a sad departure with their donkey cart, I shall never forget how Jacob leaned against our front gatepost and sobbed out his grief. Johan, you and Jacob were such close friends ever since you were small lads. It was hard for him to give you up. It was a very difficult time for all of us.

Greta and Jacob were soon married after you left and they now have a sweet baby girl named Margaret. Greta wanted her to be your namesake, Margaret. They are living in Grootvader's small cottage—where the two of you had lived. It is so good to have a kind man like Jacob close by, because there are many things we women cannot do. Jacob is also continuing your gardening job at Mynheer Voosterman's lovely home. The Lord is helping us through this rough time, but we will never stop missing you.

Hilda is doing very well with the milk route and with handling the dogs. She says she feels close to you, Johan, when she works with the dogs you trained. We have been so thankful you were willing to teach her how to do a good job. I hope she will be at home with me for several years yet, but I've been noticing some young men looking her way.

Your brother Karl and family are well. Besides their many prayers for you, they send you their love. They have another son and they named him Johan. It is so nice to hear your name, as well as Margaret's name, used often in our family, even though you are absent from us.

I'm sure you remember Dame Bowman, the old woman who sold hot water and burning peat. Hilda says she often talks of you with a thankful heart for the way you helped her to know God. Johan, it would please her if you would send some special words just for her in your next letter.

Thank you for telling us about Tommy. We're so glad the Lord made a way for you to keep him with you. I know you have given him a loving, godly home. We feel like we know you, Tommy. We would be glad for a letter from you, too. Our hearts went out to the other four boys who were also kidnapped. We shed tears when we read about the burial of the two lads and that little girl at sea.

So there were prisoners on your ship and one of them tried to steal your trunk. But God used that experience to bring Pete to Himself. I can't imagine what it must have been like to grow up never having a friend who cared. I'm so glad you could forgive the man and show him what a Christian friend was like. Pete is living proof that God can change the vilest of sinners. And to think he was willing to work another year or two to keep those two young lads, Klaus and Ben, with him. It sounds like the Lord gave them a good place to live, too. God is so good to His children.

When you told about the storm at sea, we trembled and thanked God that He kept you safe.

It was so exciting to learn that the terrible captain was converted and did his best to find good homes for you and your Christian friends, whom he had mistreated. I'm glad he kept his word and saw to it that we got your letters. Please write again. We long to hear from you.

I am well, for which I thank my God. No matter what God sends our way, let us all continue to serve Him with a pure heart fervently. It will be worth it all, when we see our Saviour face to face.

> *Jacob and your sisters send Christian greetings to you and your family. They are still missing you terribly and long to see you again. They say if it is not possible in this life, we have the assurance we will meet together in heaven with our precious Lord. Let's be faithful.*
> *My love and prayers are with you all,*
> *Your mother*

"Rachel, how can we thank you enough for being willing to read these three letters to us," said Johan, leaning over to retrieve his letter. "For years we have longed to hear from our families."

"I was glad to do it," said Rachel, with shining eyes. "If ever you would like to have them read again or if you want some letters written, I'll be glad to do it for you. Sundays would be a good day for that, because none of us will be real busy."

"That's such a kind offer!" exclaimed Margaret. "I'm sure our friend, Elizabeth Miller, would also do it for us, but since we're both working for the Morgans, it will be handier for you to do it."

"And I'll be happy to pay for the sending of your letters," offered Mr. Morgan.

"You are very kind, Mr. Morgan. I'm sure we'll want to send some letters real soon," said Johan.

Rachel said shyly, "You mentioned Elizabeth Miller; do you mean Josh Miller's wife, who lives at the mill?" At Margaret's nod, she continued, "Those good people drive two miles out of their way each Sunday, just to take me along to their church. They, as well as the Morgans, have been very kind to me."

"Rachel, since we will be attending the same church, we would be glad to spare your friends the extra drive by letting you ride with us," Johan told her. Margaret and Tommy gave nods of agreement.

"Well," said Johan, standing to his feet and looking at the Morgans, "I think it is time for us to go to our own house. Thank you for giving us a hearty welcome and sharing your delicious meal with us. I hope we didn't bore you with taking the time to read these letters, instead of visiting. We thought we couldn't wait any longer. I hope you understand."

"We certainly do understand," said Mr. Morgan, laying his big hand on Johan's shoulder. "After hearing these letters read, we feel we know you and your family much better than we would have if we had spent the time visiting. We are more convinced than ever that we did the right thing when we decided to move your family onto our farm. May your family sleep well tonight in your new home. Let's try to be at the barn, ready for work, at dawn. How does that sound?"

"Lord willing, we'll be there," promised Johan, and his words were sanctioned by a vigorous nod from Tommy.

As they walked home, they were bubbling over as they discussed their letters. Then Johan leaned down and tapped Jacob on the shoulder and said, "Jacob, those two letters that Rachel read for your ma and me were from your grandparents."

"What's grandparents?" asked Jacob.

"My mother and father and your ma's mother and father are your grandparents," explained Johan.

"You mean you have a ma and pa like me?" asked Jacob, surprised.

"Sure, all boys and girls have a ma and pa somewhere. My pa is no longer living. He fell when he was repairing a dike in Holland, but my ma is living."

"Did you cry when your pa died?" asked Jacob, concerned.

"Yes, I did, but God helped us through that hard time. I wish you could meet my mother and your ma's parents, but since that is impossible, we'll try our best to tell you about them as the days go by, because you have very wonderful and godly grandparents."

"I liked the letters, but I don't like it when it makes you cry," said Jacob.

"There are two kinds of tears, Jacob," explained his mother, "sad tears and happy tears. Those that you saw this evening were mostly happy tears."

"I'm glad. I didn't know there were two kinds." Jacob gave a relieved sigh.

When they entered their house, they lit some candles and prepared to have a time of worship.

"Tommy," Johan said, "tomorrow evening we want you to read some Scripture from our Bible again, but this evening, since it's getting late, we'll sing several songs, quote some Scripture, and pray like we did on the Hughes' farm."

After their souls were refreshed, Johan said with quiet thoughtfulness, "Just think! We are no longer indentured servants. Now we're totally free—free to serve the Lord by attending church tomorrow morning and every time our health and the weather permits. And to top it off, getting those letters was so-o-o wonderful. And now we'll be able to answer those letters. I find it hard to grasp all these wonderful blessings from God. Let us remember it was God who allowed us to be brought to America against our will, and indeed, it was a life-changing voyage. He led us so gently each step of the way—even when the way seemed most difficult. What a mighty God we serve! Let's continue to bring praise to Him, for He alone is worthy."

"Amen! That's right!" murmured Margaret and Tommy.

Bibliography

Boswell in Holland, edited by Fredrick A. Pottle, Sterling Prof. of English, Yale Univ., copyright 1952

Hans Brinker, by Mary Mapes Dodge, copyright 1963

Colonists for Sale, The Story of Indentured Servants in America, by Clifford Lindsey Alderman, copyright 1975

Mennonite Archives, Internet, Goshen College, Goshen, Indiana

Mennonites of America by C. Henry Smith, printed by Mennonite Publishing House

Scotland Farewell, The People of the Hector, by Donald MacKay, copyright 1980, printed and bound in Canada

Mennonites in Europe by John Horsch, copyright 1942, printed by Mennonite Publishing House

Information taken from the notes of Ina K. Plank, sent to Isa Ruth Plank (original compiler) by Walter Van Brocklin of Milwaukee, Wisconsin